FAITH AND THE PHILOSOPHERS

FAITH AND THE PHILOSOPHERS

EDITED BY
JOHN HICK
Stuart Professor of Christian Philosophy
Princeton Theological Seminary

WIPF & STOCK · Eugene, Oregon

Wipf and Stock Publishers
199 W 8th Ave, Suite 3
Eugene, OR 97401

Faith and the Philosophers
By Hick, John
Copyright©1964 Princeton Theological Seminary
ISBN 13: 978-1-61097-384-7
Publication date 3/28/2011
Previously published by St. Martins Press, 1964

PREFACE

THIS volume is the product of a two-day conference attended by some fifty philosophers and theologians, held at the Princeton Theological Seminary, Princeton, New Jersey, in December 1962. The conference was one of a series of events marking the Seminary's one hundred and fiftieth year of theological teaching and research.

The majority of the philosophers present — some of whom were religious believers, some sceptics — were among those who have been significantly influenced by the contemporary movement of philosophical analysis; that is to say, their aims and methods could hardly have been what they are if such men as Russell, Moore and Wittgenstein had never written. But there were also others who are critical of these modes of philosophizing. The theologians were for the most part Protestants of various denominations, but included also two Jesuit priests who contributed notably to the proceedings. It is probable that there have been few such extensive confrontations in recent times between such high-calibre representatives of Christian belief and of philosophical criticism. Perhaps it is worth recording that the discussions were as friendly as they were frank; above all they represented a co-operative search for greater clarity on some very important issues in the philosophy of religion.

The members of the conference were: Virgil Aldrich (Kenyon College); William Alston (University of Michigan); Brand Blanshard (Yale University); Richard Brandt (Swarthmore College); Norris Clarke, S.J. (Fordham University); Malcolm Diamond (Princeton University); E. A. Dowey (Princeton Theological Seminary); Joel Feinberg (Princeton University); Frederick Ferré (Dickinson College); Keith Gunderson (Princeton University); Charles Hartshorne (University of Texas); Peter Heath (University of Virginia); George Hendry (Princeton Theological Seminary); John Hick (Princeton Theological Seminary); Paul Holmer (Yale University); Paul M. Hurrell (Michigan State University); Robert Johann, S.J. (Loyola Seminary); Samuel Keen (Louisville Presbyterian Theological

Faith and the Philosophers

Seminary); Charles Kegley (Wagner College); William Kennick (Amherst College); Hugh T. Kerr (Princeton Theological Seminary); Martin Lean (Brooklyn College); Richard Luecke (Princeton, New Jersey); Alasdair MacIntyre (Oxford University); Norman Malcolm (Cornell University); James I. McCord (Princeton Theological Seminary); Kai Nielsen (New York University); Dennis O'Brien (Princeton University); George Pitcher (Princeton University); Alvin Plantinga (Wayne State University); William Poteat (Duke University); Jean A. Potter (Bryn Mawr College); Victor Preller (Princeton University); H. H. Price (Oxford University); Cyril Richardson (Union Theological Seminary); Mrs. Richard Rorty (Rutgers University); Richard Rorty (Princeton University); Paul Schmidt (Oberlin College); Fadlou Shehadi (Rutgers University); James Ward Smith (Princeton University); Elmer Sprague (Brooklyn College); W. T. Stace (Princeton University); Walter Stromseth (St. Olaf's College); Paul W. Taylor (Brooklyn College); George Thomas (Princeton University); Linwood Urban (Swarthmore College); Gregory Vlastos (Princeton University); Charles West (Princeton Theological Seminary); Walter Wiest (Pittsburgh Theological Seminary); Daniel D. Williams (Union Theological Seminary); and Willem Zuurdeeg (McCormick Theological Seminary).

The present volume includes papers which were written for the conference and which were circulated in advance of the meetings, together with some extracts from the subsequent discussions. Only limitations of space have prohibited a fuller use of the tapes on which the always interesting and often exciting discussions were recorded.

The thanks of any who profit from these pages are due to President James I. McCord of Princeton Seminary; to the Seminary's Sesquicentennial Committee, of which General Dwight D. Eisenhower was the Honorary Chairman; to the Director of the Sesquicentennial Program, the Reverend Roy Pfautch, and his staff; and to Miss Mary McAnally, who has done valuable editorial work on the manuscript.

JOHN HICK,
Conference Chairman

Introduction to the 2011 Reprint Edition

The story of the relation between Anglo-American philosophy and religion in the 20th century is a remarkable one. At the end of the 19th century, from T H Green at Oxford, through Edward Caird in Glasgow, to Josiah Royce at Harvard, Idealist philosophy of a generally Hegelian sort was prominent, and in many places dominant, in both the United States and Britain. Though often somewhat suspect in orthodox theological circles, Idealism was broadly theistic in character, and unquestionably sympathetic to religion. By the early decades of the 20th century, the position had changed drastically. Hugely impressed by the success of natural science, philosophers on both sides of the Atlantic embraced logical positivism, a conception of philosophy emanating from Vienna, which was then blended with the empiricism of Locke and Hume, recently restored to philosophical study by the scholarly production of new editions of the *Essay* and the *Treatise*. The effect of logical positivism was to deny theological assertions, and the religious language in which they were made, the sort of significance that science could claim. In kindly hands they were relegated, alongside poetry, to the realms of the expressive. More hostile treatments denied that they were meaningful at all.

By mid-century, the banishment of religion to the philosophical wilderness was almost complete. Philosophy and theology were as far apart as they had ever been in their history. For the most part philosophers with religious sympathies reserved their expression to private life, and carefully segregated questions of belief from their professional activities. In this climate, with occasional excep-

Introduction

tions, theologians came to regard philosophers as their intellectual enemies.

If we fast forward from 1960, say, to the first decade of the 21st century, the situation could hardly be more different. Philosophy of religion is flourishing and constitutes a respected part of the curriculum, not just in seminaries and religious colleges, but in all the leading secular universities. A formal Society of Christian Philosophers (begun in 1978) has many hundreds of members, and meets at major philosophical conventions. Its journal Faith and Philosophy is frequently cited as a top philosophical journal. There are prestigious and well funded research centers devoted to philosophy of religion, and the number students completing doctoral dissertations in the area has never been higher. Furthermore, the latest phase of this revival is notable for the extended intellectual exchanges it encourages been theologians and philosophers, and for dramatically revitalized philosophical interest in traditional theological doctrines such as Trinity, Incarnation, and Atonement. The deeply integrated character of these exchanges is reflected in the newly minted term 'analytical theology'.

What explains this remarkable reverse? There are some key figures, and books, that are easy to identify. In 1967 Alvin Plantinga's God and Other Minds was published in the United States. Informatively subtitled 'a study of the rational justification of belief in God', it drew compelling parallels between the philosophy of religion and topics that contemporary philosophy regarded as central. Twelve years later Richard Swinburne's courageously innovative book The Existence of God – applying probability theory to the traditional hypotheses of natural theology -- was published in Britain. Both books almost instantly generated a huge literature, and both philosophers can justly be hailed as having been instrumental in turning the philosophical discussion of religion to new and unexpectedly productive themes.

Introduction

Several years before either of these important publications emerged, however, John Hick's edited collection of essays – Faith and the Philosophers – appeared. Given the philosophical culture of the time, and what was to happen shortly after, it was an astonishingly prescient volume. Hick was at that time Stuart Professor of Philosophy at Princeton Theological Seminary. In that capacity he had contributed to the Seminary's 150th anniversary celebrations (in 1962) by organizing a conference that, unusually, brought philosophers and theologians into conversation. As well as straddling a division which had grown up between Princeton University philosophers and Princeton Seminary theologians, the list of conference participants included a number of figures then at a relatively early stage of their career. Most notable of these, perhaps, were William Alston, Norman Malcolm and Alasdair Macintyre, whose work, subsequently, would prove hugely influential in the revival of philosophy of religion. Notable too is the fact that the theology of Karl Barth, famous for his suspicion of natural theology, was given a level of philosophical attention that it was not to receive again for several decades.

The participants in the conference greatly outnumbered the papers subsequently published, but the volume also includes a record of some general discussion. This too shows it to be a remarkable forerunner of things to come. Hick's own concluding essay also has a prescient element because he identifies, and cautions against, a development in the subject – later known (not altogether accurately) as 'Wittgenteinian fideism' – which played a very large part in the philosophy of religion for the following three decades.

The republication of this volume almost 50 years on, constitutes a fine advertisement for Princeton Theological Seminary as it approaches its bi-centenary (in 2012). The book's re-appearance also provides a powerful reminder of the distinction that John Hick brought to the Stuart Chair of Philosophy. Founded in 1881 the Stuart Chair at the Seminary was first occupied by Francis Landey

Introduction

Patton, subsequently President of Princeton University, later by Emile Caillet, renowned as a scholar of Pascal, and later still by Diogenes Allen, also a scholar of Pascal and author of Philosophy for Understanding Theology, a textbook widely used in seminaries. with the publication of Faith and the Philosophers in 1964, Hick uniquely established a place for the Stuart Chair in the history of analytic philosophy of religion. Though the Chair has been vacant now for a number of years, philosophy continues to be taught at Princeton Seminary and Hick's achievement fifty years ago sets a challenging standard for philosophy at Princeton Theological Seminary to match in its 200th year.

Gordon Graham
Henry Luce III Professor of Philosophy and the Arts
Princeton Theological Seminary
October 2010

CONTENTS

Preface   i
Introduction   ii

I. RELIGIOUS EXPERIENCE AND ITS PROBLEMS

H. H. Price: FAITH AND BELIEF   3
Charles Hartshorne: IS GOD'S EXISTENCE A STATE OF AFFAIRS?   26

    DISCUSSION:
    H. H. Price: *Response to Hartshorne*   33

Virgil C. Aldrich: TINKLING SYMBOLS   38

    DISCUSSION:
    H. H. Price: *Response to Aldrich*   53
    Keith Gunderson: *Are there Criteria for 'Encountering God'?*   57
    Norris Clarke, S.J.: *Some Criteria Offered*   58

II. PSYCHOLOGICAL EXPLANATIONS OF RELIGIOUS BELIEF

William Alston: PSYCHOANALYTIC THEORY AND THEISTIC BELIEF   63
Norman Malcolm: IS IT A RELIGIOUS BELIEF THAT 'GOD EXISTS'?   103

    DISCUSSION:
    Alasdair MacIntyre: *Freudian and Christian Dogmas as Equally Unverifiable*   110

III. CAN ONE BE A BELIEVER TODAY?

Alasdair MacIntyre: IS UNDERSTANDING RELIGION COMPATIBLE WITH BELIEVING?   115
Norris Clarke, S.J.: IT IS COMPATIBLE!   134

    DISCUSSION:
    Norris Clarke, S.J.: *A Further Critique of MacIntyre's Thesis*   147
    Richard Brandt: *Critique of MacIntyre's Starting-Point*   150
    William Alston: *On Sharing Concepts*   154

Faith and the Philosophers

		PAGE
IV.	IRRATIONALISM IN THEOLOGY	
	Brand Blanshard: CRITICAL REFLECTIONS ON KARL BARTH	159
	Edward A. Dowey: 'BUT IS IT BARTH?'	201
	George S. Hendry: ON BARTH, THE PHILOSOPHER	210
	DISCUSSION:	
	Linwood Urban: *Barth's Epistemology*	218
	Malcolm Diamond: *The Pragmatic Validation of Religious Assertions*	222
	Alvin Plantinga: *The Sceptics' Strategy*	226
	C. C. Richardson: *The Sceptics' Myths*	228
	Kai Nielsen: *A Sceptic's Reply*	229
	Dennis O'Brien: *On the Limitations of Reason*	232

CHAIRMAN'S RETROSPECT
    John Hick: SCEPTICS AND BELIEVERS   235

THE CONTRIBUTORS   251

INDEX   255

I
RELIGIOUS EXPERIENCE
AND ITS PROBLEMS

FAITH AND BELIEF

BY

H. H. PRICE

It may happen to a person that he realizes, with surprise perhaps, that he cannot help believing in God. This realization may come upon him suddenly, or it may dawn on him gradually over a period of time. He may or may not be able to recall some particular experience from which this belief-state appears to have resulted. If he can recall such an experience, he will probably prefer not to talk about it except to intimate friends, or not even to them. But at any rate his present condition is that he cannot help believing in God. He would not wish to give up this belief, even if he thought it psychologically possible for him to do so. It is the most precious possession that he has, and far from wishing to give it up, he would wish anyone else to be in a similar condition.

All the same, if the person we are speaking of happens to be a philosopher, it may well seem to him that he is in a very painful dilemma. Surely he ought to have good reasons for this belief of his. But it is very difficult to think of any, and not very difficult to think of pretty strong-looking reasons against it, from the ancient ones which constitute the Problem of Evil to the modern contention that the basic propositions of theism are unfalsifiable and therefore void of content.

A clergyman, we think, ought to give up his job if he does not believe in God. It almost seems that a philosopher ought to give up his if he does. Philosophy, like other callings, has its characteristic duties. A philosopher has a duty to believe only those propositions which are favoured, on balance, by the evidence available to him. Perhaps indeed this is a duty of all rational beings. But at any rate it applies with a special stringency to philosophers. What is called wishful thinking, believing something merely because one wishes it to be true, is a weakness in anyone. But surely in a philosopher it is something worse than a weakness. It is a plain breach of professional duty. The situation is made no better when the state of affairs wished for would be good (not merely pleasant) if it actually existed; not even when this state of affairs, if it actually existed, would be the very best one which is conceivable.

One of the misfortunes of the theist is that the state of affairs which he believes to exist would indeed be the best one conceivable if it did exist. At any rate this is so if he believes not only that there is a Supreme Being who created the Universe, but also that the Supreme Being loves every single one of the persons he has created, and loves each of them for his or her own sake, with an unconditional love. This same version of theism also maintains that God invites each one of us to love him (invites, but does not compel, since love must be given freely). It maintains too that it is in our power to accept this invitation if we will, though it is equally in our power to reject it; and finally that loving him is our highest good. Indeed, this version of theism might almost be described as the metaphysics of love.

Now if there are any propositions which seem 'too good to be true', surely these do. It follows that a theist, and especially a theistic philosopher, is peculiarly vulnerable to the charge of wishful thinking. There might of course be other versions of theism. Indeed, there have been. The Supreme Being might be thought of as a God of Wrath, not as a God of Love. He might be thought of as an inflexible judge, like Rhadamanthus, who will exact the uttermost farthing from every one of us for all our offences. Again, it might be thought that so far from loving his human creatures, he treats them not as ends but as means, 'expendable' for the furtherance of some cosmic purpose. These other versions of theism cannot be accused of being 'too good to be true'. The persons who have accepted any of them are not open to the charge of wishful thinking, since what they believe is something which they and everyone else would wish to be false.

But those are not the versions of theism which I propose to discuss. I am only concerned with the type of theism whose central concept is the concept of love, the love of God for finite persons and the love of finite persons for God, since this is the only type of theistic religion with which I have any personal acquaintance. The more we consider its implications, the more astonishing it appears. For theism of this type is committed to maintaining that God loves sinners as much as saints, fools as much as wise men. More important still, we have to say that he loves those who do not love him as much as those who do. He loves atheists, agnostics and materialists as much as he loves theists — as much, in the sense that his love for each of us is without limit. His love is not only universal, but also unconditional. He loves all the persons he has created whatever they may do, whatever emotional attitudes they may have, whatever their beliefs may be; or rather he loves each of them individually, each for his own sake, as an end in himself. He is indeed *Deus Optimus Maximus*, best as well as greatest. For what could conceivably be better than universal and unconditional love?

Such a doctrine will always appear to outsiders 'too good to be true'. To be dismissed as unworthy of serious consideration, on the ground that he is a wishful thinker,[1] is an occupational risk of the theistic philosopher or theologian. The best we can expect of him, so his critics will say, is that he may be able to make his wishful thoughts a little more coherent and systematic than those of his less reflective co-religionists.

But a theistic philosopher is faced with other difficulties as well, and they too arise directly from the very nature of the religious attitude which he is trying to analyse and, if possible, to justify. The first is that there is something inappropriate, something almost blasphemous or impious, in talking *about* God at all. The proper thing is not to speak

[1] On wishful thinking see also p. 12 below.

about him, but to address him. The vocative case, not the nominative, is to be used. 'Thou' or 'You' is what we should say, not 'He', and it is what we do spontaneously say when we are inside the religious attitude itself. But unfortunately it is speaking 'about', not speaking 'to', which is the philosopher's task. *Faute de mieux*, we must fall back on the distinction between first-order and second-order speech. We can make statements about addressing, about the use of the vocative case and the mental attitude it expresses, without using that case to make them. We can discuss what it is to address someone without ourselves addressing anyone at the time, though hardly if we have never done so. The distinction between first-order and second-order speech may seem quite an easy one to make (once the possibility of making it has been pointed out to us). But in practice it is not so easy. At any rate, it is not easy at all in the very special case which concerns us now. In our attempt to talk about the attitude expressed in addressing God, we are no longer in the attitude we are trying to describe, and may well forget what it actually feels like to be in it.

There is another difficulty. It must be obvious to the reader from what has been said already. A theistic philosopher, if his theism is the type I am concerned with, cannot possibly avoid talking about love. The most characteristic expression of the theistic religious attitude is 'We love him because he first loved us'. The ancient Hindus distinguished three ways which we may follow in religion: the way of knowledge, the way of works, and the way of love or devotion (*Bhakti*). The theist chooses the third. The heart plays a central part in his religion, as it does in theistic ethics too. It follows that in a philosophical discussion of theism, love must be mentioned frequently, both God's love for us, and our capacity for loving him, and what happens when that capacity is actualized even in a small degree. But love is an embarrassing subject to all of us, and especially to a philosopher. A philosopher (at least in Anglo-Saxon countries) is not supposed to mention it, still less discuss it. This is something which is 'not done', as an old-fashioned Englishman might say. A philosopher must not wear his heart on his sleeve. Of course not. But he must not even consider what it is like to have one, or what it would be like to be without one. In this respect, a theistic philosopher is breaking the trade-union rules of his craft and must break them not once or twice, but continually. It is true that this particular trade-union rule has no inviolable sanctity. It has not been observed in all ages and in all societies, however strictly it is observed in our own, and certainly neither Socrates nor Plato felt bound by it. Still, no one likes doing what is 'not done' even when the very nature of his subject obliges him to do it.

Moreover, if we are to discuss religion at all we have to make an assumption which many will think questionable. We have to assume that each of us has an inner life, and lives through experiences which only he can describe at first-hand. Moreover, we have to assume that what goes on in the inner life is of great or even supreme importance to each of us, far more important than what we do or say overtly and publicly in the market-place. But it is commonly thought nowadays that there is no inner life at all, or that it makes no sense to say there is, or again (in practice a still more damaging criticism), that if there is an inner life what goes on in it is of no possible interest to anyone. Autobiographical reports, we are told, are just a bore, and nothing can be learned from them; they cannot throw light on any question which any rational man would think worth discussing. To this I can only answer that if there is no inner life, there is no religion either. Religion *is* a matter of the inner life. That is the seat or the locus of it, though overt and publicly observable results may follow afterwards. As a man thinks in his heart, so is he in his outward conduct. But indeed, if there were no inner life it seems to me that there would be no persons either. To have an inner life is part of what we mean by 'being a person'.

We may now return to the problem posed at the beginning. The philosopher I spoke of finds himself believing in God. He finds he cannot help it, though previously he could. What reasons, if any, could there be for holding this belief? Or rather, what reasons, if any, can he himself find for holding it? For it is not enough that there should in fact *be* good evidence for believing such and such a proposition. If a person is to believe reasonably, he must himself *have* good evidence. Some of it, or even all of it, might be the evidence of testimony (as it is, for instance, when the proposition believed is a historical one). But still the believer, if he is himself aware of this evidence, whatever type of evidence it is, must recognize for himself that it does support the proposition believed. If these are the prerequisites for reasonable believing, can the philosopher sincerely claim that his belief in God is reasonable? If he cannot, surely it is his duty to give up this belief of his, however reluctantly? It may seem to him (we have assumed it does) that he is now unable to prevent himself from holding this belief. But surely it is still his duty to try. You never know what you can do until you try. You may have to try rather hard in this case, since this particular belief is one which gives you so much joy and comfort. Well then, try your hardest. Take your courage in both hands, and sit firmly down again on the fence (you could manage it quite well before). It may not be a very comfortable position, but in this case, as in so many others, it is the only one appropriate to a rational being.

The painful dilemma of the philosopher is here represented as a conflict between duty and inclination. But it could also be represented as a conflict between two duties. For if someone does believe in God, he may well think he has a duty to God to continue believing in him, come what may, or at least to try to. And this duty, which he has (or sincerely thinks he has) as a religious person, may conflict with his duty as a philosopher to give up a belief which he can find no reason for holding, or at least to try his best to give it up.

But have we stated the problem correctly? Is there perhaps something inappropriate, out of place, in the suggestion that one should look for 'evidence' in favour of 'the theistic hypothesis'? If believing in God were just a case of believing *that*, of course the demand for evidence would be appropriate. But is it a case of believing *that*? Are we accepting a hypothesis when we believe in God, and has religion much to do with hypotheses at all?

The trouble is that the verb 'to believe' has two distinct functions. It corresponds both to the noun 'faith' and to the noun 'belief'. A man who has faith in God is called a believer, and a man who has none is called an unbeliever. But in the other sense of the word 'belief', the propositional sense as we might call it, there are no unbelievers. There is no human being who believes no propositions at all. But there are very many human beings who have no faith in God.

The philosopher said he found himself believing in God. But the attitude in which he found himself to be was one of faith, rather than believing 'that'. The difference between these two attitudes may be brought out in another way. A person might believe that God exists and that he loves every one of us. He might believe these propositions with complete conviction. Yet such a person might still be completely irreligious. He might have no faith in God at all. He might not love him at all, nor even try to, nor trust him at all, nor pray to him, nor adore him. His metaphysical outlook, one might say, is theistic. But from the religious, as opposed to the theoretical, point of view, such a person might as well be an atheist. Perhaps there is even a sense in which he *is* an atheist, despite the strength of his theistic convictions. Or shall we say that he is an 'anti-God' theist? This presumably is the position of the devils mentioned in St. James's Epistle: 'Thou believest that there is one God. Thou doest well. The devils also believe, and tremble.'[1]

A more common situation (at least it used to be) is that of the person called in Catholic countries a *pococurante* — 'one who cares little'. 'Oh, yes, of course there is a God and of course he loves every one of us, and no doubt he asks each one of us to love him. But what of it?' That is his attitude. *He* might as well be an agnostic, although metaphysically he is a convinced theist. At least, he has this in

---

[1] Chapter 2, verse 19.

common with the agnostic, that both of them are in an attitude of indifference, though in the agnostic it is a state of cognitive indifference (suspense of judgement) whereas in the *pococurante* it is an indifference of the heart or of the will.

It is not of course that the man who has faith disbelieves these theistic propositions, or doubts them. It is rather that he does *more* than believe them. He has, or he claims to have, some sort or degree of personal relationship with the Being about whom these propositions are asserted. Faith, I would suggest, is not a propositional attitude at all. It is more like an attitude of loving adherence to a person, or at least to a Being with whom one may have personal relations. It is as if (in the old feudal manner) one had given one's allegiance to someone and accepted him — voluntarily and gladly — as one's lord. It is like an act of homage, but a continuing one, repeated whenever your thoughts turn towards him. And when your thoughts do turn towards him, it is not as if you were thinking of someone absent and far away; as Blondel, in the mediaeval story, might have thought with devoted loyalty of his lord King Richard, far away in a prison somewhere in Austria. No, the lord to whom you have given your allegiance is not far away from any one of us. We can address him whenever we will, and when we do, it is not like talking to empty air on the off-chance that someone may hear. It is like speaking to someone in whose presence you are.

If this is what the attitude of faith is like, or what it feels like to be in it, does believing 'that' have much to do with it? Is it a propositional attitude at all? If you find yourself addressing someone and giving your allegiance to him, it is a little late in the day to ask the question 'Does he exist?' and look for evidence to support the hypothesis that he does. Such a question does not even occur to your mind. So if we use the word 'belief', we have to describe the man who has faith ('a believer') as one who believes *in* God, and distinguish between believing 'in' and believing 'that'. The term 'belief in' emphasizes the trust which is an essential part of the faith attitude. It does not sufficiently emphasize the love which is also an essential part of it. Still, it might be argued that one cannot trust someone unless one loves him at least a little. At any rate, it seems clear that 'faith without love' is a contradiction. Whereas 'believing *that* . . . without love' is no contradiction at all, even though the propositions believed are propositions about God.

Faith, then, is something very unlike belief 'that' and certainly not reducible to it nor definable in terms of it. Yet we should be going too far if we said that faith has no connection whatever with believing 'that'. Beliefs 'that' are usually the precursors of faith, or at any rate propositional attitudes are, as we shall see presently. Moreover, beliefs 'that' are among the results of it. Those who have faith in God believe that he will be gracious to them in future as he has been in the past, that he loves not only themselves but everyone else too, that therefore they should try to love others because he does, and that he will help them to do this if they ask him, and humbly acknowledge the lack of love which is their present condition. But if a person has faith in God, does he believe *that* God loves him, even though as a result of his faith he does believe that God loves others? Surely when a person is actually in the faith attitude, he would never say he believed that God loves him. It is rather that he *feels* God's love for him or feels the loving welcome he receives, like the Prodigal Son in the parable. It does not seem to be a matter of believing at all.

Again, even though we have actually been in the faith attitude sometimes, our faith may still be a very weak and vacillating one. (Hence it is proper to pray to God to make it firmer.) We may easily lapse out of the faith attitude even when we have occasionally been in it. In those periods of lapse — and they may be long — we have to fall back, as it were, on believing 'that', and even God's very existence may become a matter of believing 'that'. When we were actually in the faith attitude the question 'Does he exist?' did not even arise. We may remember that it did not, and how it seemed to us then that we were somehow in his presence. Or perhaps we do not remember this, because there is something in us which makes us wish to forget it. What Freud called 'active forgetting' plays a part in the lives of religious persons too, though Freud did not have them in mind when he first introduced this concept. Since it is theistic religion that we are considering, it is love which comes first, here as elsewhere. There is something in us (perhaps in everyone) which makes us wish to love God. But perhaps there is also something in us which makes us wish *not* to love him, nor to have anything to do with him, and even to wish that he did not exist. It is worth while to bear this possibility in mind when theism is described as 'wishful thinking'.[1] There may be some wishful thinking in atheism too, and in agnosticism. Denial or doubt, or even suspense of judgement, *can* be 'wishful', as much as affirmation.

But even though we do have some memory of what it felt like to be in the faith attitude, and do recall (vaguely at least) how it seemed to us then that we were somehow in God's presence and feeling the loving welcome which we received — even so, we may begin to wonder whether this experience really was what it seemed to be at the time when we had it. Then the best we can manage is to believe *that* he exists and *that* he loves us, and *that* he will give us his aid to return to the faith attitude, if we sincerely wish for his aid and ask him to give it.

In this case our evidence for our beliefs 'that' is our own rather hazy memory of what it was like to be actually in the faith attitude. It may be almost like the evidence of testimony, though not quite. It may be almost, though not quite, as if another person were telling us about an experience which *he* had had. To put it another way: a faith attitude which is weak and vacillating, so that we are in it sometimes and at other times lapse out of it, can be regarded as a symptom of a divided personality, or at least of some degree of dissociation. There are some grounds for regarding it so, if conflicting wishes have something to do with this

---

[1] *Cf.* pp. 4-5 above.

vacillation, as I have suggested they have. They are what one might call 'deep' wishes to. Both the wish to love God and the wish to have nothing to do with him are wishes which are close, as it were, to the centre of our personalities.

The beliefs 'that' which we have just been considering come *after* the faith attitude, whether as consequence of it or as substitutes for it when it has temporarily or permanently lapsed. But there are also beliefs 'that' which precede it and play an important part (normally at least) in bringing it into existence; and other propositional attitudes play an important part in this process too.

In religious literature there is a familiar distinction between 'seeking' God and 'finding' him. 'Seek and ye shall find.' 'Knock and it shall be opened unto you.' There are indeed some who find him without having to seek him, or at least without any conscious seeking. The door is opened though they never knocked. God gives his grace to whom he will, and sometimes he gives it to those who do not ask for it. But ordinarily we do not find him unless we seek him, and we may have to seek for a long time.

No doubt this seeking may take many different forms, and so may the finding which is sometimes the result of it. Perhaps no two persons seek for God in exactly the same way, nor find him in exactly the same way if they do find him. A man's religion is the most personal thing about him, and the most 'inward', if it makes sense to speak of degrees of inwardness.

Nevertheless, we can say, I think, that at least in our age and our society, the seeking for God most commonly begins with the acceptance of human testimony, the testimony of religious people; or if not with the acceptance of it, at any rate with the inclination to be interested in it and take it seriously. How does one come to have such an inclination at all? Most usually because of some personal contact one has had with religious people. In that case, a personal relationship, not necessarily a very intimate one, is what sets the whole process going, and another personal relationship — for that is what faith in God is — will be the eventual result if our 'seeking' is successful. There is a certain human quality which one can recognize sometimes when one meets with it. We call it 'spirituality' for want of a better name. It is both attractive and puzzling, and sometimes it can be awe-inspiring as well. Certain moral qualities enter into it, especially charity, but perhaps the most impressive feature of it is a certain inward peace or serenity. Spirituality is not at all the same as religiosity, nor can it be said that everyone who asserts the basic propositions of theism is a 'spiritual' person in this sense. But some of those who assert them do possess this strange, impressive and attractive human quality.

The respect which we cannot help having for these persons may well alter our attitude to the theistic propositions themselves. Of course, these propositions have long been familiar to us. But now we begin to take them seriously, and to consider it possible that there may be 'something in them' after all, since people of this kind assert them. It seems that they claim to have some grounds for their assertions. What could these grounds possibly be? Apparently, when a person of this spiritual sort asserts them he does so because he has 'faith in' the Being about whom they are asserted. According to his own account of the matter, these beliefs 'that' which his assertions express are somehow supported by a personal relationship he has or claims to have with God, a relationship of personal devotion, love, reverence and loyalty. Apparently, when he makes these strange metaphysical assertions, which in themselves seem incredible or even perhaps devoid of any clear meaning, he makes them because of some personal relationship which he has himself experienced in his own inner life. If we ask him what kind of an experience this is, he may well reply that he cannot describe it in literal language, and that only a person who has 'lived through' it himself at first-hand can know what it is like. But he will add, 'You can have this experience yourself if you sincerely wish to have it. Every human being is capable of having it. Seek for God yourself, and you will find him. It is true that you could not hope to find him by your own efforts alone. But though you cannot yet believe it, he loves each one of us, and if you sincerely seek for him, he will himself help you to find him.'

But how does one look for him? As has been said already, there may well be many different ways of doing so, and perhaps no two seekers seek in quite the same way. But still, there are certain practices which are recommended in religious literature, and we may try them for ourselves, even though each person tries in his own way. The word 'practices' must be understood literally. What is traditionally called 'seeking for God' is something that we *do*, and may have to continue doing for a long time. But further, and even more important, this doing is an inward doing. The sphere of operations is the seeker's own inner life. It is essential to insist that there is such a thing as 'inward doing'. It is something quite familiar to each one of us. We engage in such inward doing whenever we voluntarily direct our own private thoughts to one subject rather than another. The direction of our thoughts is to some extent under our own voluntary control. And despite what some philosophers have said, it is not wholly out of our power to control our emotions and wishes. We cannot do much to control them just by a voluntary effort here and now. But in the long run we can do something, because our emotions and wishes have objects (e.g. what we are afraid *of*, what we wish *for*) and thereby they have a thought-factor built into them, so to speak. For example, it is possible to try to forgive someone. We set about it by directing our attention voluntarily to certain propositions: for instance, to the proposition that it may have been our own fault as much as his; that the harm he did us was not after all so very great, that even if it was quite considerable we ourselves have often done quite as much harm to others, and very likely with less excuse. No one would say that this procedure is an easy one to follow. But we can try it all the same, and quite often it does at least something to mitigate our resentful and unforgiving attitude.

'As a man thinketh, so is he.' That is what it comes to. The spiritual practices which seekers for God are recommended to use are applications of this maxim. And it is what a man thinks privately, in his own mind or heart, that matters most, not the thoughts which he expresses overtly to others. 'Enter into thy chamber and shut the door.'

The practices recommended are of at least two kinds. First, there are what may be called meditative practices. Here we voluntarily and privately fix our thoughts on the basic theistic propositions themselves. At this stage it is quite proper to describe these propositions as the contents of 'the theistic hypothesis'; for it *is* to us a hypothesis when we set out upon the activity of seeking. At this stage it is not necessary that we should believe it, still less that we should believe it with full conviction. If we do believe it, the only evidence we have for it at this stage is the evidence of testimony, the testimony of religious persons. But all that is required of us is the suspension of disbelief; or if any more is required, it amounts only to 'suspecting that' — the traditional name for the lowest possible degree of belief, the minimum departure from the purely neutral attitude of suspense of judgement. This does not come to more than would be expressed by saying 'possibly the theistic hypothesis is not altogether false' or 'possibly there is after all something in it'.

The important thing at this stage is not the degree of belief (if any) that we have. What matters is that we should be *interested* in these theistic propositions and willing to take them seriously. What we have to do is to entertain them attentively and repeatedly, to ruminate upon them or let our thoughts dwell upon them, and to consider what it would be like if they were true. We can do this not only at set times, but at odd moments too, when we are walking in the street or sitting in the train. We may assist ourselves by reading some of the parables by which these propositions are illustrated in the Scriptures. To illustrate the proposition 'God loves every one of us' we can ruminate upon the parable of the Prodigal Son, for example. If any words have power, surely the words of the Gospel parables do. Not indeed if they just go in at one ear and out at the other (as they may, through sheer familiarity); but if they are ruminated upon, and pictured as far as possible in mental imagery, they have power to change a man's whole life. What our thoughts dwell on matters more than what we believe in the believing 'that' sense. As has been suggested already, a person might believe all the basic propositions of theism with complete and unshakeable conviction without either seeking for God or finding him.

The process I have been trying to describe may remind the reader of Newman's distinction between 'real' and 'notional' assent. We are not discussing assent at present, but only entertaining. Nevertheless, Newman's distinction applies to entertaining also, as he himself makes clear. (His name for entertaining is 'the apprehension of a proposition'.) The meditative practices I have described are intended to produce a change in our manner of entertaining the basic propositions of theism. Previously we had entertained them in a merely notional manner. But gradually, as a result of these meditative practices, we come to entertain them in a 'real' manner; or if one likes to put it so, we come to 'realize' what their import is, not indeed completely (no human being could), but to a much greater degree than we did before.

But these meditative practices, however important they are, are not the only ones which are recommended to those who wish to 'seek for God'. There are also others, equally inward, which are of a more directly devotional kind; and they raise more difficulties both for the person who is trying to practise them and for the philosopher who is trying to understand what is going on. For here we are recommended to take up emotional and conative attitudes and not merely cognitive ones. There are such forms of speech as prayers, hymns of praise and pious ejaculations.[1] These are very typical expressions of the religious life, much more so than sentences in the indicative mood. We are now recommended not merely to listen to them, or read them, thoughtfully and attentively, but also to use them ourselves. We

---

[1] For example the one attributed to St. Francis: *Deus meus et omnia!*

are to try to pray to God, inwardly, in our own hearts. Try to thank him, inwardly, for the blessings you have received. Consider such words of praise and adoration as the first few lines of the *Te Deum*. *Te Deum laudamus, Te Dominum confitemur . . . pleni sunt caeli et terra maiestate gloriae tuae.* Try to say them yourself, not just as splendid poetry, but as if you really meant what you say.

How can we possibly carry out such instructions? Surely we could only say such things if we had faith in God already, and a pretty firm faith too? But at present we are no more than 'seekers' and are not even sure that any such Being exists at all. It might not be too difficult to utter such words outwardly, just joining in with the congregation in church in public prayers, thanksgivings and praises; though even so, our 'seeker', if he is a reflective person, might wonder what on earth it is that he is doing. But saying such things inwardly, in inner speech, in the privacy of our own hearts, is a much more difficult matter, if our attitude is only one of taking a hypothesis seriously and suspecting that there might possibly be some truth in it.

Nevertheless, it can, I think, be done. So far as overt action is concerned, it is quite possible to act on a hypothesis, to do voluntarily things we should have done if we believed or knew it to be true, and to continue pertinaciously doing them for quite a long period. Sometimes we have to act in this way in order to find out whether a hypothesis *is* true. It is surely a mistake to suppose, as some do, that resolute and pertinacious action is only possible when we are already in a state of complete conviction. Human nature is not quite so weak as all that.

Now this applies to inward doing too. The inward use of these devotional expressions is a kind of inward 'acting as if'. When a man is seeking for God he can act (inwardly) as he thinks a person would who had found him. To put it another way, he can try, voluntarily, to 'assume the role' of such a person, to put himself into such a person's shoes and speak (inwardly) as such a person would speak. He is doing something like what an actor does — the kind of actor who not only says the lines which are assigned to

Hamlet in the play, but tries to feel as Hamlet may be supposed to have felt, or to 'identify' himself with the part that he is playing. It would seem that we all have this capacity for voluntarily 'assuming a role', and it could be argued, I think, that it is a more important capacity than we suppose. It enables one to experiment, as it were, with the possibility of being quite a different sort of person. The reading of imaginative literature has a rather similar function, and these devotional practices we are discussing could be regarded as imaginative exercises. One is trying to imagine what it would be like to be someone for whom the Lord's Prayer or the lines I quoted from the *Te Deum* are 'natural' things to say, the spontaneous and unforced expression of one's own emotional and conative attitudes. Such exercises are probably difficult for must of us. That is not a reason for refusing to try them. But we are not likely to have much success in them unless we have undertaken the meditative practices first, and so made ourselves able to entertain the basic theistic propositions in a 'real' and not merely 'notional' manner. In the devotional practices we have to act (inwardly) 'as if' there was a God who loves us all, and we can hardly do so unless we have ruminated for a considerable time on this proposition, and also perhaps on parables designed to illustrate it and 'bring home to us' what its import is.

So far, while we are only seeking, it is proper to speak of the theistic hypothesis and to ask what evidence we have for it. If I am right, the only evidence we have for it at this stage is the evidence of testimony. Whatever weight we give to this testimony and whatever personal respect we have for one or two of those who offer it, such evidence is nothing like conclusive. Perhaps we may think that if the theistic hypothesis were true, the evidence for it *ought* to have been conclusive. There is a story about a celebrated philosopher who was the guest of honour at a dinner of a society of agnostics. One of them asked him, 'What would you say if God himself suddenly appeared among us in this room?' The philosopher replied: 'God,' I should say, 'why did you make the evidence for your existence so inadequate?' This is indeed a problem which may trouble us. Perhaps the solution of it has something to do with the 'uncompellable' character of love. If the evidence had been conclusive and obvious to all, we should have been compelled to believe that God exists and perhaps also that he loves every one of us. But this would only be the settling of a theoretical question, no doubt a very important question, in the sense that the answers to many other theoretical questions depend on the answer given to this one. And what good would there be in settling this theoretical question, if one had no love at all for the Being whose existence was thus conclusively established? Perhaps God's will or plan was that we should love him; and love cannot be compelled, even if assent can. Love has to be given freely, if given at all. But if God must be sought for at the expense of considerable effort and trouble, and can only be found by those who wish to find him, they will love him when and if they do find him. We might even say that when of their own free will they undertook the search, and persisted in it in spite of disappointments, they were already being moved by a kind of incipient love for him. This perhaps is the interpretation of Pascal's paradox 'Thou couldst not seek me unless thou hadst already found me'.

The process of seeking may be long. There may be ups and downs in it. There may be times when it feels hopeless, when you do not seem to be making any progress at all and are tempted to give it up. There may be other times when you seem to be getting nearer, or even to have arrived just for a moment, and then you slip back again. It might also be said that the process of seeking never ends. To use a human analogy: suppose you have heard of some very wonderful person and want to meet him. You now have what you wished for; but once you have it, you wish for more. You do not have to seek for *him* any longer, but you still seek for something — to be as well acquainted with him as he will allow you to be.

So much for 'seeking'. But what of 'finding'? The 'finding', I suggest, is just the establishment of the personal relationship of faith *in* God. This, as has been said already, is not a propositional attitude at all. In the 'seeking' stage we were concerned with propositions all the time. We did not necessarily have to believe them, but our minds were continually occupied with them. In the meditational practices we tried to 'realize' the import of these propositions; in the devotional practices we tried to act (inwardly) as if they were true. These propositions purported to describe someone. We were by no means sure that there was any entity to which these descriptions applied. But now we begin to have experiences of being somehow in personal touch with One whom these descriptions fit. It is no longer a matter of speaking (inwardly) *as if* we were addressing him in a loving and reverent manner, or of voluntarily 'assuming the role' of one who does. Instead, we find ourselves actually addressing him (inwardly, in the privacy of our own minds and hearts) and now we use these devotional expressions spontaneously, without effort, just because it is the natural and appropriate thing to do. They are just the natural overflowing, as it were, of the attitude of personal devotion in which we now find ourselves to be — to our own surprise, perhaps. We use these expressions because that is how we feel towards Someone in whose presence we seem to be, Someone who seems to be giving us a loving welcome now that we are there.

Have we found him? Perhaps it might be more appropriate to say that he has found us. But even so, there is still some cognitive factor on our side. If he has found us, still, in some way or other, we are conscious that he has. The word 'encounter', which theologians sometimes use, has a similar implication. There is no encounter between A and B unless each of them is in some manner or degree *aware* of the other when they meet. If I encounter the Chief Constable in the lane, or he encounters me, it is not enough that he sees me or hears me say 'Good morning'. It is also necessary that I should see or hear *him*. Or if I am half-blind and three-quarters deaf (as this analogy would perhaps require) I must have some sort of visual or auditory perception of him, however dim and confused, or feel the touch of his hand if nothing else. And if the Chief Constable was looking for me and contrived the encounter himself, then certainly he has found me. But still in a sense I have found him too, even though he himself arranged that I should.

But if faith in God does have some cognitive factor in it, and yet is not a propositional attitude, what can this cognitive factor be? No epistemological question is more difficult to answer. But perhaps we may throw a little light on it if we are careful to put first things first. *In ordine analysandi* it is the new personal relationship which comes first, the relationship of loving and reverent devotion to God. The new awareness of him which we seem to have is just the cognitive aspect of this new personal relationship which we 'live through' or experience. If we try to pin it down and consider it in isolation, as a philosopher would naturally wish to do, I am not sure that we can. It does not exist in isolation, and perhaps it cannot. For if it could, we could be aware of God or be (consciously) in his presence without loving him at all, and surely this is impossible.

If we must try to find words to describe this cognitive aspect of a loving faith in God, it is very difficult to find any which will not claim too much. What we are discussing is only the religious experience of the ordinary religious person, not that of saints or of mystics. Saints and mystics must speak for themselves, and if we are wise we shall listen respectfully to what they say. But their experiences are not ours. In traditional language, their faith may come nearer to 'sight' than ours does. The better for them. But ours is not very like sight in any sense of that word, however stretched. True, it is not like believing 'that' either. But if this should lead us to claim that we know God by acquaintance or have come anywhere near to such a state, we should be claiming far too much. The claim to *know* the One and Only Lord of All is so enormous that one shudders at it. Perhaps it might just be allowable to use the word 'acquaintance' by itself, omitting the phrase 'knowledge by'. We might, perhaps, say that we have come to be acquainted with God — just a very, very little — whereas before, at the most, we had only believed propositions about him. But even this language seems to me somewhat presumptuous.

But indeed it is hard to find any word or phrase which will not seem presumptuous. Perhaps we might say that when we come to have faith in God we are 'with' him in a way we were not before. This might seem to be as unpresumptuous a phrase as we can find. The difficulty about it is that 'being with' is a symmetrical relation. If A is with B, it follows that B is with A. But we wish to say that God has been with us always, whereas we have not always been with him. While we were seeking him we were not as yet with him. Indeed, to be with him was the goal of our search. Still less were we with him before we had even begun to seek for him. But he is with each one of us all the time.

If we wish to use the word 'with', we shall have to say, I think, that the finding we are trying to describe is more like the removal of an illusion, the illusion of his absence, the illusion that he is 'far away', whereas in fact he has always been with us and we have always been with him. Or we might use the more interesting analogy of what is called a negative hallucination. Negative hallucinations, as well as positive ones, can be produced by hypnotic suggestion. Someone is sitting there on a chair just in front of you, but the hypnotist suggests to you that the man is not there, and the result is that you do not see him. To you the chair appears empty. In our case, however, the negative hallucination is self-induced, and the hypnotist's part is played by our own lack of love for someone who is with us always.

To put it another way, there is some cognitive capacity in all of us which is inhibited by our lack of love for someone who is its appropriate object; and the religious practices (the inward doings) recommended to us are designed to remove this inhibition. The procedure of 'seeking for God' now looks more like a therapeutic one and less like an investigation or exploration, and the word 'seek' no longer seems quite appropriate. It is a little strange to seek for someone who has been with you all the time.

Of course, it may well be that the experience of coming to have faith in God is not quite like any other (should we expect that it would be?) and the same might be said of the experiences which are the occurrent manifestations of the faith attitude when once it has been established. Perhaps we should content ourselves with parables or figurative expressions. 'Knock and it shall be opened unto you.' Well, something *can* happen for which 'it is opened' is an appropriate metaphor. Something can happen for which the return of the Prodigal Son to his home, and the welcome he receives, are appropriate metaphors. It is a matter of experience that it does happen. There is testimony that it does, and each of us can verify that testimony for himself, if he chooses to try. But he can choose not to. There is a door, but we are not compelled to knock at it. There is a way home, but we are not compelled to take it. That the possibility of 'knocking' or 'returning home' occurs to us at all may itself be the effect of God's grace. And once the possibility has occurred to us, any inclination we may have to actualize it may be the effect of his grace too. But though the possibility occurs to us, we can still refuse to do anything about it. And though the inclination to do something about it comes into our minds as well, we can still reject it.

I used the empiricist word 'verify' just now. And it is worth while to notice that the empiricist notion of 'try it and see for yourself' is by no means absent from religious literature. 'O taste and see how gracious the Lord is' is an example. A still more striking one can be found in a well-known hymn:

> O make but trial of his love,
> Experience will decide
> How blest are they, and only they
> Who in his truth confide.

'Experience will decide.' This is the voice of British empiricism. Nevertheless, the trial we are told to make is not just an experiment undertaken in a spirit of disinterested curiosity. If we are to make trial of God's love, we must do it by trying to *accept* his love, gladly and thankfully, instead of just benefiting from it passively as we have hitherto done. And if we do eventually come to 'confide in his truth' (i.e. his trustworthiness) it must be a loving confidence, analogous to the confidence we have in a human being whom we love, and not just the confidence we have in a well-supported proposition about a matter of fact.

If theism is the metaphysics of love, it is not very surprising that love should come first in the epistemology of faith as elsewhere. It might have been expected that such awareness of God as we have when we are in the attitude of faith would just be the cognitive aspect of our love for him, and that very little more can be said about it, except in metaphors and parables. And the ordinary religious person, one who is not a philosopher or a theologian, might well say, 'I do not very much mind whether it is a case of belief or knowledge or something different from either. All that matters is that one should try to love him who first loved us; and that is good enough for me.' Perhaps it is good enough for anyone.

IS GOD'S EXISTENCE A STATE OF AFFAIRS?

BY

CHARLES HARTSHORNE

UPON most of what Mr. Price says my only comment is a hearty 'Amen'! If I have any disagreement at all, it is with reference to some remarks on pages 4 and 5.

First, I do not think that such expressions as 'there is a Supreme Being who created the Universe, and [who] loves every single one of the persons he has created' describes a particular 'state of affairs'. To suppose it does is to treat the creator of the universe as himself but a certain universe, or a part or aspect of such a universe. It is to miss the very point of the concept, 'Creator of all things, visible and invisible'. I am wholly convinced that to make the existence of God contingent is an absurdity. Not only is he to be thought of as the One who has actually made the actual universe, but equally as the One who *could* have made any possible universe, his capacity to make it being what is meant by its possibility. The Ground of All Possibility is not to be treated as but the actualization of a certain possibility. The expression 'state of affairs' suggests just that. Properly used, it refers to the actualization of a possibility which might also have remained unactualized. That two and two make four is not a state of affairs; and neither is the eternal reality of deity. It is the Source of states of affairs, but not one of them.

If this is correct, if the existence of God is not a special state of reality, neither is it the best possible or most desirable of such states. It is the Principle which alone makes it possible for there to be a better and a worse, and so is not itself one of the better or worse things.

Religious Experience and its Problems

From the point just made, it follows that the conception of wishful thinking is out of place in respect to the theistic question. Wishful thinking consists in holding that a certain possibility is actualized, simply on the ground that its actualization is desirable. But the existence of God, to repeat, does not actualize a prior possibility. Back of God there is nothing, not even a possibly actualized and possibly unactualized potentiality. God as existing is a necessary feature of any actuality or inactuality whatever; or he is less even than a possibility — a bare absurdity or contradiction. Now there is something odd about the wish that a concept should be consistent, rather than an absurdity. If the concept is absurd, it could not have been otherwise; and if it is not absurd it could not have been so. So what scope for wishing is there here?

This seems the place to consider Mr. Price's reference to other and inferior forms of theism which, he suggests, are not, like the form he espouses, too good, but if anything too bad, to be true. I hold, rather, that these other forms are too vague, confused or lacking in internal coherence to be either true or false. I think there is an incompatibility between the idea of an eternal self-existence from which all other existence springs, and (for instance) the notion of a loveless employment of creatures for some cosmic purpose. As some of the deists said, the only purpose an ideally powerful and everlasting being could have is to love the creatures which are dependent upon him, and to enjoy the spectacle of their welfare. All else, I firmly believe, is either too unclear or too inconsistent to be capable even of definite falsity. So we need not 'wish' that the God of love, rather than some inferior God, might exist. Any inferior God would be derivative, at best a demon, and an addition, not an alternative, to God. Such a demon would indeed be a state of affairs, but like all such states it would have proceeded from the Source of states of affairs, and hence could not be exclusive of this source.

To prevent misunderstanding I must add that, in rejecting the statement that the existence of God is the best possible state of affairs, I am *not* denying that the idea of a

God of love is the supremely beautiful abstract idea. However, it is not one of the many beautiful ideas which may fail to correspond to reality, for this non-correspondence is possible only with ideas of contingent things. Since there are incompatible possibilities for contingent beauty, as every artist knows, whatever contingent beauty is actualized, all possible beauty could not be actualized. The beauty of a theory about the eternal or necessary principle of things is quite another matter. Any theory about *this* which is false could not possibly have been true; it must therefore be confused or absurd, and not merely false. Its lack of beauty is this very confusion. Here one may reason as follows: Of the three value-attitudes, favourable, unfavourable and neutral, only the first can be appropriate to what is necessary. The necessary cannot be correctly viewed as evil, ugly or bad, since the only justification for so viewing anything is that it be, or have once been, possible to prevent its occurrence or existence, and this by definition could not apply to the necessary. The awareness of evil being itself an evil, one requires some good to justify this awareness. The possibility of avoidance is the only justification, and it fails with the necessary. Nor can the necessary be viewed with mere indifference, for the act of taking note of a thing must, like every act, be motivated by some good. The utterly indifferent is what we fail to note at all; and when we do note it, absolute indifference has been replaced by some valuation, positive, negative or both. There remains as relevant the favourable valuation of the necessary. And we need no justification for noticing a necessary good or beauty, inasmuch as the awareness of a good or beautiful thing is itself a good. So, although we cannot value the necessary as something we would, if possible, bring into existence (since it is bound to exist whatever anyone does), we can, and all reasonable beings able to do so will, *enjoy* its existence as beautiful. And beautiful it must be, if it is to be knowable at all, since, as we have seen, a merely indifferent or an ugly object is here an absurdity. The argument then is: The necessary, being unpreventable, is not in any intelligible sense evil or ugly, and if it can be contemplated it cannot be simply neutral between beauty and ugliness; it remains that it must be entirely beautiful.

I infer from the foregoing that the supreme beauty of the metaphysics of love, compared to its metaphysical rivals, so far from raising a legitimate suspicion of wishful thinking, is rather evidence that it alone is the intelligible version of the metaphysical truth, while the others are pseudo-intelligible only. Here, and only here, beauty is indeed (inseparable from) truth and *vice versa*. If — which is doubtful — this is what Keats meant, then he was right, where many a philosopher has been wrong. Plato, I feel, was not far from the position I have just defended, in his vision of the Good as the supreme form whose reality is inherent in any intelligible reality whatever.

It is important to distinguish between the necessity of God's existence as universal loving creator, and the contingency of his reality as creator and lover of just the creatures which exist, such as ourselves. That God exists and loves all is, I have insisted, no particular state of affairs but a common truth about any and every possible such state; however, that we exist and that God has *us* as beloved creatures is indeed such a state. Thus God's actual concrete love for actual concrete creatures is precisely a state of affairs, and indeed the Supreme State of affairs. And obviously, it is a contingent fact if one of us enjoys an unusually low or high degree of awareness of the fact of our relationship to the divine love. Religion presupposes a necessary truth, the abstract reality of the God of perfect love; but it is concerned with this truth only as incarnate in a more concrete reality which is not necessary, the actual God now responding to actual creatures. Thus we may speak of the necessary 'existence' but contingent 'actuality', of the One Who is Worshipped. The positivist demand that the mere existence of God make a factual difference in experience is the unwitting demand that God be a created demon, and not the universal creator. But the demand that the acts or decisions of God make a difference (and be contingent) is legitimate. One should, however, understand that God is bound to exist, no matter what his decisions.

Faith and the Philosophers

With regard to the contingent actuality of deity, wishful thinking is not only possible, it is only too probable and pervasive. How do I and my motivations appear to the divine love? Here every kind of self-serving, self-indulgent or masochistic error is possible. For we are no longer, in raising this question, dealing with necessity. We are dealing with contingent possibilities, not all of which, and not necessarily the most desirable of which, are actualized.

I have one minor difficulty with Price. I suspect there is some ambiguity or unclarity in saying that God loves one person 'as much' as another.[1] Does this mean that he loves an insect — or indeed, an atom — as much as a man, and an imbecile as much as a rational man? Surely there is something misleading about such talk. What I should maintain is that God enters into the life of every creature, no matter how humble or distorted, as fully, with as perfect and sympathetic a comprehension, as he enters into the life of any other, however superior. In *this* sense he loves all equally. With human love it is very different. Not only do we value a man more than an insect, and some men more than others (and this I believe God also does), but we do not even bother about some creatures, including some men; no, we ignore or perversely misinterpret them. God neglects no creature and no aspect of any creature, and he never sees them in distorted perspective, or with mere indifference. If the insect wants to bite us and we want not to be bitten, God does not merely take sides for us or for the insect. To him both wishes have their reality and their aspect of validity. If either is satisfied, then God shares the sorrow of the frustrated creature as well as the joy of the satisfied one. In this way vicarious tragedy applies even to God. The life of Jesus symbolizes this truth. But I should not myself want to imply that God imputes as much value to one creature as to another. For this assertion I see no justification. And if God values men as he does not value insects, then he must also value proper men more than imbeciles. And where will you draw the line? I hope this is not a deep disagreement between Mr. Price and

[1] P. 5.

myself, for with nearly all else which he has to say I feel in intimate agreement.

As to whether or not we become 'acquainted' with the divine love, I should say, much as Price himself does, that God is always with us and we also always, in a sense, with him, and accordingly the difference between believer and unbeliever is one of levels of awareness. On some level God is always directly given. To be simply unaware of deity I hold to be impossible, even for the lower animals. They, however, are aware of him only in their non-rational animal way. They feel, but cannot think him, even in the rudimentary way in which they do think some of the things they feel. Men, however, can think as well as feel God, and they can feel him so vividly as to be also thinkingly conscious that they do this; but again, they can think so intensely, and at the same time so mistakenly, about what they feel, that they may think they do not feel God at all, on any level of awareness or with any degree, however slight, of intensity. Here I hold that they misjudge themselves. The necessary Principle of all existence cannot be simply absent, even from a single experience. To experience anything whatever is already, in some sense, to have God as *datum*. But a great deal is experienced which is not thought to be; with animals almost the whole of experience is thus unthinking, and with men, much that is experienced is not only unthought, it may even be thought to be absent from experience.

The theistic question is thus one of self-understanding. *Either* the believer *or* the unbeliever is mistaken as to what he experiences and genuinely thinks, as compared to what he thinks he experiences, or even thinks that he thinks. Error is here confusion, and only confusion, and ignorance is inadequate awareness of what is experienced.

I interpret Price as suggesting something rather like this in some of his remarks. I earnestly hope that our positions are not too far apart. For I admired and liked his paper very much.

The purport of my remarks is almost summed up in a reply of Bultmann's to the question, 'How does the God of religion differ from the God of the philosophers?' He said, approximately, 'The God of religion is my God, the God of the philosophers is anyone's and everyone's God'. The latter (I add) is God as barely existing, having and loving some creatures or others but no particular ones. This barely existing God is an abstraction from the actual one, who has particular creatures toward whom he feels a particular love. The divine existence is merely the common denominator of all possible divine actualities, correlative with possibility in general. It is therefore a grave error for theists to play the non-theist's game of asking, what difference does the bare existence of God make? or to talk as though the issue were between a Godless and Godfull world. It is the difference which the *acknowledgement* of God makes that is at stake. For while all must be 'creatures' if any are so, and not to be a creature must be inconceivable if God is conceivable, it is both conceivable and a fact that not all creatures are able to recognize their creaturely status.

The problem of faith is personal, it concerns not God but my God or your God. The impersonal aspect is merely a question of clarity and coherence. Not warm emotions but cold logic and intense intellectuality alone can ever resolve it. Here I am an ultra-rationalist. My position is that the non-theist lacks thoroughness and clarity in the intellectual framework of his position. His lack of faith, his inhibitions against adjusting his life consciously to God, may indeed lead to or partly motivate his failure to think things through. But the failure itself is just that. The fault is intellectual, whatever its ultimate causes. For a theist to grant intellectual parity to atheism is, so far as I can see, inconsistent. (I am here agreeing with many great men of the past, and with the Roman Catholic position, with which I am not generally very sympathetic.) The intellectual fault is more glaring if the atheistic position is taken (if God is treated as an unactualized possibility — just what he could not be) than if the position be positivistic (if the idea of God is held to be logically inadmissible). But that the idea of God is a mere confusion the theist cannot admit, and hence either he or the positivist must be confused. Of course he can admit that he could be mistaken. (And he freely grants that many ideas of God are logically inadmissible.) But the mistake, on whichever side it be, is intellectual, since it is a question of logic, in the broad sense. It is not essentially religious. The essential religious question is, what do I (and my friends and enemies) do about God, and what do I (we) suppose him to be doing about me (us)? Here we do need faith as well as reason. For this question is as concrete as life itself; and any response to it must be partly intuitive and pragmatic, if you will — existential. But God's existence cannot hang on this thread, either in itself or in our view, if our view is intellectually sound. If the idea of God is logically admissible, then the bare existence of God is not open to legitimate questioning; if the idea is not admissible, then the more concrete religious questions are also not admissible. Thus the intellectual question deserves an attention which our age is failing to give it. It is not the religious question; yet to suppose that there is a religious question is to presuppose an answer to the intellectual question. This answer non-theists will dispute. Thus we cannot forever shirk our responsibility to deal directly, and as honestly and carefully as we can, with the intellectual — or, if you will, the metaphysical — question. This question is precisely *not* existential; but until it is answered what the existentialists are trying to do cannot possibly be clear.

DISCUSSION

H. H. Price: Response to Hartshorne

I should like to begin by thanking Mr. Hartshorne for his kind words about my paper. I appreciate them very much, all the more so because I have never written anything on the Philosophy of Religion before, and feel much like the fool who rushes in where angels fear to tread.

I shall try to make some remarks about his comments and criticisms; and I hope, as he does, that the disagreement between us is not very serious.

Faith and the Philosophers

First, Mr. Hartshorne contends that the statement 'there exists a Supreme Being who created the universe and loves every single one of his creatures'[1] does not describe a particular state of affairs. To say that it does would be to treat the existence of God as contingent. 'The Ground of All Possibility', he says, 'is not to be treated as the actualization of a certain possibility'.[2] And it follows from this that I was wrong to introduce the notion of 'wishful thinking' at this point in my discussion, or to suggest, as I did, that the theistic metaphysics of love is very naturally rejected by tough-minded thinkers on the ground that it is 'too good to be true'. A wishful thinker is one who holds 'that a certain possibility is actualized simply on the ground that its actualization is desirable'. But since 'the existence of God does not actualize a prior possibility',[3] there is no scope here for wishful thinking.

Well, I must agree that the existence of a Supreme Being, the creator of all things, is not just one fact among others, and I am afraid I did speak as if it were. *Deus est ens a se*, and he has even been described as *Qui est* — 'He who is' — with the implication that he exists in a sense in which nothing else exists. A theist, I think, does have to accept those descriptions of him.

But I will try to explain how I was led to use these phrases, 'state of affairs', 'wishful thinking', 'too good to be true', to which Mr. Hartshorne objects. For it has also been said that *Deus noster est deus absconditus*, — 'our God is a hidden God'. In some hymn or other (by Faber, I think) I have even read the remarkable lines 'He hides himself in wondrous wise, as if there were no God'. The arguments of Antony Flew[4] could be read as a kind of anti-theistic sermon with those words as its text. But a theist could take those same words as a text for *his* sermon too. Just because our God is a hidden God (whatever it is that hides him) — just because of this, what we have to do is to seek for him. The situation of one who seeks for God was very much in my mind when I wrote my paper.

When we find him, or he finds us, we may conclude that he was very near us all the time, and what hid him was something in ourselves. But still, we do have to seek him first, or at least most of us have to. Now suppose we are wondering whether it is worth while to seek, or worth while to go on seeking if our search does not seem to be getting us anywhere. That is the time when the charge of 'wishful thinking' is likely to be most damaging, and surely it has led many a man to conclude that it is not worth while to seek at all.

[1] P. 4.   [2] P. 26.   [3] P. 27.
[4] *Cf.* 'Theology and Falsification', *New Essays in Philosophical Theology*, edited by Antony Flew and Alasdair MacIntyre.

Religious Experience and its Problems

What would Mr. Hartshorne say about this? How would he conceive the process of 'seeking'? Would he perhaps conceive of it as an activity of strenuous philosophical thinking, an effort to clear one's mind of misunderstandings and muddles, for example the muddle of supposing that the Supreme Being is a contingent entity? I think it might indeed take that form in some people. I have suggested myself that when the seeker 'finds', he may be inclined to say that the seeking was really the gradual removal of an illusion, the illusion of God's absence.

But was the illusion just a conceptual muddle? Surely emotional and conative factors also played an important part in it? Granting that there was some conceptual confusion in it, yet our wish not to admit the confusion was surely relevant as well. Hence I have suggested that when a theist is accused of wishful thinking, he can properly reply that atheists and agnostics are not free from wishful thinking either.

Now, of course, if Mr. Hartshorne is right, atheists and agnostics *cannot* wish that a Supreme Being should not exist. In his view the sentence 'A Supreme Being does not exist' is unintelligible or absurd, not even false, and it just makes no sense to say that someone wishes it to be true. Nevertheless, it does make sense to say that someone is in a state of intellectual confusion, and it also makes sense to say that he wishes to remain in this state and not to take steps to remove it. As Mr. Hartshorne remarks, there *is* something odd in the wish that a concept should not be consistent and should be an absurdity. But it is not so odd that a person should wish to remain in a state of confusion and be afraid of what he might have to admit if his confusion were removed.

But if all persons who are not in a state of intellectual confusion are bound to admit the *existence* of God (I think this is Mr. Hartshorne's thesis), are they also bound to admit that God loves every one of us? Mr. Hartshorne would answer 'Yes, they are'. But I am not quite clear what his reasons are. He does refer to an argument which some deists used in support of this crucially important proposition [1] but he does not state the argument fully.

If I am not mistaken, his view on this very important point differs from the one which many theists have held. They have often held that the existence of a Supreme Being can be proved by metaphysical arguments. But have they not also held, usually, that the existence of a *loving* Supreme Being, who loves every one of us, is something which could not be known, or even conjectured, without the evidence of testimony? Unless we have

[1] P. 29.

the testimony, it would never occur to us that the Supreme Being loves sinners like ourselves. Or if such a thought did occur to us, to try to enjoy it would be presumptuous indeed. The same could be said of the theistic doctrine that God invites us or asks us to love him. How could we dare even to try to love him, unless we first had the assurance that this is what he himself asks of us? This is why the Gospel is 'good news', εὐαγγέλιον. News is not something which is logically entailed by what is known already.

I turn now to a very interesting but rather difficult passage in Mr. Hartshorne's paper where he draws a distinction between 'the necessity of God's existence as universal loving creator' and 'the contingency of his reality as creator and lover of just the creatures which exist, such as ourselves'.[1] The existence of God, and of a loving God (he continues), is not a particular state of affairs, but God's actual concrete love for actual concrete creatures *is* precisely a state of affairs. I think that the distinction here drawn is equivalent to another one which Mr. Hartshorne draws later between the God of religion and the God of the philosophers. 'The God of religion is my God. The God of the philosophers is anyone's and everyone's God.'[2] This seems to be another version of Pascal's celebrated distinction between 'the God of Abraham, Isaac and Jacob' and 'the God of the philosophers and men of science'. The concept of 'my God' is also, I think, connected with the concept of 'the living God' which is found in some Biblical writers. The living God, I take it, is not just a self-existent necessary being, but the God who has created this particular world and loves those particular creatures he has created.

I do not intend to discuss the important distinction which is formulated in these various ways. I will only confess that I did not have it in mind, as I ought to have, when I wrote the passages which Mr. Hartshorne criticises in the first two or three pages of his paper. But I hope that Mr. Hartshorne himself, and others too, will have more to say about these two concepts of God and the relations between them. I should like to know just what this distinction between 'the God of religion' and 'the God of the philosophers' amounts to, and how far it will take us.

Finally, I should like to say a word or two about the contention that God loves one person as much as another.[3] I am afraid there was indeed some ambiguity or unclarity in my remarks on this subject, as Mr. Hartshorne points out.[4] I think we do have to say that God loves all his creatures, and I should

---

[1] P. 29.   [2] Hartshorne quoting Bultmann, p. 32, above.
[3] P. 5.   [4] P. 30.

like to express my admiration for the way Mr. Hartshorne has expounded and illustrated the implications of this universal and impartial love. (See especially the passage about the insect.[1])

I did not, however, wish to say that God loves an insect — still less an atom — as much as a man. 'You are of more value than many sparrows.' Why is this? Presumably because the sparrow, and *a fortiori* the atom, is not capable of loving God in return, whereas a person *is* capable of loving him. Hence persons, in the theistic world view, are bound to have a very special status. They are described as 'children' of God, creatures indeed, but creatures which have a very special relationship to their creator. We are even told that they are 'made in his image'. This cannot be said of sparrows or insects, and still less of atoms.

But perhaps I should not have said that God loves one person 'as much as' another, but rather that his love for each of them is without limit and unconditional; and if it is without limit, the notion of 'as much as' does not apply. I think that in the theistic view God loves each of us as an end in himself, each for his own sake, no matter who we are or what we are, wise or foolish, saints or sinners. The differences are on the recipient's side, not on the side of the giver. One person is more aware of God's love for him than another person is of God's love for *him*; we could say it is more manifest to some of the recipients than it is to others, but not that it is greater.

Are we to say then that God loves an imbecile in the same unlimited and unconditional way? Yes — if the imbecile is a person or is capable of becoming a person, either in this life or in another life hereafter. But is it in fact true that the imbecile is a person or is capable of becoming one? Perhaps we do not know the answer to the question. Perhaps we can sometimes have grounds for thinking that the answer is 'Yes' and sometimes for thinking that it is 'No', and sometimes we have to suspend judgement and can form no opinion at all. But so far as our own treatment of imbeciles is concerned, we had better err on the safe side, and treat them as ends in themselves, *as if* they were persons or capable of becoming so. It is indeed difficult for us to draw the line, as Mr. Hartshorne points out. But there may be a line all the same, though we cannot discern it. These surely are matters on which we are at present very ignorant. What I think we can safely say is this: that if any being is a person or capable of becoming one, God loves that being with an unlimited and unconditional love, in the same way as he loves each of ourselves.

[1] P. 30.

TINKLING SYMBOLS

BY

VIRGIL C. ALDRICH

May I say first that from my impression of Mr. Price's essay I confidently judge its author to be a man of rare religious sensitivity. His attitude is so right on this count that it makes me want to learn from him, all the more because in my youth I was made to practise religion much in the way that he describes and prescribes, though the affair was not taught to me as being as inward a thing as Mr. Price pictures. I devoutly hope that my reflections will not dislodge anyone from the genuine inner life which Mr. Price takes to be of the essence. I am quite sure that there is such inner experience, for occasionally my own life becomes both desperate and radiant with it. Such experience must be inward in some sense, because the people around me do not know when I am having it — unless I show it — and my trying to make sense of it to them is indeed an agonizing business. Then I tell them that right practices must precede right beliefs *and* the understanding of them. To suppose that such a principle is true only the other way around — that right beliefs must precede right practices — is a mistake. Especially in the religious case there is a reciprocity between right beliefs and right practices. They develop together in a way that makes the question, Which comes first? like this priority question applied to the chicken and the egg. On this particular count Mr. Price tends to give certain inner practices priority, of a dubious sort. And it is such mistakes in theory or in the theoretical formulation of what goes on in religion and what religion essentially is that bother me most in Mr. Price's account of the matter. I must object to some of these, after praising him for being right-hearted about religion.

Unfortunately, the best way to damn a man with faint praise is to tell him, after his *argument*, that his heart is in the right place, when the whole point was to be right-headed about the issue. I really don't want to damn Mr. Price at all, not even smoothly. But I fear that he is wrong on some theoretical counts. He *is* quite right-hearted but a bit-wrong-headed about religion.

Let me begin with a longish paragraph-condensation of the essay's main points, and then proceed to the critical assessment and constructive counter-suggestions. The essay begins by making the philosopher's job look quite like the scientist's, by asserting that a philosophy consists of a set of propositions whose truth stands objectively on evidence. Thus a theistic philosopher is hard put to it to prove the beliefs in a 'second order' conceptual or 'notional' language, beliefs which for the simple believer have a first-order sense expressed by participation and enactment and to which questions of objective evidence seem not so relevant. Such primitive language is vocative instead of descriptive, and it naturally features 'Thou' since it is not about God but addressed directly to him. Then the inwardness of such vocational practices of praying and worshipping is argued as the essence of being religious and of articulating it, thus distinguishing what the truly religious man does within himself from what he does externally as a communicant, doing what the congregation does in church, in a concerted action. The true meaning of such forms of worship lies within the human breast, the proper abode of the true love of God. The philosopher is an outsider to all this by profession and so it may look to him like wishful thinking, but if he is cagey he will notice that such wishful thinking is the starch also in a militant atheism. The question of objective evidence thus becomes acute from the philosophical standpoint. In the last analysis, the evidence of God's being is 'such awareness of God as we have when we are in the attitude of faith', since this awareness is 'the cognitive aspect of our love for him'. We are helped to such a right rapport with, or attitude toward, God by inwardly or imaginatively practising the things that would be appropriate were he to exist — or that *are* appropriate if he exists. Nothing more can be said about such grounds for believing and the referents of such beliefs, except in metaphors and parables.

Here ends the bird's-eye view of the conception the essay gives us. To say that it is simply wrong would be an immense mistake. It rings true at various points, with resonances that suffuse and save the composition as a whole. But there is a jarring note, with repercussions that are also pervasive. This is what I want to focus attention on in the short time and space left me. It has to do with Mr. Price's notion of the inner life that he is so concerned to protect against violation not only by irrelevant experiences on the outside but more especially by the dominant current conception of it which he thinks is wrong. He says that 'it is commonly thought nowadays that there is no inner life at all',[1] and that therefore 'autobiographical reports . . . are just a bore'.[2] Since he believes this, and since his main thesis is that 'religion *is* a matter of the inner life',[3] he is naturally concerned to say things that impress one with the reality of the inner life, without which there are no *persons* since, according to Mr. Price, to be a person means to have an inner life. If what is wrong in this connection were simply a misinterpretation by him of what philosophers under Wittgenstein's influence say about inwardness, I would not dwell on it. But Mr. Price's own conception of the inner life is a bit spoiled by his not having understood the current view he rejects, and this worries me. So I take a closer look now at the content of his own philosophy of the essential inwardness of being religious.

Mr. Price uses such key expressions as 'meditative practices',[4] 'spiritual practices',[5] and 'imaginative exercises',[6] stressing the notion of doing something or practising it 'inwardly'. In some places he tends to take as examples of these, things done privately or in secret, such as praying alone in a closet, instead of ostentatiously in public. Anyone can get the

[1] P. 7. [2] P. 7. [3] P. 7. [4] P. 16.
[5] P. 15. [6] P. 19.

sense of such a distinction and approve of it. Moreover, this notion of a private doing is quite intelligibly extended to two other common cases of privacy: praying and worshipping in public, say, in and with a congregation and *really meaning it*, not just going through the motions; this would involve something inner or private in a perfectly legitimate sense of the term, especially in contrast with the practice that is nothing but going through the motions. Then there is also the case of praying inwardly to God without any of the overt postures and words that one learned on one's knees at mother's knee. (Or, mothers being what they are nowadays, in Sunday school.) One can pray inwardly thus whether one is in one's closet or in church or in a Faculty meeting — though this last situation taxes the inner-praying capacities even of a truly religious person.

Now, none of these senses of 'inward practices' is ruled out by the current thinking about them in the dominant philosophy of language, sparked by the later and maturer Wittgenstein. Mr. Price would probably agree with this, since it seems that he has yet another notion of the inner life, and his complaint is that it is this notion that is being manhandled. This to him is a sad mistake because his notion is, he believes, closer to the essence of inwardness. He does not deny that there is some connection between true inwardness and external behaviour, but he feels that there is a behaviourist emphasis in the current account of the relation, an account that makes inwardness appear a more objective and observable affair than it essentially is. He thinks that this is to deny that 'there is any inner life at all'. This sets the stage for the closer examination of what he takes to be the true account.

It is hard to distinguish clearly Mr. Price's concept from the three others illustrated above because it is not so distinguished in his essay. So I approach the task with not much confidence. I will give you my impression of his picture of essential inwardness — it *is* a picture, I believe, not a concept — and I propose to do this by a teasing sort of logico-psychoanalysis of what inclines him to present such a picture.

A good way to approach the main reason for Mr. Price's introspectionist and subjectivist emphasis in the philosophy of religion is to press the question : what is it to 'really mean' something? and examine two sorts of answers that can be given, including Mr. Price's. He speaks of really meaning what you say when you utter the *Te Deum*, and makes it look as if this consists of 'inwardly' praising and adoring God while you use the external form of expression. This is an old and still viable way of answering the question. It is what I want now to examine, contrasting it afterwards with the new answer suggested — not exactly argued — by Wittgenstein and Austin.

Mr. Price's treatment of the issue gives the impression that the meanings of one's utterances are inside one in some sense, such that if a man is to mean what he says, he will take care that there are such things in him as he makes the utterance, and that a cultivating sort of introspective attention be given them. Else the utterance will be meaningless so far as the speaker is concerned, being merely an affair of going through the outward motions. In short, either these outward forms will stand for certain inner states or activities in the speaker (to which only he has direct access), or they will be meaningless since those inner elements are the meaning. And one finds out what the expressions mean, if anything, by introspecting what goes on in oneself in relation to the external expression. Moreover, what the expressions mean to another person, if anything, can be guessed only by analogy with one's own case. Thus in principle a man never quite *knows*, he only imagines, what the expression means to another, since he cannot introspect that meaning. Mr. Price does not stress this theoretical quandary in his account, but what he does explicitly say there makes a shambles of the notion that religious *community* of persons and its communal language is of *fundamental* importance. Rather, by his picture, a man is alone with himself — or perhaps alone with the Alone — in so far as he is an essentially religious person. Everything he does as such is done inwardly, in the inner life. Even the truly devotional 'attitude' is inner. Such relation as it may have to external forms of expression is itself an external relation, in the technical sense of the term.

I think that what induces Mr. Price to take this stand is the notion that, in principle, the whole inner life may be had or lived without benefit of the communal or public language of religion, the terms of which are, in course of time, incidentally appended to inner states that in principle could be what they are without the public language. Since these inner states are the meaning, and since the meaning is of the essence, the external forms of expression in the communal language have the secondary value only of establishing a precarious community of one mind with other minds. The implication is that such a language has the disadvantage of tempting people merely to *appear* religious by going through the motions of the public language whose very nature, as overt practice, is to be sounding brass and tinkling *symbols*. (I am speaking of the language, not of the hollow *men* using it for a pretence, who are the tinkling cymbals.)

Let me say again that Mr. Price's pronouncements in this vein ring a bell in all of us, and we get and accept the main idea. But still, the way he formulates it suggests that he is trying to save our knowledge and experience of God much as Bishop Berkeley tried to save our experience and knowledge of material things. The good Bishop did this by locating the essentials of stones and stars, as sensations, in the mind, where they can be introspected. Thus only the fool — meaning anyone under the spell of Cartesian dualism — will say in his heart and in his head, 'Maybe there are no material things'. Something like this foolish scepticism gets hold of the atheist, according to Mr. Price. The atheist looks outward for the evidence, and the evidence is wholly an affair of the inner life, where reside the very meanings of religious utterances. The key terms of the language of religion are based on what we are aware of in our inner life 'when we are in the (inward) attitude of (theistic) faith'. Thus, to 'really mean' what one says, using this language, is to be attentive to something inside oneself.

A subtle opposition has recently developed to such subjectivistic interpretations, mainly because of the artificial theoretical difficulties one gets into if one puts the matter that way. These difficulties do not bother the average person because he is not aware of theoretical implications. He construes 'inner' and 'inwardly' in the usual non-problematic way, with an unpremeditated art, when he comes across such statements as Mr. Price's. So they ring true. It is this usual non-problematic use of terms, especially the terms expressive of the inner life, that has been the main concern of Wittgenstein and of those under his influence. This is the other view that I wanted to examine, and to this I now turn, in the hope that Mr. Price will show more clearly just how he disagrees with it and how reasonable his disagreements are.

The point that is most commonly noticed about the new view is its concept of 'performative' meaning. Language is frequently used neither to express inner states nor to describe anything at all, inner or outer. In such cases, the act of uttering is identical with doing something that needs to be done. The saying is the doing, if the circumstances are right. And it is the sort of doing that is not feasible without the help of language in this performative use. The stock example is making a promise. One does not engage in an inner activity called promising and then, while introspecting it, report it in the words, 'I promise'. One simply says 'I promise' and this saying *is* the act of promising.[1] This sort of thing can be, and has been, said of the meaning of religious utterance. When you are chanting the *Te Deum*, you are not simply making a verbal report or show of the worshipping and adoring that is going on inside you. The chanting with these words is, in certain circumstances, the adoring and the worshipping.

But pointing just this much out about the meaning of what Mr. Price nicely calls the primary language of religion does not get us very far. It leaves unanswered the two questions that are at the heart of Mr. Price's concern. What is it for a man really to mean what he says in such utter-

---

[1] 'Illocutionary act', Austin and Alston.

ances; and, *what* is being worshipped and adored, or addressed in prayer? A man can, after all, simply go through the motions without really praying or worshipping, if he has not learned that language or if he is preoccupied with something else during the performance, or if he is expediently pretending. And he might just think or even believe that when he utters 'Thou', he is addressing something personal, while all the time he would be just imagining it if there is nothing of the sort. Then anyone using the language of religion, no matter how sincerely, would be engaged unwittingly in a kind of monologue.

We have examined Mr. Price's prescription for really meaning what one says in such cases. The activity or attitude in question must be inward to be real or genuine. In principle and in essence, it will be out of sight of, or hidden from all save the person thus engaged. Now what would the new philosophy of meaning say about really meaning what one says in a religious utterance? Let us take the case of the barren Hannah praying so hard in the temple for a child that Eli thought she was drunk. The high priest made this mistake because Hannah was praying intently in her heart and only her lips moved. (Still, if Eli hadn't been a hardened professional, he would have *seen* her praying in her mute performance.) This is as good a classical example of inward praying as I can think of, though Hannah was doing it in a place of public worship where it is usually done publicly in congregation with others, which is the sort of situation in which she had learned the prayerful use of the language of religion. But now she is praying alone and inwardly. And she is really meaning it, with a vengeance. Is this simply to say that it is inward, and what does one say when one says it is inward?

The answer of the new language philosophers is suggested by analogy with what Wittgenstein said about calculating. One learns first to calculate, and then — perhaps — to calculate 'in the head'. That is, 'calculating' in its primary sense is an affair of operating with pebbles, or abacus, or pencil and paper, or computer, and a man first learns 'really to calculate' with these as instruments. When he is calculating this way, he is really calculating but *not* calculating in his head. He is doing it in this primary sense *with* his head, if you like, along with the other instruments, but still this is not doing it *in* his head; as one walks with one's legs, but not in them.

Now, the difference between overt calculation and inner calculation is the difference between doing it *not* with the head alone on the one hand (overt), and with the head alone on the other (inner). But whether done outwardly or inwardly in this sense, it is calculating that is really being done; and — this is the crux — its being done inwardly, or with the head alone, does not make it any the more real or essential, though being able to do it this way is usually a sign of expertise in calculation. More important yet, it should be noticed that a man gets the sense of calculating first in the outward performance. If, afterwards, the terms of this external operation become strictly meaningless to him, such that he does not any longer understand what is going on in the outward performance; if this should happen, the alleged inner calculating would become a pretence. He would have to act as if he really meant it inwardly. This could take the form of unwitting self-deception or deliberate deception of others. Such histrionics commonly occur in cases where there is an obligation to understand and to do something, and where the ability to do this has waned or is simply lacking. In such situations one takes to imagining that one is performing the required action, perhaps with the false impression that one is inwardly really doing it or with the intention of making it appear that way to others.

Now there *is* something 'essentially inner' about practices which a man simply imagines he is engaged in. 'Simply imagining' here means picturing oneself going through the motions, without *really* performing the action, *not even inwardly*. Examples of this are the imaginings in day dreaming and night dreaming. Simply to imagine thus that calculating is going on is to picture some creature — it could be a chimpanzee — going through the motions with the usual instruments of calculation, without any real calculating going on anywhere. This holds precisely for one who is simply imagining *himself* to be calculating. He is not thereby calculating, not even inwardly; though he can be said to be doing something inwardly, namely, imagining that he is calculating. And he can do this without knowing how to calculate either outwardly or inwardly. To do this sort of thing outwardly — the imagining it — would be *pretending* to calculate, or to be putting on an act.[1]

It is time to apply all this, in conclusion, to Mr. Price's case. I fear that the way he puts it does not distinguish a real inward worshipping or adoring or praying from inwardly imagining these and the like religious performances. He is of course aware of some difference. He speaks of inner 'imaginative exercises' and inward 'meditative practices' that he takes to be a prelude to the real thing, not the real thing itself. But it is just this that worries me. The picture he gives is of one who, having lost the ability really to do these things or wanting to acquire it for the first time, will learn how to do them by *simply imagining* that he is doing them, in the inner recess of his being, as far away as possibly from the tinkling symbols employed in the outward performance, or at the greatest possible remove from all the public instruments of a worship service. This is to overlook how he learned really to be religiously active in the first place if he ever was as a child, or, if he wants to learn the language of religion later on, telling him to imagine himself using it is like telling him to learn to calculate by assiduously and repeatedly imagining that he is. It is like asking one who cannot use language in communication with others to practise communicating inwardly in an imaginative exercise 'as if' communication with others

---

[1] In these last few remarks on 'simply imagining' I have been agreeing with Mr. Malcolm, in his book *Dreaming*. Moreover, I am *not* agreeing with behaviourism in *any* of my remarks about the 'inner life', if behaviourism consists of propositions that *identify* such inward doings with movements of *any* parts of the agent's body. My suggestion is, rather, that the body and its parts are expressive of the mental activity and that this action, if 'really' engaged in, is more or less visible by another person as, say, the duck-aspect of the duck-rabbit picture is visible in the picture. Or, as the aspect 'animates' the picture *for perception*, so does what the agent is mentally doing animate his body-in-action or some part of it.

were really going on, without the help of the linguistic externals that in principle are dispensable anyway according to this view of the matter.

My point is that one's ability really to do something inwardly — not simply to imagine one is doing it — depends on being able really to use a language and really to mean it in forms of expression whose *significance* is never simply private, howsoever private some of the *experiences* are that being a language-user enables him to have. Thus there is no such thing as really meaning what you are doing in your inner life if for you there is no form of outward expression that occasionally is animated with the performatory meaning of the utterance. If there is for you no external symbol that, as a part of the language, ever becomes too full of meaning to tinkle, in an outer performance that you really mean, you will not be able to realize an inner life that rings true or where things are really done and meant. Thus the final prescription for such a realization, for one who is at a loss, is to come out of subjective imaginings into participating in forms of religious expression, in active communion with other communicants. Then, as the sense of what you are doing in the concerted enactment begins to dawn *via* the forms of the language of liturgy, you will know how to retire into the inner meditative practices to reinforce the meaning. Then, like Hannah, you will be able really to pray in your heart, and to mean it. Such are the practices in the framework of which religious belief takes shape and gets defined. Its further exposition and elaboration is in metaphor and parable, as Mr. Price has noticed. If this procedure fails to give one some sense of the language of religion in its primary use, then the inner 'imaginative exercises' also must fail, since one is not really doing at all what one simply imagines oneself to be doing; and so one does not learn how to do it that way.

So much for the concept of a person's taking action inwardly. There remains the other question, for which I have no space or time left here, of what it is that a man addresses when he gets thus engaged, be the performance inner or outer. This can be, and is, answered in the primary language itself of myth and parable, the cosmic symbols of which themselves have an etherealized or refined sort of performative meaning, grounded in the sense of the religious practices at base. They prescribe attitudes and things to be done, while *also* telling the sacred story of the beginning, the middle and the end of things.

But this would be to miss the sense of the question as philosophically asked, in what Mr. Price calls the 'notional' or conceptual language. Though he is much concerned to answer the question in this idiom, he devoted the bulk of his essay to an account of the inner life, as if this were the way to get as much evidence as possible for propositions about God's nature and existence, philosophically construed. I think this is a mistake. The answer to the question in the notional sense will be more clearly indicated when we know more than we do about the logic of pronouns. Mr. Price showed some feeling for this when he mentioned the 'vocative' language of religion whose key term is not a noun, not even the noun 'God', but the pronoun 'Thou'. Present-day philosophers of language have noticed what a tricky business it is to give a proper account of the use of 'I'. The logic of naming, reference, designation and description is at a loss here, as is the logic of emotives and imperatives, even performatives. This can be said for 'You' as well. And for 'Thou'. This logic of pronouns and its cautions against looking for what they 'stand for', either as subjects or objects, is perhaps what I should have explored in this essay. A sensitive understanding of this logic suggests a metaphysics not of pure being but of being-in-the-presence-of-something-personal, where the workaday distinctions between subjects and objects, minds and bodies, break down. This would also clear up the concept of evidence for statements in which 'You' and 'Thou' occur. But Mr. Price's emphasis on the inner life tempted me to concentrate on the concept of inward doings.

Still, lest the suggestion about pronouns, first and second person, be left quite empty, I want to conclude with a few more remarks about the core of my idea and what the development of it would be like.

In the first place, these words have a use or make sense only in the presence of something personal. I say 'something personal' instead of 'persons' because sometimes one addresses an animal or a flower or a house or a car in this dialogic way. In short, this I-you relation may supervene even where one is not addressing what is strictly called a person. But one will never engage in such dialogue except in cases where one experiences the addressee as 'something personal' or where this has 'something personal' about it, even though it is not a person. Moreover, any such nonperson that is being experienced and addressed in this personal way is felt to be not only a listener but also a potential speaker — something that possesses an unexercised capacity to respond in answers beginning with 'you'. You live, for example, in the presence of a blue mountain that looms up above you. Sometimes you say privately to it, 'I love you, and wish I had some of your immutability and strength'. It remains mute but, in that personal rapport, you are not mouthing words at a blank wall. And this is a condition of its being a potential speaker. It is in an answering relation to you, even if it does not answer. Or, put this phenomenon in a way that reminds one of what Spinoza said about God. You love and address the mountain. It does not respond with love and speech because it is not a person. But there is 'something personal' about it, appropriately to be spoken to and loved.

A philosopher might grant all this as a phenomenon, a kind of experience, but he would then wonder about its objectivity. Before I consider that question, let me draw attention to some other features of the logic of 'you'.

Notice that 'you are wonderful' is not equivalent to (1) your body is wonderful, (2) your mind is wonderful, (3) your person is wonderful, (4) your personality is wonderful, (5) you are a wonderful person. The first four of these expressions contain not 'you' but the possessive 'your' which makes them into remarks *about* something possessed to which the attention of both speaker and listener is directed; and this sets the stage for empirical considerations of and checks on the statements. In them, the key terms are nouns. But in 'you are wonderful', nouns are dispensed with and by-passed in favour of a personal pronoun as the key word. The expression then ceases to function in the 'aboutish' way and becomes a bedrock acknowledgement of the presence of something personal, not a statement about it. The conceptual distinction between possessor and what it possesses breaks down in the direct address by means of the personal pronoun without the noun. What you then say is such that an empirical procedure of confirmation becomes irrelevant. Yet, it is not just a venting of a feeling of approval, since the person addressed may agree or disagree with what you say thus, or a third person overhearing it might also do this. But this sort of agreement or disagreement would be resolved by the disputants getting into the bedrock rapport of the personal relation, in some cases of which it becomes a puzzling question whether 'I' and 'you' stand for distinguishable entities of any sort. For example, 'I love you'. What is the lover and what is the beloved? Tom Jones loving Helen Smith? Not only do the mystics reject such an interpretation — they do it in too wholesale a manner — but so does the sensitive phenomenologist (Buber, for example) who also sees the subject-object and subject-predicate distinctions dissolving away in such cases, without implying, however, the nihilistic monism of mysticism. Not that the first person and second person pronouns cease to have distinctive logical functions, but what these are becomes puzzling here, since they are not simply referential or simply emotive or simply imperative. Perhaps a commitment of some special sort is involved in such expressions, so a refinement on the concept of 'performative' might get us closer to the answer.

The long paragraph above considers only the first four of the five cases listed. What about the equivalence of 'you are wonderful' with 'you are a wonderful person'? The answer to this has already been indicated in view of such cases as that of, say, the blue mountain. When I say to the mountain, 'You are wonderful', I *mean* exactly what I say when I address the expression to Helen Smith, who is a person. But the mountain is not a person. I do not *mean* 'You are a wonderful person' when I say 'You are wonderful' to the mountain. So the two expressions are not equivalent. The use of 'you are wonderful' is appropriate, I have argued, as an acknowledgement of the presence of something personal, and this need not be a person, though perhaps it usually is.

Finally, about the 'objectivity' of the experience and why I have called it 'bedrock'. Having just argued that the subject-object distinction is *aufgehoben* in such cases, it would be silly for me to argue that the experience is simply objective. My whole point has been that there are bedrock experiences to which neither 'objective' nor 'subjective' can do justice, especially in view of what these terms have come to mean with the encroachment of the secular or scientific model that MacIntyre and Alston mention.[1] But why 'bedrock'? The considerations that influence me on this count are partly like Strawson's in his treatment of the concept of person as somehow back of, or presupposed by, 'mind' and 'body' and their distinction, though the bearing of this point on mine is devious; and partly like the age-old notion that any clear-cut distinction between the subjective and the objective is shown to be conditioned by a truly penetrating analysis of either one or the other, in the sense that such a distinction emerges and crystallizes only under special sets of controls. Even logical positivists, Schlick for example, have talked in this vein. So has William James. One may, and does, relax out from under these into the more personal rapport with things — *any* thing, — but *this* thought is not pressed by the positivists. A third consideration is that 'at first', in the chronological sense of 'primitive', this sort of bedrock experience of 'something personal' in things was less disrupted by the abstractive techniques which now set the stage for the various more sophisticated and distinctive ways of looking at things, under categories.

I suggest that Christian religious experience is this sort

---

[1] They might have made more of the evidence that at present the stranglehold of the scientific world-picture is being loosened, thanks mainly to a freer, saner or less partisan consciousness of the manifold functions of language.

of rapport with the world *as a whole*, and this is the experience of God. Then 'something personal' is prehended in the world in a diffuse and pervasive way, without the world itself or the something personal being experienced *as a person*. (Remember the blue mountain.) 'We worship Thee' would then *not simply* mean 'We worship Thy Person'. Taken absolutely or without qualifiers, the expression is addressed to Godhead, which is the something personal in things at large, not itself a person. (Neither can we accurately say that it is 'impersonal' in view of what this term connotes.) But we can say, as Christians do, 'We worship Thee in the Person of Jesus Christ'. Christ then would be the supreme Person symbolizing the 'something personal' in the world as a whole, which is God. To believe this is to be a monotheist and a Christian.

It is true, as Alston and MacIntyre suggest, that in our time of exclusive ways of secular looking and thinking, we can no longer 'relax' into such an experience. It is, rather, something now to be cultivated; an achievement. Yet, I suspect that we have the *experience* more often and more naturally than we *think*, precisely because our *thinking* is strait-jacketed by those empirical modes of thought that have taken on the force of dominant customs during the last three centuries. There is nothing in the fundamental nature of things that exclusively demands or sanctions this. We still have our moments of loving the scheme of things, or getting angry at it, even adoring or cursing it in the 'vocative' language that Mr. Price noticed without giving it the study that is so full of clues for the purpose of this symposium.

DISCUSSION

H. H. Price: *Response to Aldrich*

I hope that the disagreement between Mr. Aldrich and myself is much less than he supposes. Certainly there *is* some difference between us (I shall come to it at the end), but I think it is not a philosophical disagreement.

Faith and the Philosophers

I do not deny of course that there may *seem* to be a philosophical disagreement between Mr. Aldrich and myself; and if it is really there, it is undoubtedly an important one, because it concerns the philosophy of language and the analysis of the concept of meaning. But I do not want to hold the theory of meaning which he attributes to me in his paper,[1] and I hope I have not committed myself unwittingly to holding it.

The trouble arises from the dangerous phrase 'really mean', which is incautiously used in my paper. I spoke of really meaning what you say, when you say the first few lines of the *Te Deum* privately.[2] Now dangerous as this phrase is, I would point out that it is a perfectly good piece of ordinary language. Mr. Aldrich is willing to use it himself and even admits that 'praying and worshipping in public, . . . and *really meaning it*', does 'involve something "inner" or private in a perfectly legitimate sense of the term'.[3] And presumably the notion of 'really meaning' what you say is also applicable to inner speech, when the words are not overtly and publicly uttered. For I am sure he does not want to maintain that praying and worshipping *have* to be done in public, either in a logical or a psychological sense of 'have to'.

But still, perhaps I should have used another phrase instead of 'really mean'. Should I have said 'try to say it *ex animo*' or 'try to put your heart into saying it' or even just 'try to say it seriously'? These surely are things which we can try to do. And there is need for such trying. The trouble with religious language is that it has become too familiar. Sentences and phrases which one utters over and over again, or which one reads or hears read over and over again, do tend to become 'mere words', as we say. Of course, those words still have their rules of usage and their appointed role in the language game. *They* have not lost their meaning, but *we* may cease to use them meaningfully: or perhaps we have slipped into using them in a different sort of language game, a game of 'vain repetitions'. Or when we read them, or hear them read, we tend to take them as mere literature, which is all the easier to do because they are often beautiful. (There is a book on my shelves at home whose title has always shocked me deeply: *The Bible Designed to be Read as Literature*. I hasten to add that its contents do not correspond with the title.)

What shall we do when religious language loses its force for us in this kind of way? We must try to change ourselves, to alter our inward attitude. The fault is in us, not in religious language itself. We must try to take a fresh look at these reli-

[1] Pp. 42-3. [2] P. 18. [3] P. 41.

gious utterances so that they 'come alive' for us again. That is why the practice of meditation is recommended. If I may put it so, some of us (not all) have fallen into the way of using religious expressions in an uncashed manner, and then we must try to put the cash back into them or realize again what their cash value is. This is the point of Newman's distinction between 'notional' and 'real'. And this is the context in which I incautiously used the phrase 'really mean'. Perhaps I still have not succeeded in saying unambiguously what I was trying to say, but I do think it is something important which needs to be said.

Now none of this, so far as I can see, commits me to an 'inner life' theory of meaning. All I commit myself to is the rejection of a purely behaviouristic analysis of human personality (for I do think that if such an analysis were correct, there could be no religion at all). As a student of the philosophy of religion, I am content with any theory of meaning which allows me to say that there is an inner life and that there are private experiences, and to attach importance to them; and the theory of meaning which Mr. Aldrich holds does allow me to do this.

In his paper Mr. Aldrich offers the ingenious analogy of imagining that you are calculating.[1] But I do not think it applies at all to what I was trying to say. When you are saying the first few lines of the *Te Deum* privately, you do not just imagine that you are saying them. You do actually produce the words, though you do it in the form of inner speech. You do, if you like, imagine that you are a pious or devout person, which you are not, or not as yet, though you hope you are on the way to becoming one. As I put it in my paper, you voluntarily assume the role of such a person. You try to speak (inwardly) as if you were one, by putting your heart into what you say. But this does not at all imply that you are using or trying to use a private language or assigning a private sense to the words you use. You are certainly using a public language, Latin or English, which you learned from others. Moreover, it is still possible for some of the things you say privately to have a performatory character. '*Te Deum laudamus*' can still be a performatory sentence, in which one is not stating that one praises, but actually praising. Similarly if I say 'forgive us our trespasses', I am making a request or a petition, not stating that I make it; and this is still so if I say the words privately.

Mr. Aldrich could properly point out that *laudamus* is in the first person plural, that in the Lord's Prayer God is addressed as 'Our Father', and that we ask him to forgive *us our* trespasses. Well, when I use those words privately, in inner speech, I am

[1] Pp. 46-7.

joining myself in thought with 'the company of all faithful people', and I find nothing at all incongruous in doing so. Only it seems to me that if God is *our* Father in heaven and if *we* praise him and acknowledge him to be the Lord, this is because he is *my* Father in heaven, *my* God and *my* Lord, to each one of us. The truth is, I am suspicious of any theory which treats societies (religious or secular) as if they were entities; or if in some sense they are entities, they are not entities which think and feel. It seems to me that only an individual person can pray to God or praise him or love him, though of course individual persons can and should and do have personal relations with one another, and the 'warmer' these relations are, the better.

So much for the difference which Mr. Aldrich thinks there is between himself and me concerning the philosophy of language and the theory of meaning. I hope I have shown that it is more apparent than real, or at any rate much smaller than he supposes.

But there still is some difference between us, as I said at the beginning, a difference of a non-philosophical kind. It is concerned with what one might call religious or spiritual procedures. I tried to make allowances for differences of this kind in my paper, when I suggested that no two people seek for God in quite the same way and that there are some people who find him without having to seek at all.[1]

It has been said that there are many ways up the mountain, but they all meet at the top. I think that this is an apt analogy. In what I said about 'seeking' in my paper, I tried to describe just one of the ways. It might be described as the 'inward' way. This way suits some people, but not others. To seek for God, I go off into a cave, like a hermit, and there I sit and meditate all by myself, in the hope of altering my inner life so that the inhibitions and blind spots which prevent me from being aware of God may be removed. That is the method which happens to suit me. Mr. Aldrich does something very different. He goes to church and seeks God there. Both ways are perfectly legitimate, if they work; that is, if they do eventually result in the 'finding' which is the aim of both of us. And both these methods do seem to work, one for this person, the other for that one. It is a question of temperament.

Moreover, the difference between them is less sharp than it may look, for it is partly a question of 'timing' as well as of temperament. Before I went off to my cave I had sometimes been to church and joined in the service, and I shall go there again when I come back; and then perhaps I shall be able to

[1] P. 13.

join in the service *ex animo*, in a way I could not before. And Mr. Aldrich, after he has sought and found by his own very different method, a communal or socio-liturgical one, is willing to go off into a cave himself and meditate there and thinks it will then be profitable for him to do so. At least, that is what I infer from what he says near the end of his paper.[1]

DISCUSSION

Keith Gunderson: Are there Criteria for 'Encountering God'?

I would like to raise one or two points in connection with Mr. Price's paper. In general I'm wondering how far Mr. Price (and others) would wish to push the claim that the cognitive factor in someone's faith in God is not propositional but more of the order of some sort of awareness of, as Price says, a 'personal relationship' which we 'live through' or 'experience'.[2] I am not inclined to think that one can clarify or justify a belief in God by comparing it to ways in which we come to 'believe in' our friends — which we may all admit cannot be reduced, as it were, to *simply* believing that certain propositions are true. At least this comparison raises a number of difficulties of its own.[3] In virtually all of our personal relationships with other *people* there seem to be many sets of criteria one could resort to in order to justify our 'belief in' this or that person. For example, in Mr. Price's example of encountering the Chief Constable it is possible to imagine (as I'm sure Mr. Price would admit) that though we thought the subject encountered was the Chief Constable, it later turns out to be a robot carefully and cleverly constructed to deceive us. Similarly we might find out that though we thought so-and-so was a good friend, he wasn't a friend at all. Thus we would come to alter our beliefs about him *as well as* the sorts of belief we would have in him. But in these respects, so far as I am able to tell, there is no parallel in the case of belief in God. In other words, it's not at all clear that one could make available various sets of criteria for determining whether or not one has had or does have a well-grounded belief

[1] P. 48. [2] P. 14.
[3] As Ronald Hepburn has pointed out in his discussion of Divine Encounters in *Christianity and Paradox*.

in God. In short it seems obvious that we need some way of telling whether or not our belief in God is well-grounded, or whether we've been duped, self-deceived, and so on. But I do not think Mr. Price (or anyone else here) has been able to tell us what this 'way of telling' would be — though I am aware that Price's paper did not attempt to meet this point head-on. I am wondering if perhaps he has some further suggestions in connection with this?

Of course one might argue instead that the case of encountering God is only *like* a personal encounter with another person in such-and-such respects, and that it differs from it in others. In particular it might be argued that encounters with God wear their truth on their sleeve, as it were, are self-verifying, self-authenticating, or what you will. But this move, I believe, drags in a number of new problems. It is like stepping out of the swamp into the quicksand. For no one, so far as I know, has been able to make much sense out of 'self-authenticating' or 'self-verifying' experiences of God. But either one is left trying to make some sense out of the latter, or one has to tackle the problem of setting forth the criteria needed to distinguish 'true' experiences of the Divine from 'bogus' ones. I actually doubt whether either has been or could be done. But in that case nothing seems left to undergird theology but the traditional proofs. And they don't exactly inspire confidence.

DISCUSSION

Norris Clarke, S.J.: Some Criteria offered

Mr. Gunderson and others have made a strong — and to my mind justified — plea for a criterion of objectivity that can be applied to the inner experience of passing from seriously entertaining the hypothesis of God and praying to him as if he were there, to positively believing in him as a loving Presence actually there. I think we should try to meet this demand as fully as the subject matter allows, not just because we are philosophers but because we are reflective religious persons who take seriously the exigency of rationality as something that should pervade their whole lives. Hence I would like to indicate what seems to me a method of going a little further than the point where Mr. Price left us in his beautiful description of the inner experience of coming to believe in God.

Religious Experience and its Problems

The crucial point in his description was this: I find myself passing from the attitude of one reaching out for God and praying to him *as if* he were there to the conviction that I am engaged in loving discourse with a personal Presence *actually* there. In a word, the whole spiritual tonality of the experience has quietly undergone a change from that of hopeful seeking to interpersonal presence, though of a very veiled and mysterious kind. Now the question is, what kind of evidence can I find within this experience which gives it intellectual respectability, the sense of being objectively grounded and not merely arbitrarily projected.

It seems to me that the crucial new element is a certain awareness, elusive and intangible though it may be, that I am no longer experiencing merely my own *activity* of pondering and reaching out for God, but also a new strand of *passivity*, as though I am *being* acted upon, *being* stirred to my depths and changed, *being* awakened and drawn by some hidden Presence not out in front of me but somehow deep 'within', or just 'beyond', my own profoundest centre (the directional images can vary). The conviction grows upon me that such a profound stirring, awakening, bringing to light and drawing (sometimes even imperious summoning) of what I now recognize as my deepest, most authentic and most 'full' or total self cannot be merely the effect of my own efforts, but exhibits rather the character of a tidal pull on my soul from some greater force beyond. This is not an abstract deduction but a responsible intellectual (though not necessarily conceptual or self-consciously analytic) weighing or estimation of the quality of an experience and its implications. We find something analogous in the experience of becoming suddenly aware by some slight clue that someone else is with us in a dark room in which we first believed ourselves to be alone.

The criterion here is the difference in quality between the inner experience of acting and that of being acted upon. And the same criterion operates analogously, it seems to me, in all *experiences* of another — person or thing — as other, including the basic skill of discriminating between the inner representations of my own imagination, which I am aware of controlling from within, and those of the external senses, which I experience as beyond my control but controlling and determining me willy-nilly as long as I remain attentive to them. Under the light of this criterion I can become convinced that I have now sufficient reason for affirming that I have come to 'know', 'to be aware of', the presence of God in some meaningful sense, in an obscure but convincing interior way, not indeed as an object seen by vision out in front of me, or grasped by clear conceptual comprehension, but as a hidden 'magnet' revealing itself by its pull deep within me, so that I feel it would be a betrayal of my deepest self and my most authentic desires and needs to hold out beyond a certain point and refuse to yield to this gentle but powerful drawing that presents itself more and more clearly as an invitation to free personal response and commitment.

We could also frame a second kind of informal inference (Newman's terms) from the same experience by reflecting directly on the effects arising in us as we reverently and hopefully entertain the hypothesis of God. Since the effects (mentioned briefly above) are so profoundly beneficient on us, we judge it reasonable to infer that the object whose contemplation produces them cannot be a mere illusion, a pure mental construction spun entirely out of our own resources, with no real, existentially efficacious goodness behind it. Illusions do not nourish so richly, so powerfully, so deeply. The inference, of course, contains an experiential premise whose evidence is insuperably private: how good must 'very good, very beneficent' be in order to carry conviction that it must be real to be so good? Only the individual can put flesh on these formal bones and make them come alive, but he may well be able to do so quite decisively — and reasonably to him — from his privileged vantage point.

Another type of inference can also be drawn from the same experience. Seriously contemplating the possibility of God as real can operate as a profound uncovering, a revelation, of what we might call the ultimate dynamism of our authentic selves, and show that only in God could it receive adequate fruition. Thus my own meaningfulness becomes solidary with the reality of God. I can then reasonably choose to believe in God because I believe in my own intelligibility, that I am not a radical absurdity, a 'useless passion' on the face of the earth. If I make sense, and I believe I do, then God is.

II
PSYCHOLOGICAL EXPLANATIONS OF RELIGIOUS BELIEF

PSYCHOANALYTIC THEORY
AND THEISTIC BELIEF

BY

WILLIAM ALSTON

IN this paper I am going to attempt to determine just what bearing, if any, the existence of an adequate explanation of theistic religious belief exclusively in terms of factors within the natural world would have on the acceptability of such beliefs; more particularly I shall examine the claims to the effect that such explanations render theistic belief unacceptable. It would be possible to proceed immediately to a consideration of this problem with no more specification of the sort of explanation in question than what I have just given. I believe, however, that the discussion will be more likely to be firmly anchored and that there will be a greater chance of focusing the discussion on real issues if the treatment of the philosophical issues is prefaced by a fairly detailed presentation of an actual example of the sort of explanation I have in mind. Indeed there may be those who, in the absence of such documentation, would suppose that the chance of success for such explanatory ventures is so remote as to render consideration of my problem useless. But I should not like to justify my prolegomenon in this way, for I fear that there is nothing in developments to date which could be relied upon to remove such a doubt.

If a man accepts a given belief that is widely accepted he is not likely to feel a need to explain the fact that it is widely accepted. But if he does not accept it, especially if it seems to him to be plainly false, he may well come to wonder why so many people do accept it. From ancient times there have been many attempts on the part of religious sceptics to answer this sort of question. To the question, 'Why do people believe in the existence of supernatural personal beings?' some of the simpler answers which have been given are:

1. Man has a natural tendency to personify things in his environment.
2. Believing that the course of events is controlled by one or more personal beings which can, by suitable devices, be persuaded to direct it in a way favourable to man, serves to alleviate man's fear of the dangers in his environment.
3. These beliefs are a survival from the earliest human attempts to explain natural phenomena.

More elaborate attempts which have been made in the last 150 years include:

4. The Marxian theory that religion is one of the ideological reflections of the current state of economic interrelations in a society.
5. Durkheim's similar but more extensively developed theory that religious belief represents a projection into another realm of the actual structure of the society. This approach has recently been considerably elaborated by G. E. Swanson.[1]
6. The Freudian theory that belief in gods arises from projections which are designed to alleviate certain kinds of unconscious conflicts.

I have chosen the Freudian theory for detailed presentation for several reasons. First, it is the only theory which attempts to spell out in any detail the psychological mechanisms involved. Although Swanson in supporting the Durkheimian theory shows by statistical studies that there is a considerable correlation between certain features of the structure of a society and certain features of its theology, neither he nor any other protagonist of this point of view has, to my knowledge, done anything to indicate what psychological processes effect the transition between one's awareness of the structure of one's society and one's readiness to accept a certain theology. Second (though this point does not distinguish this theory from *all* the others), this theory is a live issue at present; there are men who are working to develop and extend it (though not, un-

[1] In *The Birth of the Gods*, University of Michigan Press, Ann Arbor, 1961.

fortunately, to test it) and so long as psychoanalytic theory continues to develop, this explanation of religious belief will have considerable growth-potential. Third, although it should be clear that no theory which proceeds in terms of one sort of factor can possibly be a complete explanation of religious belief, I am inclined to think, without really being able to support this, that Freudian theory is in possession of a larger segment of the complete explanation than any other.

I

A

To get the fundamentals of Freud's theory, we should look first at his great work, *Totem and Taboo*,[1] and I think it will be worth our while to retrace briefly the main stages of his investigation as he sets them out there. He began by considering the notion of taboo, which is very widely diffused in primitive societies. Certain things, persons, places, etc., are credited with a mysterious sort of sanctity or uncleanness (the two are not clearly distinguished) and from this character springs a strict prohibition against contact with them, except perhaps in very special circumstances. Freud noted some strong analogies between these taboos and certain compulsion neuroses, particularly those in which prohibitions are prominent. They are alike in the following striking features. (1) The prohibition has no rational explanation, or at least its violation will give rise to anxiety out of all proportion to the reasons against violating it. (2) The prohibition has to do chiefly with the act of touching and secondarily with other sorts of contact. (3) The prohibitions are readily displaced from their primary objects to others associated with them in some way. For example a person who has violated a taboo himself becomes a taboo, and a neurotic who finds it impossible to pronounce a certain name will also find it impossible to have any dealings with anything on a street which bears that name. (4) Violation can be expiated by carrying out certain stereotyped

[1] In *The Basic Writings of Sigmund Freud*, tr. A. A. Brill, The Modern Library, New York.

procedures such as repeated washings. Now the existence of these analogies gives us some hope of explaining taboos, for psychoanalysis, Freud thinks, has discovered the explanation for compulsion neuroses of these sorts. In early childhood the individual has a strong impulse to touch, look at, or otherwise come into contact with something, e.g., his mother or certain parts of her body. Some external authority (his father) prohibited him from doing so and backed the prohibition with strong sanctions. These threats plus the authority which the father's position gave him stopped the overt actions, but the desires were not destroyed — they were merely repressed, driven into the unconscious, from which they seek satisfaction in all sorts of disguised ways. The compulsion is a result of this psychic constellation of forces. The desire, blocked from its initial object, seeks substitute objects which are connected along various paths of association with the original object; but the prohibition, which has itself become unconscious as well, opposes each substitute in turn, the opposition now being manifested as a strange and inexplicable anxiety over the carrying out of the act. Thus both the tendency to touch the object and the fear of doing so are derived from sources which have been forgotten.

To give an analogous explanation of taboos we should have to show that at some earlier period of the race man had certain strong desires which were forcibly suppressed by external authority in such a way that both the desires and their suppression were forced into the unconscious, to emerge in the form of simultaneous desires for and fears of handling certain objects which are somehow associated with the original objects of desire. But where are we to find such phenomena? At this point totemism is brought into the picture. A totemic group is one which is bound together by a special regard for a certain species of animal or plant, the totem, which is regarded somehow as the original ancestor of the group and hence of one blood with it. If we make the assumption that totemism is the oldest form of religion and social organization, then we can take the fundamental totemic taboos as the basic ones, out of which all the others are derived by various associations. These are: not to kill the totem animal, and to avoid sexual intercourse with other members of one's totemic group. But even if we can somehow derive the other taboos from these, how does that help? These taboos themselves seem as inexplicable as can be. To what primordial trauma could they be related?

At this point two important clues present themselves. First the phenomenon of the totemic feast. In many totemic societies, the first taboo is cancelled on a solemn yearly occasion on which a member of the totemic species is killed and eaten in a rigorously prescribed way. The interesting thing is that this is both an occasion of mourning (for the slain totemic ancestory) and a joyful celebration. This clearly indicates that the ambivalence typical of the compulsion neurosis is present here; there are strong tendencies to both commit and abstain from committing (and hence regret committing) the tabooed act. The second clue comes once again from psychopathology, this time from the animal phobias of children. Freud's analysis of these, particularly his famous 'Analysis of a Phobia in a Five-Year-Old Boy',[1] where the boy was afraid to even look at horses, convinced him that in each case the animal feared was a symbolic substitute for the father. If we can take the totem animal as a father substitute, then the desires against which the fundamental totemic taboos are in fact directed are those which Oedipus realized — to slay one's father and sexually possess one's mother, — and we come within sight of the possibility of explaining totemism on the basis of the Oedipus complex, which, according to Freud, is at the root of all or most neuroses.

But we still need a racial analogue of the individual's infantile conflict with the father over his mother. At this crucial point in the argument I shall quote Freud's own summary of his position, in *Moses and Monotheism* and *Totem and Taboo*:

> The argument started from some remarks by Charles Darwin and embraced a suggestion of Atkinson's. It says that in primaeval times men lived in small hordes, each under the domination of a strong male. . . . The story is told in a very

[1] Sigmund Freud, *Collected Papers*, ed. Ernest Jones, Vol. III (London: Hogarth Press, 1956), pp. 149-242.

condensed way, as if what in reality took centuries to achieve, and during that long time was repeated innumerably, had happened only once. The strong male was the master and father of the whole horde: unlimited in his power, which he used brutally. All females were his property, the wives and daughters in his own horde as well as perhaps also those robbed from other hordes. The fate of the sons was a hard one; if they excited the father's jealousy they were killed or castrated or driven out. They were forced to live in small communities and to provide themselves with wives by robbing them from others. Then one or the other son might succeed in attaining a situation similar to that of the father in the original horde. . . . The next decisive step towards changing this first kind of 'social' organization lies in the following suggestion. The brothers who had been driven out and lived together in a community clubbed together, overcame the father and — according to the custom of those times — all partook of his body . . . we attribute to those primaeval people the same feelings and emotions that we have elucidated in the primitives in our own times, our children, by psychoanalytic research. That is to say: they not merely hated and feared their father, but also honoured him as an example to follow; in fact, each son wanted to place himself in his father's position. The cannibalistic act thus becomes comprehensible as an attempt to assure one's identification with the father by incorporating a part of him.[1]

After they [the brothers] had got rid of him, had satisfied their hatred and had put into effect their wish to identify themselves with him, the affection which had all this time been pushed under was bound to make itself felt. It did so in the form of remorse. . . . The dead father became stronger than the living one had been — for events took the course we so often see them follow in human affairs to this day. What had up to then been prevented by his actual existence was thenceforward prohibited by the sons themselves, in accordance with the psychological procedure so familiar to us in psycho-analyses under the name of 'deferred obedience'. They revoked their deed by forbidding the killing of the totem, the substitute for their father; and they renounced its fruits by resigning their claim to the women who had now been set free. They thus created out of their filial sense of guilt the two fundamental taboos of totemism, which for that very reason inevitably corresponds to the two repressed wishes of the Oedipus complex.[2]

[1] *Moses and Monotheism*, Hogarth Press, London, 1951, pp. 130-133.
[2] *Totem and Taboo*, translated by James Strachey (London: Routledge and Kegan Paul, 1950), p. 143.

Thus the dictates of the father return in a disguised form in the totemic taboos, and their strength is based not only on the original power of the father, but on the enhancement of the power of his memory, as a result of the guilt felt for his murder.

However ingenious all this may be as an explanation of totemism, what does it have to do with religion as we know it today? Well, Freud tries to use these same principles to explain the development of religion up through Christianity. The basic point is that the memory of the primaeval murder(s), together with the ambivalent tender and hostile impulses toward the father associated therewith, have been repressed, and that like all repressed material, it is constantly seeking expression; but in order that the repression be maintained, this expression must be more or less disguised. The first step in the development is the replacement of the totem animal with a person deity; in transitional stages, he still bears the countenance of the animal, or the animal may be his inseparable companion; he may sometimes transform himself into the animal, or he may have attained his status, according to the myth, by vanquishing the animal. To represent the father as a personal deity is obviously closer to the truth of the matter, closer to an actual reinstatement of the father, and Freud suggests that this development was abetted by the fact that in the course of time the bitterness against the father abated and his image became a more ideal one, especially since, as none of the brothers could attain to his power and status, that status came to be an unattainable ideal for them. But the hostility had not disappeared. Just as the totem animal was ritually killed and eaten once a year, so the practice of sacrificing divine kings, gods in human form, grew up in many forms. This side of the picture was also reflected mythically in widespread stories of the divine son who committed incest with the mother in defiance of the divine father, only first to be killed by an animal and then resurrected amid joy and celebration.

The primaeval father is most fully restored in all his grandeur in monotheism, the worship of the one and only father-deity whose power is unlimited. In *Moses and Monotheism* Freud explains the fact that it was the Jews who most decisively attained this stage as a people by supposing, with some off-beat heterodox Old Testament scholars, that Moses was an Egyptian who tried to impose monotheism on the Jews and was murdered by them for his pains. The murder of this godlike figure formed such a close parallel with the primaeval murder that the Jews were, so to say, sensitized for a more complete return of the repressed material, and so gradually came to accept the doctrines of their great leader. But this pure ethical monotheism is unstable; it tries to achieve a reconciliation with the father without taking into account the guilt of the sons, and as a result it cannot deal with the hostile tendencies and the guilt accruing therefrom; it offers them no expression. This deficiency is remedied in Christianity which takes as its starting-point man's original sin, and proclaims that the Son of God has suffered death to atone for that sin. (From Freud's standpoint, the attribution of innocence to the Son is part of the disguise.) But though the Son dies he rises again and henceforth occupies the centre of attention and worship so that the hostility to the father is triumphant after all.

Such is Freud's theory as we have it in his two major works on religion. There is no doubt that as historical explanation it is fantastic. There seems to be little basis for the assumption of the primaeval horde and its violent dissolution, other than its usefulness for a psychoanalytic explanation. And other features of the account have found as little acceptance among anthropologists and historians. For example, it is not generally thought nowadays that totemism is the earliest form of religion, or that every group passed through a stage of totemism. And practically no Old Testament scholars accept the thesis that Moses was murdered by the Israelites. An even more serious difficulty concerns the way Freud treats the race, or a society, like an individual man. By analogy with individual case-histories he supposes that cultural behaviour at a certain period of history can be viewed as a disguised manifestation of impulses and memories which had been repressed because of traumatic experiences in an early stage of the race or society. This presupposes that mental contents can persist in a

Psychological Explanations of Religious Belief

repressed form over many generations, indeed over many millenia, and can from time to time profoundly influence people's behaviour. Being repressed, they cannot have been transmitted from one generation to another by oral teaching or anything of that sort. Despite Freud's disclaimer of Jung's concept of the collective unconscious, it seems that he is committed to something like that.

But really these objections do not strike at the root of the matter. We can look on this prehistoric 'I was a Teen-Age Oedipus' story, and its unconscious sequels, as so much window-dressing to Freud's basic ideas. If we remember that, according to Freud, what the primaeval sons did is what every son wants to do but usually fails to carry out, and if we remember that, according to Freud, in the unconscious the wish is equivalent to the deed and gives rise to an equivalent guilt, we can see that the Oedipean conflict which each individual goes through in his childhood is for him an emotional equivalent of such a prehistoric deed persisting in the racial memory. Or to turn it around, we may look at Freud's narrative as a mythical exposition of the unconscious complex which every individual gets from his own early relations with his parents. By this revision we can consider Freud's theory in a form in which it can be taken more seriously as an account of the role played by individual development, rather than cultural evolution, in the formation of religious belief.

B

Unfortunately there is no canonical presentation of this more sober version of the Freudian theory. We shall have to rely on scattered and relatively undeveloped remarks in Freud, particularly in *The Future of an Illusion*,[1] supplemented with works by other psychoanalytic theorists, particularly T. Reik's *Dogma and Compulsion*[2] and *Ritual*,[3] J. C. Flugel's

---

[1] Tr. W. D. Robson Scott, Liverright, New York, 1949, *also* Hogarth Press, London, 1928.
[2] Tr. B. Miall, International Universities Press, New York, 1951, *also* Bailey Bros., London.
[3] Tr. D. Bryan, W. W. Norton, New York, 1931.

Faith and the Philosophers

Man, Morals, and Society,[1] and M. Ostow's and B. Scharfstein's *The Need to Believe*.[2]

Translating Freud's pseudo-historical narrative into an account of those factors in the development of the individual which render him susceptible to belief in a theistic God, we get something like this. In his early life a boy's relations to his parents typically develop in such a way as to present grave problems to him. (To keep things within manageable length we are restricting ourselves to the male believer. Perhaps the religious beliefs of females cannot be causally explained!) His parents, particularly his father, appear to him as almighty all-knowing beings, and as such they are regarded as mysterious and responded to with awe. The child is dependent on them in all sorts of ways and, of course, he normally develops a close attachment to them, feeling gratitude to them for their providential care and protection and vastly enjoying their company (a great deal of the time). But, of course, they also function as disciplinarians, restricting him in various ways and punishing him for transgressions, and so they are also regarded as stern judges and harsh taskmasters whose wrath is likely to be provoked at any moment, and this harshness naturally arouses resentment and hostility. (Of course there are wide variations between different sets of parents in these regards, but these differences may loom larger to the adult observer than to the child.) Thus we have a striking surface similarity between the standard attributes of the theistic God — omnipotence, omniscience, inscrutability, providential concern and the small child's view of his parents and feelings toward them — and between the standard ways of relating oneself to the theistic God — utter dependence, awe, fear of divine punishment, gratitude for divine mercy and protection. Of course this similarity in itself is no evidence for a causal connection; at best it furnishes a clue.

So far, there is nothing to provide a decisive distinction between the parents in these regards, although it is generally

---

[1] International Universities Press, New York, 1947, *also* Duckworth, London, 1955.
[2] International Universities Press, New York, 1954.

assumed that the father is usually regarded as the chief source both of frustration and protection. Freud's main reason for regarding the father as the chief model for God (still restricting ourselves to the male child) comes from the Oedipean situation, and this is the chief point at which the theory of individual development parallels the 'historical' account. As all the world knows, Freud supposes that the male child at around the age of four comes to desire the mother sexually and to regard the father as a rival. Depending more or less on actual indications, the child becomes so afraid of the father's hostility that he not only abandons his sexual aims but also represses the entire complex of desires, fears, etc. (Love for the father plays a role here too.) This complex remains, in greater or less intensity, in the unconscious, and it is because the theistic God provides an external figure on which to project this material that men have as much inclination as they do to believe in such a Being and to accept the attitudes and practices that go along with this belief.

This rough sketch of the theory leaves many questions unanswered. The most important of these is: Just what does 'projecting' this unconscious material do for the individual? To answer this question we must first get a fuller idea of the nature of the material and the conditions of its existence in the unconscious.

Normally the termination of the Oedipean situation leaves the individual with a number of conflicts, the exact nature of which are hidden from him because of the repression. There is the conflict between tendencies to rebel against the father and tendencies to submit to the father. And of course there is the conflict between the desires which his father opposed and the prohibitions against satisfying these desires; many of these prohibitions have now become internalized in the form of the 'super-ego'. Since these desires, fears, prohibitions, conceptions, etc., are excluded from consciousness, they are largely unavailable for further development and so retain their childlike form. But they also retain their strength; the desires press for some sort of satisfaction and the fears and prohibitions oppose this.

And the lack of satisfaction and the continual vacillation manifest themselves in various kinds of conscious distress.

The projection of the childhood father-image onto a supernatural being serves to alleviate, or at least reduce this distress in several ways. First, the mere fact of externalizing the problem is some relief in itself. Instead of mysterious discomfort with only vague intimations of its source, the individual has a clear-cut opposition between various desires of his own on the one hand and a forbidding external person on the other. At least he can understand the problem. Second, there is much less conflict because the balance has been tipped decisively in the direction of the prohibiting tendencies. (Perhaps the theory should hold that this decisive shift has to have already occurred in the unconscious before there is a very strong tendency to believe in the theistic God. See the detailed analysis from Freud below.) The external figure is so overpowering as to seriously weaken the rebellious tendencies, and on the other hand he is so idealized morally and credited with such perfect love as to render resentment and hostility much less appropriate. Third, as is suggested in our summary of Freud's historical account, the theology tends to be shaped in such a way as to give some vicarious satisfaction to the rebellious tendencies as well. Reik in *Dogma and Compulsion* carries out an elaborate analysis of the development of the Christian doctrine of the Trinity as a series of shifts in the balance of rebellious and submissive forces in the son-father conflict. And even if there are no female deities available there are feminine aspects of God, or perhaps the Virgin Mary, and in relation to these the individual may achieve some substitute satisfaction of the Oedipean desires.[1]

The Oedipean situation leaves a heavy deposit of guilt, as well as conflict, in the unconscious — guilt both for the continuing sexual desires for the mother and for the hostility against the father. Projection onto a supernatural deity can also serve to alleviate this guilt, for religion not only

---

[1] It is worth noting, however, that satisfaction of sexual desires in fantasy plays a very small role in Freud's account of religion, although, of course, it is primarily conflicts over sexual impulses that underlie the relationships to the father which he does take as crucial.

gets out into the open a figure, transgression against whom gave rise to the guilt and to whom reparations will have to be made, but also provides means for making the reparation and otherwise dissipating guilt — confession, penance, restrictions and renunciations of various kinds. Some Freudian writers, especially Ostow and Scharfstein, have placed the chief emphasis on this function of the religious projections in relieving guilt.

In *The Future of an Illusion*, a very chaotic work, the only clear suggestion made as to the psychological basis of theistic belief seems to be rather different from all the foregoing. There Freud speaks of the various dangers and frustrations of life, and says that the adult, in the face of these conditions, tends to regress to the infantile state in which he could rely on the love and protection of his almighty father. And since the adult can only carry this off by positing an invisible cosmic counterpart of the infantile image of the father he proceeds to do so.[1] Now in itself this suggestion differs from the old-age idea that belief in God is a wish-fulfilment only by invoking the well-attested mechanism of regression and calling attention to the fact that the infantile attitude toward the father provides an appropriate goal of regression. But it can also be viewed as a supplement to the Freudian theory as sketched above. In the concept of regression in the face of emotional difficulties it provides a possible way of answering questions as to the timing of conversion to or revivification of religious beliefs. The regression has three important features. First, it tends to reinstate various earlier modes of feeling toward, thinking about, and relating to, persons and things. This is the point made in the passage from *The Future of an Illusion* alluded to earlier in this paragraph. Second, it tends to strengthen the childhood desires, etc., already existing in the unconscious, thereby increasing the need for some sort of relief. Third, it lowers resistance to projection, since the further back we go in individual development the less sharp the distinction between oneself and the external world. All these factors are conducive to the sort of projection posited by the theory. We should also note

---

[1] *Op. cit.* pp. 41-42.

that the difficulties which set off regression can themselves be intimately connected with the relevant unconscious material; for example, anxiety over intimate involvement with a woman unconsciously identified with the mother can play this role.

To sum up, Freudian theory can be construed as regarding an individual's tendency to accept belief in a supernatural personal deity (of the sort envisaged in the Judæo-Christian tradition) as partly due to a tendency to project a childhood father-image existing in the unconscious, this projection normally following on a regression set off by emotional difficulties of one sort or another and serving to alleviate, at least in part, unconscious conflicts and unconscious guilt. It would seem that *contra* many psychoanalytic writers the conflicts and guilt so alleviated need not be restricted to the Oedipean situation. It does seem that only conflicts between the super-ego and forbidden tendencies could be alleviated by this method, rather than conflicts between different morally neutral tendencies; but this still leaves a very wide field. And it would seem that unconscious guilt arising from any source could be interpreted by the individual as due to transgressions against divine commands. Hence I do not believe that this theory of religious belief is necessarily tied to the thesis that the Oepidean situation has the absolutely central importance attributed to it by Freud; although if we are to hold that projection of an unconscious father-image underlies theistic religious belief we have to suppose that relations to the father are extremely important in the life of the young child and that in the course of these relations difficulties arise which result in considerable repression.

What reason is there to suppose that this theory is correct? There is no scientifically respectable evidence for it. Such evidence might conceivably be gathered. If we could develop reliable measures of such factors as degree of unconscious conflict, degree of unconscious guilt, strength of tendency to regress under difficulties and strength of tendency to project, we could then determine the extent to which these correlate with degree of belief in a theistic God, provided we had some reliable way of measuring the latter. But we are a long way from this. Meanwhile the only backing for the theory consists of speculative extensions to religious belief of mechanisms like regression and projection, the existence and (to some extent) the conditions of which have been established elsewhere. These extensions are supported by analogies between cases of religious belief and cases of neurosis in which the operation of these mechanisms is fairly well established.' The analogies are sometimes developed in great detail, as in Reik's analysis of the development of the doctrine of the Trinity, but no matter how elaborate, they remain suggestive rather than evidential. Nevertheless, the analogies and extrapolations seem to me impressive enough to make them worth taking seriously.

It may be in order to append to this rather abstract summary an actual example of an analysis by Freud of a particular case of coming to believe in God. Freud once received a letter from an American physician who had noted in a published interview with Freud a reference to the latter's lack of religious faith, and who communicated to Freud an account of his conversion experience. The account ran, in part, as follows: [1]

... One afternoon while I was passing through the dissecting-room my attention was attracted to a sweet-faced dear old woman who was being carried to a dissecting-table. This sweet-faced woman made such an impression on me that a thought flashed up in my mind, 'There is no God: if there were a God he would not have allowed this dear old woman to be brought into the dissecting-room.'

When I got home that afternoon the feeling I had had at the sight in the dissecting-room had determined me to discontinue going to church. The doctrines of Christianity had before this been the subject of doubts in my mind.

While I was meditating on this matter a voice spoke to my soul and said that 'I should consider the step I was about to take'. My spirit replied to this inner voice saying, 'If I knew of a certainty that Christianity was truth and the Bible was the Word of God, then I would accept it'.

In the course of the next few days God made it clear to my

[1] Sigmund Freud, *Collected Papers*, 'A Religious Experience', translated by J. Strachey (London: Hogarth Press, Vol. 5, 1950), pp. 243-246.

soul that the Bible was his Word, that the teachings about Jesus Christ were true, and that Jesus was our only hope. After such a clear revelation I accepted the Bible as God's word and Jesus Christ as my personal Saviour. Since then God has revealed himself to me by many infallible proofs.

I beg you as a brother physician to give thought to this most important matter, and I can assure you, if you look into this subject with an open mind, God will reveal the truth to your soul, the same as he did to me and to multitudes of others. . . .

Freud proceeded to subject this account to psychoanalytic interpretation, with the following results.

We may suppose, therefore, that this was the way in which things happened. The sight of a woman's dead body, naked or on the point of being stripped, reminded the young man of his mother. It roused in him a longing for his mother which sprang from his Oedipus complex, and this was immediately completed by a feeling of indignation against his father. His ideas of 'father' and 'God' had not yet become widely separated; so that his desire to destroy his father could become conscious as doubt in the existence of God and could seek to justify itself in the eyes of reason as indignation about the ill-treatment of a mother-object. It is of course typical for a child to regard what his father does to his mother in sexual intercourse as ill-treatment. The new impulse, which was displaced into the sphere of religion, was only a repetition of the Oedipus situation and consequently soon met with a similar fate. It succumbed to a powerful opposing current. During the actual conflict the level of displacement was not maintained: there is no mention of arguments in justification of God, nor are we told what the infallible signs were by which God proved his existence to the doubter. The conflict seems to have been unfolded in the form of an hallucinatory psychosis: inner voices were heard which uttered warnings against resistance to God. But the outcome of the struggle was displayed once again in the sphere of religion and it was of a kind pre-determined by the fate of the Oedipus complex: complete submission to the will of God the Father. The young man became a believer and accepted everything he had been taught since his childhood about God and Jesus Christ. He had had a religious experience and had undergone a conversion.

C

I have been presenting the psychoanalytic explanation as an example of an explanation of theistic belief in terms

Psychological Explanations of Religious Belief

of factors within the natural world. My central concern in this paper is to determine what bearing the adequacy of an explanation of this sort would have on the acceptability of theistic belief. But before settling down to this task, we must try to be clearer as to the defining features of the sort of theory in which we are interested and as to the extent to which the psychoanalytic explanation does or does not exemplify these features.

First, let me make more explicit what I mean by the adequacy of such an explanation. In saying of such an explanation ('causal' explanation, if you like, though I do not wish to import anything into 'causal' other than what is specified here) that it is adequate, I simply mean that it specifies conditions which are such that whenever those conditions are satisfied theistic belief exists in some specified relation to the conditions. It might be argued that in order to explain the occurrence of a belief we need something further, e.g. some intelligible relationship between the antecedent conditions and the belief. Thus it might be said that even if we found an absolutely unexceptionable correlation between theistic belief and level of blood sugar, so that on the basis of this we were convinced that wherever blood sugar is at a certain level theistic belief exists, that would not serve to *explain* such belief or to show that blood sugar *produces* such belief, for it is impossible to understand how there could be any connection between them. But if we did have a perfect correlation over a wide range of cases, then I would suppose that we should first look for intermediate factors which would bridge this conceptual gap, or, if persistent search should fail to uncover any, we should have to revise the basic principles in terms of which blood sugar level and theistic belief cannot be directly connected. This raises problems in the philosophy of science into which I cannot go.

One must recognize that Freudian theory, as it actually exists, is just not a theory of this sort. By this I do not mean that it has not been established as a theory of this sort, but that it is not put forward, and cannot plausibly be put forward, as a theory which specifies conditions sufficient to give rise to theistic belief. Remember that when I summed up the theory I presented it as claiming that an individual's *tendency* to accept belief in a supernatural deity is *partly* due to a tendency to project a childhood father-image. . . . It can aspire to explain only a *tendency* to accept the belief, rather than simply the belief, because the theory in the form in which we are considering it is dealing with a situation in which the individual finds the belief ready-made in his culture, rather than dealing with the problem of the cultural origin of the belief. Therefore the cultural configuration with which the individual is faced and the learning processes by which he assimilates this will have to form part of the explanation of the fact that a given individual acquires theistic belief. Psychoanalysis can aspire only to explain the differential readiness of different people to accept what is thus proffered. And I have said '*partly* due' because even with this restriction there are obviously many other factors which play a part in determining the degree of this readiness. Both from everyday observation and from various systematic investigations there is every reason to suppose that such things as intellectual capacity, temperamental factors such as a generalized enthusiasm or the reverse, the associations that he has formed with things religious, and the kinds of religious believers with whom he has been in personal contact, will affect an individual's readiness to accept certain beliefs with a given degree of assurance and a given sort of integration with other aspects of his personality. (Moreover, we should not lose sight of the possibility that theistic belief has very different psychological roots in different sorts of people and that psychoanalysis might give part of the explanation for some but not for all.) Given this obvious diversity in the determinants of theistic belief, if we try to inflate any of the current theoretical approaches into a theory which claims to provide a specification of sufficient conditions it becomes hopelessly implausible. And thus far no one has made any plausible suggestions as to how we might develop a theory which integrates all the relevant factors. Therefore, in the absence of any genuine actual example, I am going to take the psychoanalytic

Psychological Explanations of Religious Belief

explanation as one which might, with suitable supplementation, be developed into the sort of theory in which I am interested, and in referring to it as an example I shall be pretending such supplementation has actually been carried out.

There are various other questions which might be raised concerning the boundaries of the kind of theory in which we are interested. Just what are we to count as theistic belief? For example, does the sort of religious belief which Paul Tillich says he has count? More generally, to just what extent does a Supreme Being have to be conceived as a person in order for the belief to be classified as theistic? And are we considering simply the bare belief that there exists an omnipotent perfectly good personal Being, or are we also including other typical components of a theistic theology, such as the doctrines of creation and predestination, and certain sorts of beliefs concerning human nature and destiny? Again, will the theory try to account for variations in the strength and/or persistence of such beliefs in terms of variations in the factors, or will it be simply an explanation of presence-or-absence, defined by some cut-off point? There are many such issues which would have to be settled by someone setting out to refine and develop such theories, but for our purpose we can leave these alternatives open. We shall simply suppose that a theory has been established which defines theistic belief in a way which makes it possible to reliably determine when we have it and when we don't, and in a way which does not significantly jar with the established use of the term; and that the theory relates the existence and/or degrees of such belief to certain factors in the natural world.

There is one further restriction on the theories in which we are interested which must be made explicit. Let us suppose that there are one or more cogent arguments for the existence of God, and let us suppose that it can be shown that a grasp of one of these arguments, plus acceptance of the premises, is always sufficient to bring about theistic belief, unless certain specifiable and enumerable forms of irrationality are present. The fact that someone understands a certain argument and the fact that someone accepts certain propositions are surely facts within the natural world. Yet I suppose that no one would have the slightest inclination to say that the adequacy of this sort of explanation would have any tendency to show the belief to be unacceptable. I want to restrict my attention to possible explanations with respect to which there would be an inclination to say this. This restriction can be carried out by including a proviso that the theories specify conditions which do not include acquiring, considering or possessing good reasons for theistic belief. I shall put this by saying that these theories specify 'reason-irrelevant' conditions. This will still leave us with a wide range of examples, including the psychoanalytic theory.

II

We can now turn to the central question of this paper: Would the success of an explanation of religious belief in terms of natural factors have any tendency to show such belief to be unacceptable? We may as well begin by considering the most extreme claim which could be made on this matter, viz., that such explanations of religious beliefs as the Freudian show that these beliefs can no longer be considered serious candidates for acceptance. We can distinguish different versions of this view, depending on just what aspect of the explanation is supposed to give it this force. Presumably it will be either the general point that theistic belief is due to some reason-irrelevant natural causes[1] or others, or it will be the more specific point that it is due to the particular sort of natural causes specified in the psychoanalytic explanation. I shall consider each of these possibilities in turn.

A

Why should anyone suppose that the fact that there are casual factors within the world of nature which are responsible for theistic belief constitute any reason for rejecting the belief? One cannot appeal here to a general principle

[1] Henceforth when I use the phrase 'natural cause' or even simply 'cause' the appropriate qualifications are to be understood.

that any belief can be refuted by showing that it is due to natural causes. For if we accept causal determinism within the psychological sphere, and those whose positions are being considered presumably would, then such causal determinations could, in principle, be exhibited for any belief whatsoever. There would have to be something special about the belief in a theistic God which would render it specially liable to such refutation. Now there are undoubtedly some beliefs which could be refuted by showing them to be causally determined, e.g., the belief that no beliefs are causally determined (assuming that we can get around self-referential difficulties here). Similarly it might be supposed that theism has implications which are incompatible with a causal determination of theistic belief. For example, it might be claimed that it would not be in keeping with the character and/or purposes of a theistic God to allow belief or non-belief in his existence to be determined by any natural factors; that he would reserve such a sacred matter as this for his own direct jurisdiction.

I do not suppose that anyone would claim that such causal determination is *logically* incompatible with the existence of God. Surely there is nothing in the theistic notion of God which would make it impossible that God should set up the natural world in such a way that belief in his existence would be produced by certain natural mechanisms. The fact that such belief is especially important to him does nothing to establish any such conclusion. For there is no reason to doubt that he could so arrange things that the operation of such mechanisms would be such as to be in line with his purposes. Indeed there are many other things in the universe which are presumably very important to God's plans (indeed, what isn't?) which everyone admits to be causally determined, e.g. the revolution of the earth around the sun and the biological processes responsible for the functioning of plants. The most that could be claimed with any plausibility is that one would not *expect* a theistic God to arrange things so that theistic belief is so controlled. I will resist the temptation to oppose this on the grounds that no human being can have any grounds for expecting an omnipotent Creator to act in one way rather than another. For if that is the way the game is played we are also prevented from having any *a posteriori* grounds for deciding whether such a Being exists, and I would take that to be a severe blow to theistic belief. Moreover, in so far as our concept of God has any content we have some reason, on some level of generality, for expecting one thing rather than another; and if the concept has no content then religion evaporates. However, in this particular case I would like to say that I do not see that the great importance or sanctity of this matter carries any strong presumption that God would not tie the belief to natural causes. I suppose I would admit to some mild surprise at finding a theistic God operating in this manner. But if anything is clear, it is that there are many features of the world which are not quite what one would initially expect from such a deity, and that if the belief can survive those that are repeatedly brought out in discussions of the problem of evil, it has nothing to fear from the present point.

There is one stronger reason for regarding such causal determination as discordant or even strictly incompatible with theism. This is the idea that it is part of God's plan to leave decision on belief or non-belief (in this matter) to the free choice of the individual. God has created man as a free moral agent and has left him to work out his own destiny. And among the most crucial choices which each individual has to make for himself is this one — whether to recognize the divine existence, with everything that this entails, or to blind oneself to it. (This line of thought requires the assumption that the divine existence is obvious to anyone who does not *avoid* it.) But if such belief is causally determined, then the individual does not have a free choice in this matter. *Ergo*. . . . This line of argument, even if sound, does not show that causal determination of theistic belief is incompatible with certain views as to the divine purpose that are firmly entrenched in theistic thought.

This issue cannot be considered here because it raises all the fundamental problems about free will. The line of argument just sketched presupposes that if a certain belief is causally determined then one can't make a free choice as to whether to accept it or not. (I am leaving aside the further difficulty that it may be a mistake to use notions like choice and decision with respect to belief.) But whether this is so is perhaps the chief issue in discussions about free will, and there are powerful reasons for doubting that it is the case. In any event, if psychoanalytic theory comes into conflict with theism on this ground, it does so together with any view which regards human actions as causally determined. And so we are not faced here with a difficulty for theism which is in any way special to the causal determination of *theistic belief*.

But let us remember that we are dealing, not with explanations in terms of *any* natural factor, but specifically with those in terms of reason-irrelevant factors. And it might be thought that this restriction would put us in a better position to demonstrate an incompatibility. Can we suppose that a deity which is the source of rationality would structure things in such a way that theistic belief is produced by irrational factors; i.e., in such a way that those who have the belief are (or may be) without any real basis for the belief? Well one can easily construe a concept of God which would rule out such causal determination, but it is not at all clear that the concept of God in, e.g., Christianity, always or even usually is of this sort. References in Christian literature to God as the source of reason are far outnumbered by apostrophes to the inscrutability, mysteriousness or downright irrationality (by human standards) of the divine activity. God as a cosmic mathematician is a modern invention. And of course to a religious thinker like Kierkegaard rationality is the last thing in the world God is interested in promoting.

There seems, then, to be little reason to suppose that the fact, if it is a fact, that theistic belief is causally determined directly furnishes any *evidence* against theistic belief. And this is not surprising. For psychological investigations into the causation of beliefs, even this belief, is the wrong quarter in which to look for such evidence. One looks for evidence for and against the Darwinian theory of evolution not in the factors which make people accept it or the reverse, but in the results of palaeontology, comparative anatomy and the experimental production of mutations in fruit flies. And the fact that Kepler developed his heliocentric theory of the solar system under the influence of his quasi-religious sun-worship is not thought to be a relevant consideration if we are trying to determine whether his theory is correct. Of course in attempting to transfer these points to the theistic case we run into the fact that it is much more difficult here to say what would be relevant evidence. But in spite of all the problems that can be raised about the traditional arguments for the existence of God, I feel confident in saying that the order, or lack thereof, in the world, the existence of evil and the facts of human morality, are the right sort of thing to consider in a way that factors productive of theistic belief are not — if we are looking for positive or negative evidence.

I have still done nothing to rule out the possibility that a theory of the sort we are considering could do something in a more indirect way to weaken theistic belief, e.g., by showing that certain supposed reasons for acceptance are not sound ones, or by providing reasons for doubting that any adequate supporting reasons can be found. Something of the former sort is suggested by Freud in *The Future of an Illusion*.

Now, it is quite true that if anyone should argue that the existence of religious belief could only be explained by supposing that God himself had communicated it to men (that men could never have thought of all this by themselves, that the conceptions are too lofty to be initially formed by men, etc.), then showing another way in which such belief can be, and is, brought about disposes of this argument. It would nullify, e.g., the argument put forth by Descartes in his *Meditations* to the effect that the presence of the idea of God in the human mind can only be explained by supposing that God himself is ultimately responsible for putting it there. (Of course this does nothing to show that God has not in fact revealed truths to men; it only shows that we cannot hold that he has done so on *these* grounds.

Note too that the sort of theory we are considering takes as one of the factors to be used in explaining the occurrence of theistic belief in the individual the existence of certain conceptions and certain beliefs in the culture to which that individual is exposed. This means that the ultimate origin of that cultural tradition is still unexplained, and as long as this is the case, a wedge is left for the revelationist.) But this is hardly a serious consequence; theism is not usually defended in this way.

There is one important way of supporting theistic belief which would certainly be adversely affected, perhaps fatally, by causal explanations. I am referring to the claim that one can be sure of the existence of God because one has directly experienced the presence of God.[1] Of course there are different sorts of experiences which have been so construed, and a complete discussion would have to take account of these differences, but for purposes of illustration we can once more revert to Freudian theory and consider a Freudian explanation of certain very pervasive features of mystical experience — (1) a breakdown of the usual boundaries of the self, a sense of a merging of oneself into the object, loss of separateness; (2) joy, which sometimes reaches rapturous intensity, combined with a profound sense of peace. If we look, as a Freudian would, for analogues of this in the development of the individual, we can find it in the experience of the infant. As reconstructed by psychoanalysis the infant's experience lacks the self-world distinction. He has to learn by hard experience what is part of him and what is outside him. Thus his consciousness is, in Freud's apt terminology, 'oceanic'. He feels an inseparable connection between himself and his environment; or rather he just feels, without referring contents to different sources. Moreover, if we consider the fed, satisfied baby on the edge of sleep, we may find the prototype of the profoundly peaceful rapture with which the mystic is suffused.

Then, by invoking the familiar concepts of fixation and

[1] General explanations of theistic belief would not have any bearing on the force of this reason, except for the way in which a specification of necessary and sufficient reason-irrelevant conditions cuts off the possibility of any adequate reasons, as explained below.

of regression we can suppose that such experiences arise as follows. People differ in the extent to which they outgrow the desires, modes of thought, etc., of a given stage of development, and this certainly seems to be the case with respect to the early infantile stage; consider the well-established concept of the 'oral personality'. When an adult who still has strong but repressed desires to be in the infantile situation runs into severe difficulties and frustrations, a regression will ensue. One of the things this means is that the desires appropriate to that stage will be strengthened and press even more insistently for some sort of satisfaction. One form such satisfaction could take is an hallucinatory experience in which the individual feels himself to be in something like the infantile situation, suitably reinterpreted (as immediate union with God) so as to be acceptable to one's consciously held standards. Thus we find Ostow and Scharfstein quoting the following from Porphyry's *Life of Plotinus*: 'Plotinus would tell his disciples how, at the age of eight, when he was already going to school, he still clung about his nurse and loved to bare her breasts and take suck: one day he was told he was a "perverted imp" and so was shamed out of the trick'. The authors then go on to say, 'The tendency to retreat and demand the love and security granted an infant had already been established, and his later longing to join God in a union of love was a reappearance on a new level of the old desire'.[1]

I do not want to suggest that there is any strong reason to believe that this is a correct explanation of such experiences. (There is, again, no direct evidence at all.) I simply present it as an example of the sort of explanation I wish to consider. Supposing that some such theory were established, what bearing, if any, would this have on claims that in such experiences one is directly apprehending God? There are those who maintain that the success of such explanations would constitute a refutation of the claim. So far as I can see the strongest way to support this position is to say that if we can show that there are natural factors which are

[1] Mortimer Ostow and Ben-Ami Scharfstein, *The Need to Believe* (New York: International Universities Press, 1954), p. 118.

sufficient to produce experiences of this sort, then one is unwarranted in claiming that divine activity or influence must be at least partly responsible for their occurrence, and hence that one has no basis for supposing that one is in contact with God when one has such an experience. To this it will, no doubt, be replied that causal origin is one thing and epistemological status another, and that answering questions about one does not suffice to answer questions about the other. More specifically, to say what one perceived on a given occasion is not to say what produced one's perception (or the sensations that were involved in the perception), and *vice versa*. Hence the fact that one's experience is produced by certain psychological factors, independently of any supernatural influence, leaves completely open the question whether one is perceiving God in that experience.

Clearly this raises fundamental questions concerning the concept of perception. There are those who affirm and those who deny that a necessary condition of perceiving x is that x be among the factors which produce the experience (sensation, awareness of sensa, etc.) involved in the supposed perception. (It is a further question whether the notion of perception can be completely analysed in such terms.) The parties to the above dispute will, of course, take opposite positions on this issue. I am unable to go into these matters here. I will only say that it seems to me plausible to say that the presence of x somewhere (not too far back) in the chain of causes giving rise to a certain experience is one necessary condition of that experience being involved in a perception of x. This principle seems to be supported by some of the procedures we use in determining whether or not someone has directly perceived something. If a thick brick wall was so placed as to prevent light waves from a house from reaching my eyes, then I could not have seen that house at that time.

It seems reasonable to take principles which are well established with respect to sense-perception, an area where we pretty much know what to say under a given set of conditions, and extend them to the discussion of purported direct experiences of God, an area where it is not at all clear what one should say. Thus I am inclined to agree that a successful explanation of certain mystical experiences in terms of purely natural factors would enable us to disallow claims that in these experiences one is directly apprehending God.

But even if there are certain ways of justifying theistic beliefs which could be discredited by psychological explanations — either of theistic belief in general or of the way in question — there would always remain the possibility that there were other modes of justification which would turn out to be valid. To do any real damage the Freudian theory would have to provide reason for supposing that no adequate justification could be given.

Construed in a certain way Freudian theory will have this consequence. Up to now I have been interpreting a causal theory in such a way that it purports to specify *sufficient* conditions of religious belief. But suppose we understand our imaginary enriched Freudianism to put forward its factors as both sufficient and necessary for religious belief. Then it follows that no adequate reasons could be given. For if there were such reasons, the grasp of them by a rational man would itself be a sufficient condition of his accepting the belief.

I am sure that many will oppose this thesis on the grounds that reasons are one thing and causes quite another. Hence to say that someone has adequate reasons for a certain belief is to say nothing about the causes of his coming to have the belief, and to say that someone's belief is due to certain causes is to say nothing about the reasons that he might or might not have for it. But this seems to me to be mistaken. Of course a reason cannot be a cause, nor can a cause be a reason. They exist in logically different realms. But that does not mean that a statement about reasons cannot have implications concerning causes and *vice versa*. It seems quite clear to me that to say that A's reason for thinking that his lawn-mower is in his garage is that he saw it there in the morning, or that B's reason for thinking that the Republicans will show gains in the 1962 elections is that the party which does not have control of the presidency generally gains in off-year elections, is to imply something about the causes which have (or might have) given rise to his having this belief, or at least something about the causes which maintain his belief. It would be absurd to say 'A has every reason to believe that x, but I can't imagine what led him to believe that'. Conversely, to say that A's belief that there exists an omnipotent personal Being is *wholly* due to cultural conditioning in early childhood plus a projection of an unconscious father-image onto the Being envisaged in that cultural training is to deny that he has any reason for the belief. For if he had a reason, the psychological processes involved in becoming aware of the considerations involved in the reason, and in connecting them to the belief in question, would be at least part of what led him to have or retain the belief.

But this is a hollow triumph for the psychoanalytic critic of theistic religion. For the psychoanalytic factors could be established as necessary as well as sufficient conditions only if we could be sure that no one could acquire sufficient reasons for the belief; for if he could the belief could be produced in some other way.[1] Since the establishment of reason-irrelevant necessary and sufficient conditions presupposes that no sound reasons can be given, it can hardly be used to warrant that claim.

Now if we are dealing only with an established claim that there are reason-irrelevant causal factors which are sufficient to produce that belief (and furthermore are in general what is responsible for producing it), then what? Of course it follows that anyone whose belief is produced in this way lacks any sound basis for the belief. But what implication should I draw from it for *my* state of religious belief? Well, if I have adequate reasons for the belief myself it will do nothing to shake my confidence in those grounds. And justifiably. Why should I abandon what I can see to be sound reason for the belief just because it has been shown that many other people hold the belief without

[1] It is significant that in *The Future of an Illusion* Freud prefaces his presentation of his explanation of theistic belief with a chapter in which he argues that there is no sound ground for the belief. Though if I am correct he should have gone further and argued that there *could be* no sound ground.

Faith and the Philosophers

having any such grounds? It may be said that the demonstration that the belief is generally held as a result of unconscious projections might well make me suspicious of the cogency of my reasons. My belief might be caused by similar projections and I might be deceiving myself into thinking that I have good reasons in order to put a good face on the matter. And so I might. I would agree that the psychoanalytic results would properly make me suspicious and that in the light of this the reasonable thing for me to do would be to scrutinize my reasons very carefully. But if I have looked on them and have seen that they are good, what more is there for me to do.[1] And if I do not have adequate reasons for the belief, we have already seen that the existence of reason-irrelevant sufficient conditions does nothing to show that there could not be adequate reasons for the belief.

There still remains one way in which the success of a theory of the sort we are considering might have some relevance. If a man has no grounds of any magnitude for deciding the question of the existence of God one way or the other, he might be faced with the question of whether this is an issue which is worth considering further. After all, there are many important theses which at present we are unable to either prove or disprove, and we only have a limited amount of time and energy to devote to such matters. In this instance, he might take note of the fact that there are many people, including many intelligent and thoughtful people, who accept this belief, and this might lead him to conclude that it is a matter which should be looked into further. But now if it could be shown that, so far as we can tell, what leads these people to adopt this belief is something which is quite irrelevant to its truth or falsity, this would nullify the above reason for taking the issue seriously. Thus a causal explanation could, under these conditions, properly have the effect of counteracting a possible reason for regard-

---

[1] There is also the case in which I came to the belief *via* the Freudian route and then subsequently found really adequate reasons. In this case we should not say that in the later stages the belief is *really* due to the psychoanalytic factors alone. For now the situation has changed in such a way that even if the unconscious pressures should cease to operate I would still have a strong tendency to retain the belief.

ing the question as one which is worth exploring further. Not much of a consequence, but something.

Thus I am forced to conclude that the fact, if it is a fact, that reason-irrelevant causal factors are sufficient to produce theistic belief has little or no tendency to show that the belief is false, unlikely to be true, or not worthy of serious consideration. And remember that we have arrived at this conclusion with respect to an imagined theory which would present at least sufficient conditions for the belief. As for theories of the sort we actually have, which can reasonably claim nothing more than a certain degree of correlation between theistic belief and certain factors, the case would be even worse. For such theories leave ample room for the operation of awareness of reasons in the production of the belief. And here there is even less reason to think that a theistic God would not set things up so that such partial correlations would not obtain.

B

Thus far we have simply been considering Freudian theory as an example of the general claim that theistic belief is in general due solely to reason-irrelevant causal factors. But the Freudian theory has some special features which distinguish it from some of the other theories of this class and some of these might be relevant to our problem. More specifically, the theory tends to assimilate religious belief to infantile modes of thought and to neurotic manifestations. Remember that, according to the theory, theistic belief, like many neuroses, is based on a regression to infantile modes of psychic organization and that it bears traces of this regression in the way it conceives God and in the ways it leads men to feel toward God. Moreover, as Reik points out in elaborate detail in his two books on the subject, religion exhibits many of the features of neurotic compulsions both in its ritual and in its doctrinal aspects. Michael Argyle summarizes the points of similarity as follows:

(a) . . . obsessions and compulsions simultaneously allow some substitute gratification both of the desire and of its prohibition. . . . Reik . . . similarly traces the development of ideas about the Trinity as a compromise between ideas of filial rebellion and veneration for the father.

(b) The neurotic's rituals have a compulsive character, in that he must carry them out conscientiously and experiences guilt if he fails to do so : this is to some extent true of religious rituals too.

(c) In religion there are taboos — of Sunday work, food before communion, and so forth : neurotics also have things which they must avoid touching or thinking about. . . . Reik . . . points out that the taboos surrounding religious dogma develop as a defence against scepticism : at the same time the dogma is developed in absurd detail, reflecting an underlying contempt for it.

(d) The real conflict in neurotics becomes displaced on to trivial details and verbal matters; this is also the case with religion, where the dogmas and rituals become elaborated in enormous detail, minute parts of which may become the basis for schisms and persecutions.[1]

On the basis of all this it is argued, or more often suggested, that beliefs which have this status, which are essentially infantile and/or neurotic in character could not be taken seriously by rational, adult individuals. This sort of claim is clearly different from the one based on the mere existence of *some* sort of causal determination, and it must be examined separately.

But first note that it is not at all clear that *this* argument requires that we suppose the psychoanalytic theory inflated into a complete statement of causal conditions. It would seem plausible to suggest that the existence of substantial correlations between theistic belief and such factors as degree of unconscious conflict, tendency to regression, etc., would do as much, or almost as much, to show that theistic belief has an infantile and/or neurotic *character* as would the development of a complete theory integrating these factors with others. For presumably the other factors that would have to be included — degree of intelligence, cultural training, etc., would not add anything to the force of the

[1] Michael Argyle, *Religious Behaviour* (London: Routledge and Kegan Paul, 1958), p. 165.

diagnosis. Hence in this section we can work with the theory as we actually have it.

In evaluating this claim we must first make some important distinctions which are generally overlooked. First we must, as noted earlier, distinguish between the existence of similarities between the *forms* taken by theistic belief and the *forms* of infantile and neurotic behaviour, and the existence of causal factors for theistic belief of an infantile or neurotic kind. A great deal of the psychoanalytic discussion of religion consists simply of pointing out similarities, as with the similarities between obsessional neurosis and theistic belief listed above, and supposing that this shows that the two are fundamentally the same sort of thing. But such surface similarities are radically insufficient to bear the weight of such a conclusion. A man 'obsessed' with a radically new idea, who is constantly preoccupied with thinking it through, seeing its implications, devising ways to test it, etc., exhibits striking similarities to obsessional neurotics, but it would be a great mistake to dismiss his theorizing on this basis. And in fact, despite the obvious similarities in patterns of overt behaviour, his 'obsession' with the idea may be psychologically quite a different thing and may have very different psychological roots from the obsession of the neurotic. When I look at a snake in a zoo my experience may be phenomenally quite similar to that of a man suffering from hallucinations in delirium tremens, but it would be a great mistake to conclude from this that my experience is really an hallucination, or that this shows that there are really no such things as snakes. Surface similarities can be misleading.

But with respect to the charge that religion is a neurosis, the Freudian theory goes beyond these similarities and posits similar underlying mechanisms. But here, too, we must distinguish between two views which are not always distinguished. (1) Among the important causal factors producing theistic belief is always some neurosis of a commonly recognized sort. (2) Some of the important causal factors here are the same as some which play a crucial role in producing certain neuroses. There seems to be no evidence at all for (1), not even if we restrict our sample to neurotic believers! I shall confine my attention to (2).

If the Freudian theory as presented earlier is to be adequate, there are common causal conditions for neurosis and theistic belief — a substantial amount of unconscious conflict, a tendency to regression, etc. But the question remains as to whether this justifies Freud in terming religion 'the universal obsessional neurosis of humanity'.[1] Why should we not rather say that given these common causal conditions there are two ways in which the individual may respond — either by a neurosis or by religious faith? Of course we could say with Freud that this is just the difference between an idiosyncratic neurosis and a socially approved neurosis. But we might also say, with Jung, that a religious orientation is an alternative to neurosis, or even constitutes a prophylaxis against, or cure for, a neurosis. How can we choose between these positions?

In considering this question we are forced to get clearer about the term 'neurosis', and more particularly about the sense of this term, if any, in which there would be any plausibility in saying that the fact that a belief arises out of a neurosis shows that we do not have to take it seriously. There are various ways of defining 'neurosis' and more general terms like 'psychological abnormality'. If we define a neurosis in terms of underlying causal factors, as is often done, e.g., in terms of the amount of conflict which is unconscious and therefore not resoluble by rational deliberation, then in order to show that a belief can be dismissed from serious consideration on the grounds that it arises out of a neurosis we would need a supplementary argument to the effect that any belief so produced is unlikely to be correct. But we know too little about the effects of unconscious processes to have any confidence in any such principle. Moreover, if we widen the sphere to cover kinds of disguised resolutions of unconscious conflicts other than beliefs, we can think of many such cases which would not

---

[1] Sigmund Freud, *The Future of an Illusion*, translated by W. D. Robson-Scott (New York: Liveright, 1953), p. 76

Psychological Explanations of Religious Belief

be classified as harmful or undesirable — e.g. (to take a couple of favourite textbook examples) the resolution of unconscious conflict over aggression by developing skill as a surgeon or resolution of unconscious conflict over love of one's mother by specializing in painting madonnas.

Therefore it seems that if we are to draw negatively evaluative implications from connection with a neurosis we shall have to build some negative evaluations into the concept of neurosis. And I believe that this is usually what is done. Included in the commonly-used working criteria for calling a state a neurosis is the requirement that this state have the effect of hampering the individual in his 'adjustments to the environment' or in his attempts to achieve his aims in life. If that is part of the definition of a neurosis, then there is some plausibility in holding that a belief which arises from a neurosis is, *ipso facto*, unlikely to be correct. For if a neurosis has the effect of hampering the individual's attempts to get along in his environment, then the hampering would presumably involve among other things, producing false beliefs about the environment, or suppressing or warping true beliefs. And in fact this is one of the prominent features of neurosis. But now what happens is this. As people develop confidence in a theory of the causal basis of states which satisfy the initial criteria for neurosis, we get the familiar phenomenon of transition from synthetic to analytic connections; the underlying causal mechanisms come to be themselves used as criteria. It is then easy to assume unquestioningly, with respect to anything which satisfies these latter criteria, that it will have the unfortunate effects which were among the initial criteria. But, of course, the proposition that anything which results from certain sorts of unconscious processes will hamper the individual's pursuit of his goals is a generalization which must be tested separately for each new range of cases.

Hence the matter stands as follows. In order to argue that theistic belief, since neurotic, is unworthy of serious consideration, one must be holding the term 'neurosis' subject to the evaluative criteria mentioned earlier. But so long as all we have shown is that this belief is due to certain unconscious processes, we have no right to call it neurotic in this sense. To gain this right we would have to show that a person who has a theistic belief is less able to function effectively than he would have been without it. And no one has ever begun to show this.

Moreover, there are some profound difficulties which intrude themselves when we consider the possibility of establishing such a conclusion. A psychoanalytically-minded writer who set out to do so would, presumably, proceed by determining whether religious believers were less able to establish satisfying personal relations, get ahead in their professions, etc., than non-religious believers who were identical in other respects. But even if this could be established the theist might complain we have been too restrictive in our survey of the 'environment' and of what constitutes 'success' or 'effective functioning' therein. If we include the 'supernatural environment' in our survey, it would seem plausible to suppose that theistic belief would be a powerful, or rather indispensable, aid to effective functioning with respect to *it*. And if we did not include it, our opponent might accuse us of stacking the cards against him. 'You are', he would say, 'using a criterion of effective functioning which already presupposes that my beliefs are false. For if they are not false, it would be quite reasonable to suppose that the conditions which were conducive to effective functioning and accurate apprehension with respect to two such different realms would be radically different.' As James put it, 'If there were such a thing as inspiration from a higher realm, it might well be that the neurotic temperament would furnish the chief condition of the requisite receptivity'.[1]

It is hard to know what to say about this issue. This may be one point at which there is, in the nature of the case, a complete *impasse* between the theist and his psychoanalytic critic.

To sum up, even if the psychoanalytic theory of the causal basis of theistic belief is correct, there seems to be no

[1] *The Varieties of Religious Experience* (Longmans, London, 1952, *and* New American Library, New York, 1958).

reason to say that therefore religion is a happy alternative to a neurosis; and therefore there is no reason for suggesting, on these grounds, that theistic belief is false, probably false, or unworthy of serious consideration.

The charge that theistic belief can be dismissed as infantile in character can be handled more briefly. This is based solely on the surface similarities between the theistic conception of God, and the believer's feelings and attitudes toward him, and the child's conception of, and feeling and attitude toward, his father. (The matter of regression to an infantile orientation has already been handled as part of the grounds for regarding religion as a neurosis.) Such similarities may be admitted. But the theist might well reply that whether such conceptions, attitudes, etc., are warranted is wholly a matter of whether his beliefs are true. It would be unworthy of an adult human being to take up such attitudes toward another human being. But if theism is correct, we do as a matter of fact, stand in a relation to God very similar to that in which we stood to our fathers in early childhood, and therefore, if theism is correct, such attitudes and feelings are quite appropriate. In view of this fact one could hardly use such similarities as a basis for rejecting theistic claims. In general, a set of facts which are perfectly compatible with a theory can do nothing to weaken the plausibility of that theory.

We should note that here too it makes a difference whether the theory is asserting only sufficient, or necessary and sufficient, conditions. If it is the former (and we have seen that this is the only form of the theory which is not clearly unjustified), then in addition to the moves already considered it is open to the theist to hold that although many people may hold religious beliefs as the result of the unconscious mechanisms in question, the belief can and sometimes is, held as a result of other factors. That is, it is open to him to distinguish between quasi-neurotic and non-quasi-neurotic ways of being religious. Of course he may not be able to show any sufficient conditions of the latter sort, but at least the theory in the weaker form does nothing to indicate that this would be impossible.

III

In this paper I have been considering the possible bearing of causal explanations of theistic belief on the question of whether there are, or might be, adequate reasons for or against such beliefs. What emerges from the foregoing discussion is the, by no means novel, conclusion that in religion as elsewhere there is no substitute for the detailed examination of evidence which has a direct bearing on the truth or falsity of a given belief, and that, in particular, investigations of the factors which generally produce the belief is no such substitute. As I say, this conclusion is nothing new; if the present discussion has added anything to previous discussions it is by way of considering more thoroughly and patiently some of the relevant distinctions.

But there is another way in which causal theories might be relevant to a decision on the acceptability of theistic belief. Consider the position of James in *The Will to Believe*, or the more extreme position of Kierkegaard, according to both of whom believing in God is somehow justifiable, even though no adequate reasons can be presented either for or against the proposition that God exists. (That is, even though we cannot discover adequate reasons in support of the proposition that God exists, we can discover adequate reasons for the proposition that it is justifiable to believe that God exists.) Such support may be of different sorts. In *The Will to Believe* James says that we are going to take some position on this problem without having adequate reasons for it in any event, so that we may as well recognize the inevitable and accept it with good grace. Kierkegaard supposes that if he presents the stance of faith and contrasting stances in sufficient concreteness, the reader will see that the former is the only possible stance for one who resolutely faces the facts of the human situation. One might wonder whether a psychoanalytic explanation of theistic belief, if established, would properly have any bearing on one's response to the position of these authors. That is, would an acceptance of the psychoanalytic explanation properly influence my decision as to whether or not it is justifiable to believe in God without adequate evidence for his existence?

This question presents very different problems from those already considered, problems that I cannot really discuss at the tail-end of a paper that is already too long. To settle the question we would have to decide what sorts of considerations properly influence a decision as to the justifiability of accepting a proposition under these conditions. I do not know how to lay down a criterion which will separate proper from improper considerations here, and perhaps no such separation can be made. Perhaps if we have abandoned the attempt to show that the proposition is true or false and are still trying to decide whether it is all right to believe it, then anything goes. But even if there still is a distinction between relevant and irrelevant considerations, it is hard to see how facts about the usual causal basis of the belief could be excluded. If one is to admit as relevant facts about the psychological consequences of accepting the belief, about the relative or absolute inevitability of taking some stand or other on a question, and about the way acceptance of the belief will have logical implications for the way various enquiries can and cannot be carried out (and facts of all these sorts have been adduced by philosophers who have discussed this sort of question), it is hard to see how facts about the causal basis of the belief can be excluded. Thus it might be quite pertinent, if not conclusive, in this sort of context to deny that theistic belief is justifiable, on the grounds that it involves acquiescing in a regression to an infantile mode of thought.

IV

There is one other sort of way in which causal explanations might be relevant to the status of theism, but, although I feel that this dimension of the problem is quite important, I am unable to formulate it clearly enough to even begin to determine just how much it does come to. It is often remarked that the general climate of thought in which supernaturalistic theology flourishes is very different from that in which intellectual endeavour is largely devoted to searching out empirically testable causal generalizations. Not that there is any logical incompatibility between a sophisticated theism and the search for such generalizations, or even between theism and a dogmatic determinism. It is just that the general cast of thought which naturally lead to taking the one or the other very seriously are quite different. So long as the search for natural causes shies away from human thought, experience and behaviour, it is relatively easy to distinguish the physical world, investigated by science, from the supernatural realm, which makes contact with man through religion. But when the search for natural causes extends to man, including religious thought, experience and behaviour, such compartmentalization is not so easy. It is still possible, as we have seen in the various moves made in the body of this paper, to distinguish causal explanation of a belief from a disproof of that belief. But to carry it through introduces more and more strain. Therefore it seems that the thorough-going success of a theory like the Freudian would help to render the climate of thought even more antithetical to full-blooded theistic belief. But what implications, if any, this has on the justifiability of theistic belief, I do not know.

IS IT A RELIGIOUS BELIEF THAT 'GOD EXISTS'?

BY

NORMAN MALCOLM

I ADMIRE the strategic plan of Alston's paper, and also the skill and thoroughness of his execution. I think his main results are entirely sound. I agree with his conclusion that even if it is a fact that 'reason-irrelevant' factors are sufficient to produce a belief in God's existence, this could have little or no tendency to show that the belief is false, or probably false, or unworthy of serious acceptance.

I agree also with Alston's comments on the Freudian view that religious belief is a form of neurosis, especially with his observation that we are likely to use the word 'neurosis' ambiguously, sometimes defining a belief as neurotic in terms of its supposed causation, sometimes in terms of its supposed injurious effect on a person's adjustment to reality.

It might be worth remarking that one could not expect a religious man to be well-adjusted to the world, if it is a teaching of his religion that he must cast off worldly considerations. A man who desired to be perfect was enjoined by Jesus to sell his possessions and give to the poor (Matthew 19:21). If any one of us were to believe in his heart that this is necessary and had the courage to act on it, he would thereby begin to live an abnormal life. This would have no tendency to prove that he had a neuropathic temperament, but rather that he was a doer of the word and not a hearer only.

At the same time it could be the case that certain forms of neuropathic disposition do contribute to an acute religious sensitivity. William James has put the point better than I can:

As regards the psychopathic origin of so many religious phenomena, that would not be in the least surprising or disconcerting, even were such phenomena certified from on high to be the most precious of human experiences. No one organism can possibly yield to its owner the whole body of truth. Few of us are not in some way infirm, or even diseased; and our very infirmities help us unexpectedly. In the psychopathic temperament we have the emotionality which is the *sine qua non* of moral perception; we have the intensity and tendency to emphasis which are the essence of practical moral vigour; and we have the love of metaphysics and mysticism which carry one's interests beyond the surface of the sensible world. What, then, is more natural than that this temperament should introduce one to regions of religious truth, to corners of the universe, which your robust Philistine type of nervous system, forever offering its biceps to be felt, thumping its breast, and thanking Heaven that it hasn't a single morbid fibre in its composition, would be sure to hide forever from its self-satisfied possessors. (*The Varieties of Religious Experience*, Lecture I.)

The points of my disagreement with Alston occur only on the periphery of his paper. Although he thinks there is no logical impossibility in the supposition that belief in God could be produced by some 'reason-irrelevant' natural causation, yet he also thinks there would be something unsuitable about it. He would be 'mildly surprised' to learn that God did allow the belief in himself to be produced in this manner.[1] I do not think I have any inclination to feel that this sequence of cause and effect would be somehow inappropriate. If such a causal explanation were true, then that is the way (or one way) God does it! Suppose we learned that the dividing of the Red Sea, which permitted the Israelites to escape from the Egyptians, was probably caused by a strong wind. Would there be anything inappropriate in the thought that this is how God accomplished his purpose? I cannot see that there would. Suppose there was a certain stimulation of the brain that produced a belief in God, and another that made one believe in one's country, or in science, or in psychoanalysis. Would this form of causation be more unsuitable in the first case than in the others?

A possible source of confusion may be the assumption

[1] P. 84.

Psychological Explanations of Religious Belief

that if belief in God was produced by reason-irrelevant natural causes, then the belief would have no rational content: one would not be able to expound or discuss one's belief in an intelligible way. I should agree that this would be a pretty poor sort of belief in God, hardly worthy of the name. But why would it have to be like that? Why could not some form of purely natural causation, even physiological, cause a man to have a belief in God that was full of intelligible content, so that he could relate this belief to Scripture, to the theological structure of his particular faith, and to the problems of human life?

Another objection which may be felt is that if a reason-irrelevant natural cause produced a belief in the existence of God, then the man who held this belief would not have any reasons or grounds for it. At least it would be true that reasoning did not help to produce his belief, this being so by hypothesis. One may think that the belief in God's existence, if one has it, *ought* to be, in part at least, derived from *grounds* of some sort. Does Alston think this? I suspect that he is pulled in opposite directions. On the one hand, he explicitly declares that there is nothing logically wrong with the idea that God might arrange that the belief in his existence was produced by reason-irrelevant natural causes. On the other hand, Alston confesses that he would be (mildly) *surprised* at such an arrangement. It is evident that his inclination to assume that God would not operate in that way is *a priori*: it is not based on some knowledge of how he normally does things. Thus it seems to me that Alston is inclined to deny, but also has some inclination to accept, the *a priori* proposition that if things were the way they ought (ideally) to be, the belief in God's existence would be derived, in part at least, from *grounds* for believing in his existence.

Behind the inclination to accept this proposition there stands the assumption that it must be *possible* for a person to have grounds for believing in the existence of God. Alston makes this assumption whole-heartedly. He says, for example, that if we could not have any '*a posteriori* grounds for deciding' whether God exists, this would be 'a severe blow to theistic belief'.[1] He says that he feels confident that 'the order, or lack thereof, in the world, the existence of evil, and the facts of human morality, are the right sort of thing to consider . . . if we are looking for positive or negative evidence' of God's existence.[2] Toward the end of his paper he draws the conclusion that 'in religion as elsewhere there is no substitute for the detailed examination of evidence which has a direct bearing on the truth or falsity of a given belief'.[3]

Although I am in nearly perfect agreement with every detail of Alston's attack on the idea that a natural causal explanation of religious belief would or could undermine its truth or respectability, there is in the background of his work an assumption that seems to me to be unrealistic. The assumption is that there is a particular belief, namely, the belief that God exists, and with this belief as with any other we must make a distinction between causes of the belief and grounds or evidence for its truth.

What is unrealistic about this assumption? First of all, I must confess that the supposed *belief that God exists* strikes me as a problematic concept, whereas *belief in God* is not problematic. Some people believe in God and some do not. Some believe in God more (or less) strongly at one time than another.

Belief in God is partly, but only partly, analogous to belief in one's friend or one's doctor. Belief in another human being primarily connotes trust or faith in him. You believe in your friend: that is, you trust him to keep his word or to defend your interests. You believe in your doctor: that is, you trust his skill or his humane interest in his patients. You might trust someone *as* a typist but not *as* a translator. When you believe in a person what it is that you trust him to do (or to say or to think) would depend, of course, on the particular circumstances of the case.

Belief in a person primarily connotes trust or faith: but this is not so of belief in God. A man could properly be said to believe in God whose chief attitude toward God was *fear*. ('A sword is sent upon you, and who may turn it back?')

[1] P. 84.   [2] P. 86.   [3] P. 100.

Psychological Explanations of Religious Belief

But if you were enormously afraid of another human being you could not be said to believe in him. At least you would not believe in him *in so far* as you were afraid of him: whereas the fear of God is one form of belief in him.

I am suggesting that *belief-in* has a wider meaning when God is the object of it than when a human being is. Belief in God encompasses not only trust but also awe, dread, dismay, resentment and perhaps even hatred. Belief in God will involve some affective state or attitude, having God as its object, and those attitudes could vary from reverential love to rebellious rejection.

Now one is inclined to say that if a person believes in God surely he believes that God exists. It is far from clear what this is supposed to mean. Of course, if 'believing that God exists' is understood to mean the same as 'believing in God' (and this is not an entirely unnatural use of language) then there is no problem. But the inclination we are discussing is to hold that you could believe *that* God exists without believing *in* God. As I understand it, we are supposed to think that one could believe that God exists but at the same time have no affective attitude toward God. The belief that he exists would come first and the affective attitude might or might not come later. The belief that he exists would not logically imply any affective attitude toward him, but an affective attitude toward him would logically imply the belief that he exists.

If we are assuming a Jewish or Christian conception of God I do not see how one can make the above separation. If one conceived of God as the almighty creator of the world and judge of mankind how could one believe that he exists, but not be touched *at all* by awe or dismay or fear? I am discussing logic, not psychology. Would a belief that he exists, if it were completely non-affective, really be a belief that he exists? Would it be anything at all? What is the 'form of life' into which it would enter? What difference would it make whether anyone did or did not have this belief? So many philosophers who discuss these matters assume that the first and great question is to decide whether God exists: there will be time enough later to determine how one should regard him. I think, on the contrary, that a 'belief that God exists', if it was logically independent of any and all ways of regarding him, would be of no interest, not even to God.

The second thing which leads me to believe that Alston's assumption is unrealistic, is that even if the belief that God exists is a non-problematic concept, we seem to have no clear conception of what would be reasons, grounds or evidence for this belief. Arguing for the existence of God, especially when it is from *a posteriori* grounds, such as the existence in the world of order, good or morality, appears to be an activity in which people make up the rules as they go along, in accordance with their inclinations. Since there are different inclinations, there is no agreed-upon right or wrong in this kind of reasoning.

A good many years ago I was told about a public discussion in which one philosopher repeatedly threw at another philosopher the question, 'But how do you *know* that God exists?' At last the latter replied, 'Because my father told me so!' It was a long time before I saw what was impressive in this reply. My first reaction was to think it was absurd; it did not offer anything which could be considered a *good reason*. But do we know what a good reason would look like? I do not believe so. Discussions of grounds for believing in the existence of God typically end in frustration.

Nothing is put forward in the Old or New Testament as evidence for the existence of God. Someone whose religious concepts were formed exclusively from the Bible, might regard this question of evidence as an alien intrusion. It would have no contact with the religious ideas he had learned. It is my impression that this question of evidence plays no part in workaday religious instruction and practice, but puts in an appearance only when the language is idling.

I am not taking Freud's view that 'religious doctrines . . . do not admit of proof'.[1] It is false that there cannot be evidence for or against any religious doctrine. One might support the doctrine of the Apostolic Succession, for

[1] *The Future of an Illusion*, Hogarth Press, London, 1928.

Psychological Explanations of Religious Belief

example, by citing Matthew 16:18-19, or the belief in the Third Person of the Trinity, by citing John 15:26. There is a genuine place for reasoning for or against various religious doctrines from *a posteriori* grounds. Of course, this kind of justification can take place only within the framework of belief in God and acceptance of the testimony of the prophets, of Jesus, and of the apostles, as authoritative in the determination of dogmatic questions. But when it comes to adducing evidence for or against the existence of God, there is no agreed-upon framework.

Alston makes a remark which is pertinent to this question of evidence. He says that 'in so far as our concept of God has any content we have some reason . . . for expecting one thing rather than another'.[1] This remark comes immediately after his assertion that it would be a severe blow to belief in God's existence if we could not have *a posteriori* grounds for deciding whether God exists. I imagine that there is a connection of thought between the two remarks. My surmise would be that the connection is this: Alston is thinking that our concept of God must have some content; and this implies that we shall have some expectations as to how things will be in the world; and the fulfilment or non-fulfilment of those expectations will be evidence for or against the existence of God.

This is a difficult point to discuss. I agree that if my concept of God has any content then I must have some *beliefs*, and some of these beliefs might be called 'expectations'. For example, as part of my concept of God I might have the belief that faith in God will cause this mountain to be cast into the sea (Mark 11:23-24). But if the mountain does not move shall I conclude that the belief is false; or that God does not exist? It need not be so. I might conclude instead that my faith was not strong enough. If I drew this latter conclusion, would that be evidence that I did not really believe that faith will move mountains? Quite the contrary. The belief might be held by me in such a way that no fact of experience could falsify it. Another item of content in my concept of God might be the belief

[1] P. 84.

that if I am truly repentant my sins will be forgiven. Does this belief have to be held in such a way, or is it generally held in such a way, that it is verifiable or falsifiable in experience? Certainly not.

There are beliefs and beliefs. Some of them do not issue in expectations in such a way that their fulfilment or non-fulfilment would be a verification or falsification of the beliefs.

One may have the feeling that unless religious belief somewhere involved empirical consequences which can provide verification or falsification of the belief, then it does not 'get a grip' on the world; it does not really deserve the name of 'belief'. But a belief can get a grip on the world in another way. The man who believes that his sins will be forgiven if he is truly repentant, might thereby be saved from despair. What he believes has, for him, no verification or falsification; yet the belief makes a great difference to his action and feeling.

I think, therefore, that although a genuine concept of God will involve some beliefs, and the beliefs will make a difference, it does not follow that they will have consequences which could be grounds for or against the existence of God.

DISCUSSION

Alasdair MacIntyre: Freudian and Christian Dogmas as Equally Unverifiable

My difficulty is not that I do not believe in the God who is being discussed, but that I do not believe in the Freud who is being discussed. For when Mr. Alston says that to ask for the reasons for belief is one thing and to ask for the causes of a belief is another, this seems true but misleading when we are concerned with Freud. How does Freud characteristically explain the facts of belief, not in *Totem and Taboo*, but when he is dealing with a patient? Take the case of an adolescent who experiences guilt and explains the guilt by saying, 'I was responsible for my parents' marriage breaking up,' when this is in fact false. Freud explains this belief as a misconstruction of the facts of childhood. Freud's reasons for saying that the child misunderstood are in part that what he now believes is false. In other words, it is only when Freud knows how the adolescent's belief stands

Psychological Explanations of Religious Belief

in relation to the appropriate justificatory reasons or lack of them that Freud knows where to begin to look for causes. The enquiry into the causes of belief only takes off the ground when you have already settled how the belief stands in relation to reasons. Asking for the causes of someone's belief, anterior to asking independently how the belief stands in relation to possible reasons for holding it, would be very odd indeed. Freud himself muddies the water at this point because when he treats of religion he treats it as a form of belief known independently to be false, and therefore to be explained as a misconstruction, and this is what directs him to look where he does for causes. A problem here is that someone who holds the total psychoanalytic view moves within a circle of justifying reasons in relation to religious belief which is analogous to the one in which the Christian moves. Freudianism exists on the same level as a religious system because the Freudian, although he assesses matters differently in his own terms, accepts a great deal that the Christian says about belief in God, for example all the things about the uselessness of looking for evidence and the like; the Freudian may also accept all the things the Christian says about the consequences of belief. In his paper Malcolm said that believing in the forgiveness of sins may save a man from despair. The Freudian would say, 'Yes, this is just what we want to say of religion; this is just the sort of thing that may save a man from despair'. And on the basis of this he gives an elucidation, but this elucidation depends upon a prior attitude towards religion.

The issue which has been with us since our discussion of Price's paper is not in fact between people who say 'We want evidence' and other people who point out that one is being absurd in asking for it. The trouble is that there are *too many* beliefs around of which it is possible to point out the logical inappropriateness of asking for evidence. The Freudian explanation of religion appears to me to be another of them. For Freudianism, in the sense in which it provides a ground for rejecting Christianity, is more, far more than a theory.

If we accept the Freudian explanation of religion we are already moving inside the Freudian circle. The key difference is not between those who think it is absurd to ask for evidence and those who think it is realistic, but between those of us who find ourselves very puzzled by both alternatives and cannot see how one can assent either to Freudianism or to Christianity, and those who apparently find no difficulty in talking clearly from within Freudianism or within Christianity, but have not yet given the rest of us any clear criterion for deciding where one can start.

III
CAN ONE BE A BELIEVER TODAY?

IS UNDERSTANDING RELIGION COMPATIBLE WITH BELIEVING?

BY

ALASDAIR MACINTYRE

BEGIN with an elementary puzzlement. In any discussion between sceptics and believers it is presupposed that, even for us to disagree, it is necessary to understand each other. Yet here at the outset the central problem arises. For usually (and the impulse to write 'always' is strong) two people could not be said to share a concept or to possess the same concept unless they agreed in at least some central applications of it. Two men may share a concept and yet disagree in some of the judgements they make in which they assert that objects fall under it. But two men who disagreed in *every* judgement which employed the concept — of them what could one say that they shared? For to possess a concept is to be able to use it correctly — although it does not preclude mishandling it sometimes. It follows that unless I can be said to share your judgements at least to some degree I cannot be said to share your concepts.

Yet sceptic and believer disagree *in toto* in their judgements on some religious matters; or so it seems. So how can they be in possession of the same concepts? If I am prepared to say *nothing* of what you will say about God or sin or salvation, how can my concepts of God, sin and salvation be the same as yours? And if they are not, how can we understand each other? There are parties to the discussion who would cut it short precisely at this point, both Protestants who believe that only saving grace can help us to understand the concepts of the Scriptures or the creeds, and sceptics who believe that religious utterances are

I owe a great deal in this paper to conversations with Professor Ernest Gellner and Mr. Peter Winch, neither of whom will agree with the use I have made of what I have learned from them.—A. M.

flatly senseless. But each of these is presently convicted of paradox. For the Protestant will elsewhere deny what is entailed by his position, namely that nobody ever rejects Christianity (since anyone who thinks he has rejected it must have lacked saving grace and so did not understand Christianity and so in fact rejected something else); and the sceptic of this kind has to explain the meaning of religious utterances in order to reject them (that is, he never says — as he would have to if they were flatly senseless — 'I can't understand a word of it'). So it seems that we do want to say that a common understanding of religious concepts by sceptics and by believers is both necessary and impossible. This dilemma constitutes my problem.

Someone might argue that this dilemma is an entirely artificial construction on the grounds that the concepts used in religion are concepts also used outside religion and that sceptics and believers agree in the non-religious judgements which make use of such concepts. Since I have said that it is far from necessary for two men who share a concept to agree in every judgement which they make in which they make use of the concept, there can be no objection to saying that sceptics and believers share the same concept and, *a fortiori*, no difficulty in mutual understanding. But this objection rests upon two mistakes. First of all it ignores those specifically religious concepts which have no counterpart in non-religious contexts; and the concepts I have already cited such as those of God, sin and salvation belong to this class. Secondly, when secular predicates such as 'powerful' and 'wise' are transferred to a religious application, they undergo a change. Certainly they are used analogically; but just this is the point. A new element is introduced with the analogical adaptation of the concept. The transition from 'powerful' to 'omnipotent' is not merely quantitative. For the notion of 'supreme in this or that class' cannot easily be transferred to a being who does not belong to a class (as God does not).[1] And thus a new concept has been manufactured. But if the understanding of this new concept can lead theologians to make one set of

[1] *Summa Theologica*, Part I, Q. 3, Art. 5.

judgements and the understanding of what is apparently the same concept can lead sceptics to make quite another set of judgements, then how can it be the same concept which is in question? The dilemma stands. If by any chance examples were to be produced from religions which turned out to use no specifically religious concepts, and only to use secular predicates, without change of meaning, then certainly we should have no problems of meaning with them. And with them for that very reason I am not concerned.

An indirect way of approaching this dilemma as it arises for the philosophy of religion would be to enquire whether the same dilemma arises in any other field; and at once it is clear that there is at least one field in which it *ought* to arise, namely the study of so-called primitive societies. For anthropologists and sociologists (I intend to use these terms interchangeably) claim to understand concepts which they do not share. They identify such concepts as *mana*, or *tabu*, without themselves using them — or so it seems. If we could discover what anthropological understanding consisted in therefore, we might be in a stronger position to restate the problem. And if, as I shall claim, we could also show that the variety of positions taken up by anthropologists reproduce a variety of positions already taken up in the philosophy of religion, the sense of relevance would be even stronger. I want to distinguish four different positions, each of which has defects.

(A) There is the now unfashionable view of Levy-Bruhl that primitive thought is pre-logical. When Australian aborigines asserted that the sun is a white cockatoo [1] Levy-Bruhl concluded that he was faced with a total indifference to inconsistency and contradiction. From the standpoint of rational discourse we can study primitive thought much as we study natural phenomena. It obeys laws as particles obey laws; but in speaking, primitives do not follow rules as we do. Therefore we cannot elucidate the rules that they use. In an important sense therefore, although we can describe what primitives say, we cannot grasp their concepts. For they do not possess concepts in the sense of recognizing

[1] *Les Fonctions mentales dans les sociétés inférieures*, pp. 76 et seq.

that some uses of expression conform to and others break with rules for the use of such expressions. It is of course consistent with this view that we might by a kind of empathy imagine ourselves to be primitives and in this sense 'understand'; but we might equally understand by imaginative sympathy what it is to be a bear or a squirrel.

The counterpart in philosophy of religion to Levy-Bruhl is the kind of position which wants to interpret religious language (or metaphysical language — see R. Carnap, *Philosophy and Logical Syntax*) as expressive of attitudes rather than as affirming or denying that anything is the case. On this view religious language simply does not function as *language*; for it is used either causally to evoke or aesthetically to express feelings or attitudes, and Carnap thinks that language can do these things in precisely the same way in which 'movements' can. We can thus study religious language, as in Levy-Bruhl's writings, only as a natural phenomenon; we cannot grasp its concepts for they cannot, on this view, be conceptual. The problem for writers like Levy-Bruhl and Carnap is that they have to treat their own conclusions as palpably false in order to arrive at them. For unless Levy-Bruhl had grasped that 'white cockatoo' and 'sun' were being used with apparently normal referential intentions, he could not have diagnosed the oddity of asserting that the sun is a white cockatoo; and unless Carnap had grasped the assertive form of religious or metaphysical statement, he would not have had to argue that this language is not assertive but expressive. That is, in Levy-Bruhl and Carnap we find a tacit acknowledgement that primitive *language* and religious *language* are *language*. And that therefore something is there to be construed and not merely described or explained.

(B) At the opposite extreme from Levy-Bruhl is the practice of Professor E. E. Evans-Pritchard in his book *Nuer Religion*, which is of course offered as an explicit refutation of Levy-Bruhl. Like the Australian aborigines, the Sudanese Nuer appear to fly in the face of ordinary rules of consistency and contradiction. 'It seems odd, if not absurd, to a European when he is told that a twin is a bird as though it were an obvious fact, for Nuer are not saying that a twin is like a bird but that he is a bird.'[1] Evans-Pritchard begins from the Nuer concept of the divine, *kwoth*. The difficulties in the notion of *kwoth* spring from the fact that *kwoth* is asserted both to be sharply contrasted with the material creation and to be widely present in it. It is both one and many: and the many, as aspects of *kwoth*, are one with each other. In order to tease out the notion Evans-Pritchard has to allow full weight to the social context of practice in which the assertions about *kwoth* are used. By doing this he is able to show that the utterances of the Nuer are rule-governed, and on this rests his claim to have refuted Levy-Bruhl. But Evans-Pritchard takes this to be the same as having made the utterances of the Nuer intelligible. Certainly he has shown us what the Nuer idea of intelligibility is. He has shown why the Nuer think their religion makes sense. But this is not to have shown that the Nuer are right. 'When a cucumber is used as a sacrificial victim Nuer speak of it as an ox. In doing so they are asserting something rather more than that it takes the place of an ox.'[2] When we have grasped the whole of Nuer practice have we grasped what more this could be? Or is there anything left over that we have not understood? Evans-Pritchard would have to answer this last question by 'No'. In doing so he brings out the parallels between his position and the kind of Wittgensteinianism in philosophy of religion exemplified by Mr. Peter Winch.[3]

Winch argues that 'intelligibility takes many and varied forms'; that there is no 'norm for intelligibility in general'.[4] He argues that 'criteria of logic are not a direct gift of God, but arise out of, and are only intelligible in the context of, ways of living or modes of social life as such. For instance, science is one such mode and religion is another; and each has criteria of intelligibility peculiar to itself. So within

[1] E. E. Evans-Pritchard, *Nuer Religion* (Oxford: Clarendon Press, 1956), p. 131.
[2] Evans-Pritchard, *op. cit.* p. 128.
[3] *The Idea of a Social Science and its Relation to Philosophy* (London: Routledge and Kegan Paul, 1958).
[4] *Op. cit.* p. 102.

science or religion actions can be logical or illogical; in science, for example, it would be illogical to refuse to be bound by the results of a properly carried out experiment; in religion it would be illogical to suppose that one could pit one's own strength against God's; and so on. But we cannot sensibly say that either the practice of science itself or that of religion is either illogical or logical; both are non-logical.'[1] It follows from this that anything that counts as a 'way of living' or a 'mode of social life' can only be understood and criticized in its own terms. Winch indeed argues that so far as religion is concerned, a sociologist can only identify religious actions under their religious descriptions and if he answers any questions about them of the form 'Do these two acts belong to the same kind of activity?' the answer will have to be 'given according to criteria which are not taken from sociology, but from religion itself. But if the judgements of identity — and hence the generalizations — of the sociologist of religion rest on criteria taken from religion, then his relation to the performers of religious activity cannot be just that of observer to observed. It must rather be analogous to the participation of the natural scientist with fellow-workers in the activities of scientific investigation.'[2] That is, you can only understand it from the inside.

Winch therefore points to a theoretical justification for Evans-Pritchard's practice, and in so doing exposes its weakness. For there are not two alternatives: *either* embracing the metaphysical fiction of one over-all 'norm for intelligibility in general' *or* flying to total relativism. We can elicit the weakness of this position by considering the conceptual self-sufficiency claimed for 'ways of living' and 'modes of social life'. The examples given are 'religion' and 'science'. But at any given date in any given society the criteria in current use by religious believers or by scientists will differ from what they are at other times and places.[3] Criteria have a history. This emerges strikingly

[1] *Op. cit.* pp. 100-101.   [2] *Op. cit.* pp. 87-88.
[3] Consider Kepler using as a criterion in selecting from possible hypotheses what could be expected from a perfect God whose perfection included a preference for some types of geometrical figure as against others.

if we ask how we are to think of magic on Winch's view. Is magic a 'mode of social life'? Or is it primitive religion? Or perhaps primitive science? For we do want to reject magic, and we want to reject it — in the terms which Winch has taken over for polemical purposes from Pareto — as illogical because it fails to come up to our criteria of rationality. An excellent case here is that of the witchcraft practised by the Azande.[1] The Azande believe that the performance of certain rites in due form affects their common welfare; this belief cannot in fact be refuted. For they also believe that if the rites are ineffective it is because someone present at them had evil thoughts. Since this is always possible, there is never a year when it is unavoidable for them to admit that the rites were duly performed, but that they did not thrive. Now the belief of the Azande is not unfalsifiable in principle (we know perfectly well what would falsify it — the conjunction of the rite, no evil thoughts and disasters). But in fact it cannot be falsified. Does this belief stand in need of rational criticism? And if so by what standards? It seems to me that one could only hold the belief of the Azande rationally *in the absence of* any practice of science and technology in which criteria of effectiveness, ineffectiveness and kindred notions had been built up. But to say this is to recognize the appropriateness of scientific criteria of judgement from our standpoint. The Azande do not intend their belief either as a piece of science or as a piece of non-science. They do not possess these categories. It is only *post eventum*, in the light of later and more sophisticated understanding that their belief and concepts can be classified and evaluated at all.

This suggests strongly that beliefs and concepts are not merely to be evaluated by the criteria implicit in the practice of those who hold and use them. This conviction is reinforced by other considerations. The criteria implicit in the practice of a society or of a mode of social life are not necessarily coherent; their application to problems set within that social mode does not always yield *one* clear and unambiguous answer. When this is the case people start

---

[1] E. Evans-Pritchard, *Witchcraft, Oracles and Magic Among the Azande*.

questioning their own criteria. They try to criticise the standards of intelligibility and rationality which they have held hitherto. On Winch's view it is difficult to see what this could mean. This is to return to the point that criteria and concepts have a history; it is not just activities which have a history while the criteria which govern action are timeless.

What I am quarrelling with ultimately is the suggestion that agreement in following a rule is sufficient to guarantee making sense. We can discriminate different types of example here. There are the cases where the anthropologist, in order to interpret what people say, has to reconstruct imaginatively a possible past situation where expressions had a sense which they no longer bear. Consider theories about what taboo is. To call something taboo is to prohibit it, but it is not to say that it is prohibited. To say that something is taboo is to distinguish it from actions which are prohibited but are not taboo. We could say that it is to give a reason for a prohibition, except that it is unintelligible what reason can be intended. So some theorists have constructed [1] from the uses of taboo a sense which it might once have had and a possible history of how this sense was lost. One cannot take the sense from the use, for the use affords no sense, although the temptation to tell anthropologists that taboo is the name of a non-natural quality would be very strong for any Polynesian who had read G. E. Moore.

In the case of 'taboo' we can imagine a lost sense for the expression. What about cases, however, where the sense is not lost, but is simply incoherent? According to Spencer and Gillen some aborigines carry about a stick or a stone which is treated *as if* it is or embodies the soul of the individual who carries it. If the stick or stone is lost, the individual anoints himself as the dead are anointed. Does the concept of 'carrying one's soul about with one' make sense? Of course we can re-describe what the aborigines are doing and transform it into sense, and perhaps Spencer and Gillen (and Durkheim who follows them) mis-describe what occurs.

[1] See F. Steiner, *Taboo*.

But if their reports are not erroneous, we confront a blank wall here, so far as meaning is concerned, although it is easy to give the rules for the use of the concept.

What follows from this is quite simply that there are cases where we cannot rest content with describing the user's criteria for an expression, but we can criticise what he does. Indeed, unless we could do this we could not separate the case where there are no problems of meaning, the case where now there is no clear sense to an expression, but where once there may well have been one (as with 'taboo') and the case where there appears never to have been a clear and coherent sense available. What matters for our present purposes is that these examples suggest that sometimes to understand a concept involves not sharing it. In the case of 'taboo' we can only grasp what it is for something to be taboo if we extend our insight beyond the rules which govern the use of the expression to the point and purpose which these rules once had, but no longer have, and can no longer have in a different social context. We can only understand what it is to use a thoroughly incoherent concept, such as that of a soul in a stick, if we understand what has to be absent from the criteria of practice and of speech for this incoherence not to appear to the user of the concept. In other words we are beginning to notice requirements for the elucidation of concepts which are necessarily absent from the kind of account given by Evans-Pritchard or by Winch.

We have not only to give the rules for the use of the relevant expressions, but to show what the point could be of following such rules, and in bringing out this feature of the case one shows also whether the use of this concept is or is not a possible one for people who have the standards of intelligibility in speech and action which we have. But do we have to be thus self-centred in our application of criteria? Can we, as it might appear from this, only understand what makes sense to us already? Can we learn nothing from societies or modes of social life which we cannot understand within our present framework? Why dismiss what does not fit easily into that framework? Why not revise the framework? To find a clue to the answering of these questions

Faith and the Philosophers

let us examine yet a third doctrine of intelligibility in anthropology.

(C) Dr. E. R. Leach [1] commits himself to a version of the philosophical theory that the meaning of an expression is nothing other than the way in which the expression is used. Myth is to be understood in terms of ritual, saying in terms of doing. To interpret any statement made by primitive people which appears unintelligible, ask what the people in question do. So Leach writes that 'myth regarded as a statement in words "says" the same thing as ritual regarded as a statement in action. To ask questions about the content of belief which are not contained in the content of ritual is nonsense.' [2] Leach, that is, adopts an opposite standpoint to Evans-Pritchard. Evans-Pritchard insists that the anthropologist has to allow the Nuer to make sense in the Nuer's own terms; Leach insists that his Burmese society must be made sense of in Leach's own terms. What is impressive here is that both Evans-Pritchard and Leach have written anthropological classics and this may be thought to be inconsistent with what I have just said. But the reason why we get insight both into Evans-Pritchard's *Nuer* and Leach's *Kachin* is that both are so explicit in presenting us both with their philosophical assumptions and with the field-material to which they apply those assumptions. Each furnishes us not merely with a finished interpretation but with a view of the task of interpretation while it is being carried out.

In Leach's case, although his attitude is the opposite of that of Evans-Pritchard, the results are oddly similar. In the case of the Nuer everything made sense, for the Nuer were judged on their own terms. In the case of the Kachin everything makes sense, for the rules of interpretation provide that every statement which appears not to make sense is to be translated into one that does. So Leach insists that metaphysical questions about the spirits in whom the Kachin believe (*nats*) are out of place. We cannot ask if *nats* eat or where they live for we are not to treat statements about *nats*

[1] *The Political Systems of Highland Burma*, Ball, London, 1954.
[2] *Op. cit.*

as statements at all, but as ritual performances which can be performed properly or improperly, but which are scarcely true or false.

The counterpart to Leach in the philosophy of religion is perhaps Professor R. B. Braithwaite's reinterpretation of the meaning of religious utterances. Braithwaite sets out a classification of utterances derived from his philosophical empiricism and asks where religion can be fitted in.[1] The answer is that the room left for religion is in providing a specification and a backing for ways of life. I do not want to discuss Braithwaite's position in this paper. I only want to point out that Braithwaite's way of giving a sense to religious utterances distracts us from the question. What sense do these utterances have for those who make them? And because Braithwaite deprives us of this question, he makes it unintelligible that anyone should cease to believe, on the grounds that he can no longer find a sense in such utterances. So also it seems difficult to see what view Leach could take of a Kachin who was persuaded, for example by a Christian missionary, that his belief in *nats* was false and idolatrous.

It is therefore true that if the criteria of intelligibility with which we approach alien concepts are too narrow we may be liable not only to erroneously dismiss them as senseless but even more misleadingly we may try to force them to a sense which they do not possess. It must seem at this point that my attempt to illuminate the original dilemma has merely led to the formulation of the second one. For it seems that we cannot approach alien concepts except in terms of our own criteria, and that yet to do this is to be in danger of distortion. But in fact if we are careful we shall be able to set out some of the necessary prerequisites for an adequate understanding of beliefs and concepts without this inconsistency.

Against Winch and Evans-Pritchard I have argued that to make a belief and the concepts which it embodies intelligible I cannot avoid invoking my own criteria, or rather the established criteria of my own society. Against Braithwaite

[1] *An Empiricist's View of the Nature of Religious Belief.*

and Leach I have argued that I cannot do this until I have already grasped the criteria governing belief and behaviour in the society which is the object of enquiry. And I only complete my task when I have filled in the social context so as to make the transition from one set of criteria to the other intelligible. These requirements can be set out more fully as follows:

(1) All interpretation has to begin with detecting the standards of intelligibility established in a society. As a matter of fact no one can avoid using clues drawn from their own society; and as a matter of exposition analogies from the anthropologist's society will often be helpful. But we have to begin with the society's implicit forms of self-description. Malinowski is contemptuous of the account which, so he says, a Trobriander would give of his own society; but Malinowski's own account of the Trobrianders is curiously like that which he puts in the mouth of his imagined Trobriand informant. And, had it not been, there would have been something radically wrong with it, since how a man describes himself is partially constitutive of what he is. It does not follow from this, as I have already suggested, that the descriptions used or the standards of intelligibility detected will always be internally coherent. And, if they are not, a key task will be to show how this incoherence does not appear as such to the members of the society or else does appear and is somehow made tolerable.

(2) But in detecting incoherence of this kind we have already invoked *our* standards. Since we cannot avoid doing this it is better to do it self-consciously. Otherwise we shall project on to our studies, as Frazer notoriously did, an image of our own social life. Moreover, if we are sufficiently sensitive we make it possible for us to partially escape from our own cultural limitations. For we shall have to ask not just how we see the Trobrianders or the Nuer, but how they do or would see us. And perhaps what hitherto looked intelligible and obviously so will then appear opaque and question-begging.

(3) We can now pass on to the stage at which the

difficult and important question can be put. How is it that what appears intelligible in one social context can appear not to make sense in another? What has to be underlined is that answers to this question are not necessarily all going to be of the same form.

There is the type of case where a concept works very well, so long as certain questions are not asked about it, and it may be that for a long time in a given society there is no occasion for raising such questions. The concept of the divine right of kings will undergo a strain which reveals internal incoherences only when rival claimants to sovereignty appear, for it contains no answer to the question Which king has divine right? Then there is the type of case where incoherence and intelligibility are to some extent manifest to the users of the concept. But the use of the concept is so intimately bound up with forms of description which cannot be dispensed with if social and intellectual life is to continue that any device for putting up with the incoherence is more tolerable than dispensing with the concept. A third type of case is that in which the point of a concept or group of concepts lies in their bearing upon behaviour. But changed patterns of social behaviour deprive the concept of point. So that although there is no internal incoherence in the concept, the concept can no longer be embodied in life as it once was, and it is either put to new uses or it becomes redundant. An example of this would be the concept of honour detached from the institutions of chivalry. 'It is difficult', a British historian once wrote, 'to be chivalrous without a horse'. And the change in the importance of the horse in war can turn *Don Quixote* from a romance into a satire.

(D) I must seem to have come a very long way round. And it is therefore perhaps worth trying to meet the charge of irrelevance by saying what I hope the argument has achieved. I first posed the question: in what sense, if any, can sceptic and believer be said to share the same concepts, and so to understand one another? I then tried to show how the anthropologist might be said to grasp concepts which he does not share, in the sense that he does not make the same judgements employing them as do the people whom he studies. I now want to use my answer on this point to pose a new question which will begin the journey back to the original enquiry. This is still an anthropological question. Up to the seventeenth century we should in our society all have been believers and indeed there would be no question of our being anything else. We should not merely have believed that God existed and was revealed in Christ but we should have found it obvious and unquestionable that this was so. Since the seventeenth century, even for those who believe, the truth and intelligibility of their beliefs is not obvious in the same sense. What accounts for the fact that what was once obvious is now not so? What accounts for the fact that nobody now believes in God in the way that mediaeval men did, simply because men are aware of alternatives? And more importantly still, what makes some of the alternatives appear as obvious to modern sceptics as belief in God did for pre-seventeenth-century Christians?

I pose this question as a background to another. If we can understand why one group of men in the past found Christian beliefs obviously true and intelligible and another group now find them opaque, and we can locate the difference between these two groups, perhaps we shall also be able to locate the difference between contemporary believers and contemporary sceptics. And if we do this we shall have solved our original problem. This brief excursus may make clear the relevance of my apparently rambling procedure. So it becomes urgent to attempt an answer, at least an outline, to the anthropological question. And the form of this answer will be to ask which of the different types of answer to the question How is it that what appears intelligible in one social context can appear not to make sense in another? is applicable in the case of the transition from mediaeval belief to modern scepticism.

It is obvious that the internal incoherences in Christian concepts did not go unnoticed in the Middle Ages. The antinomies of benevolent omnipotence and evil, or of divine predestination and human freedom, were never more clearly and acutely discussed. But it is not the case in general that mediaeval thinkers who were dissatisfied with the solutions offered to these antinomies differed in their attitude to belief in God or belief in Christ from thinkers who believed that they or others had offered satisfactory solutions. So the problem becomes: why do the same intellectual difficulties at one time appear as difficulties but no more, an incentive to enquiry but not a ground for disbelief, while at another time they appear as a final and sufficient ground for scepticism and for the abandonment of Christianity? The answers to this question are surely of the second and third types which I outlined in the last section. That is, the apparent incoherence of Christian concepts was taken to be tolerable (and treated as apparent and not real) because the concepts were part of a set of concepts which were indispensable to the forms of description used in social and intellectual life. It is the secularization of our forms of description, constituting part of the secularization of our life, that has left the contradictions high and dry. To take an obvious example, Christianity does not and never has depended upon the truth of an Aristotelian physics in which the physical system requires a Prime Mover, and consequently many sceptics as well as many believers have treated the destruction of the Aristotelian argument in its Thomist form as something very little germane to the question of whether or not Christianity is true. But in fact the replacement of a physics which requires a Prime Mover by a physics which does not secularizes a whole area of enquiry. It weakens the hold of the concept of God on our intellectual life by showing that in this area we can dispense with descriptions which have any connection with the concept.

Some Christian theologians such as Paul Tillich have welcomed this process of secularization, describing it in Tillich's terms as a transition from heteronomous to autonomous reason. But the counterpart to secularization is that the specific character of religion becomes clearer at the cost of diminishing its content. Primitive religion is part of the whole form of human life. Durkheim in *The*

Faith and the Philosophers

Elementary Forms of the Religious Life tried to show, and had at least some success in showing, that the most primitive modes of our categorical grasp of the world are inextricably embedded in religion. Thus it is even difficult to talk of 'religion' in this context, as though one could identify a separate and distinct element. But it is just this distinctiveness which can be identified in our culture. Religious apologists, not sceptics, stress the uniqueness of religious utterance. The slogan 'Every kind of utterance has its own kind of logic' finds a ready response from theologians.

The counterpart to this is an easy toleration for contradiction and incoherence, through the use of such concepts as 'the absurd' (Kierkegaard), 'paradox' (Barth) or 'mystery' (Marcel). We can in fact reach a point at which religion is made logically invulnerable. The attempt in the controversy over the falsification of religious assertions to show that if religion were irrefutable religious utterances would be deprived of sense failed for the same reason that attacks on Azande witchcraft would fail. Religious believers do know what would have to occur for their beliefs to be falsified — they can specify some occurrences with which the existence of omnipotent benevolence is incompatible ('utterly pointless evil' is one commonly used example). But just as the Azande can state what would falsify their assertions about witchcraft — but we could never know that such an occurrence had taken place — so the Christian will leave us in the same difficulty. For the after-life, that which we do not see, may always lend point to otherwise pointless evil, or absurd happenings. This line of argument is certainly open to attack; but the invocation of concepts such as 'mystery' or 'paradox' is always there in the background. Thus the logical invulnerability of Christianity seems to me a position that can be maintained.[1] But only at a cost. The cost is emptiness.

I have already produced reasons to explain why incoherences which only presented problems to an Occam could present insuperable obstacles to a T. H. Huxley or a Russell.

---

[1] As I myself did maintain it in 'The Logical Status of Religious Beliefs' in *Metaphysical Beliefs*.

Can One be a Believer Today?

But now I want to argue that the form of Christian apologetic on moral questions itself exhibits Christian concepts as irrelevant in the modern world in much the way in which the concepts of chivalry became irrelevant in the seventeenth century. For what Christian apologists try to show is that unless we live in a certain way certain ill consequences will follow (broken homes and delinquency, perhaps). But this turns Christianity into a testable nostrum. For we can always ask empirically: do particular religious practices in fact produce higher standards of behaviour? Again we return to the very simple point — are Christians in fact different from other people in our society, apart from their ritual practices? And if they are not what is the point of Christian belief, in so far as it issues an injunction? Now, whether Christians are different or not is an empirical question. Certainly empirical enquiry cannot tell us whether Christianity is true or not. But if Christian beliefs belong now to a social context in which their connection with behaviour has ceased to be clear (as it was clear in the Roman empire, say) the question of the truth of Christianity is put into a different perspective.

Christians here will perhaps want to point to the distinctively Christian forms of behaviour of the Confessional Church under Hitler, and this is certainly relevant. For the regressive primitivism of National Socialism with its idols provided a context sufficiently alike to that of early Christianity to make Christianity once more relevant. The Nazis desecularized society with a vengeance. But while to be asked to choose for Christ has a clear meaning when the practical choices are those of the Nazi society, does this injunction have a clear meaning also in our society? And if it had would we not in fact find Christians united on ways of behaving in a way that they are not?

From an historical point of view, of course, it is most unfair to present Christianity as only the victim of secularization. Christianity, especially Protestant Christianity, was itself a powerful secularizing agent, destroying in the name of God any attempt to deify nature, and so helping to rid the world of magic and making nature available for scientific enquiry. The kind of negative theology which refuses to identify any object with the divine (God is not this, not that) has its final fruit in the kind of atheism which Simone Weil and Tillich both see as a recognition of the fact that God cannot be identified with any particular existing object. But what is left to Simone Weil or Tillich is in fact a religious vocabulary without any remaining secular content. Hegel's irreligion consists in his insight into the possibility of extracting truth from its religious husks. Kierkegaard's answer to Hegel is the assertion of a religion defined entirely in its own religious terms, uncriticizable *ab externo*. Together Hegel and Kierkegaard reflect accurately the status of religion in a secularized environment.

(E) For a sceptic to grasp the point of religious belief, therefore, he has to supply a social context which is now lacking and abstract a social context which is now present, and he has to do this for the mediaeval Christian, just as the anthropologist has to do it for the Azande or the aborigines. But in dialogue with contemporary Christians the sceptic is forced to recognize that they see a point in what they say and do although they lack that context. And therefore either he or they are making a mistake, and not a mistake over God, but a mistake over criteria of intelligibility. What is at issue between sceptic and Christian is the character of the difference between belief and unbelief as well as the issue of belief itself. Thus the sceptic is committed to saying that he understands the Christian's use of concepts in a way that the Christian himself does not, and presumably *vice versa*. The discussion is therefore transferred to another level, and a Christian refutation of this paper would have to provide an alternative account of intelligibility. If I am right, understanding Christianity is incompatible with believing in it, not because Christianity is vulnerable to sceptical objections, but because its peculiar invulnerability belongs to it as a form of belief which has lost the social context which once made it comprehensible. It is now too late to be mediaeval and it is too empty and too easy to be Kierkegaardian. Thus sceptic and believer do not share a common grasp of the relevant concepts any more than anthropologist and Azande do. And if the believer wishes to he can always claim that we can only disagree with him because we do not understand him. But the implications of this defence of belief are more fatal to it than any attack could be.

IT IS COMPATIBLE!

BY

NORRIS CLARKE, S.J.

THERE is no doubt that Mr. MacIntyre has given us a very intelligent paper to discuss. It brings up a key problem of our contemporary pluralistic culture, that of mutual understanding between believers and non-believers in a living religion (specifically the Christian religion for our culture) and the possibility of intelligent discussion between them, and it presents a type of answer, clothed in sophisticated terms, which is not merely private to the author but perhaps the one most widely accepted or lived implicitly in our day by intelligent non-believers (or sceptics, as the author more accurately calls them, to distinguish them from simply disinterested agnostics). In my own comments I would like first to summarize briefly the essentials of the author's position taken in the paper and then assay the strength of its challenge to the reasonableness of Christian belief. I intend to do this by making fully explicit the hidden or not fully expressed premises of his argument from analogy, which I find both partially illumines and partially obscures the issue.

The problem is that of the difficulty of mutual understanding between sceptics and believers when, as is the case, they differ totally in their judgements about most, if not all, of the key concepts of the Christian religion, such as God, salvation, Providence, sin, etc. Now, total disagreement about a given concept is a pretty sure indication that the parties in disagreement do not really share in common the concept about which they are making judgements.

But unless they agree to some extent on the meaning of the concept under discussion it is impossible even to disagree meaningfully in judgements about it. The parties are not even talking the same language. Hence a common understanding of Christian religious concepts by both sceptics and believers seems at once necessary and impossible — surely a strange state of affairs. And it is clear that the onus of solving the problem falls principally on the sceptic, since it is hard to see how one can be a positive sceptic or disbeliever if one does not understand what it is that one disbelieves in. The case is not the same, we might add, for a pure agnostic.

After disposing — quite successfully to my mind — of certain over-facile ways of trying to escape the dilemma, the author proposes his own very ingenious and fruitful suggestion of a way out of this embarrassing *impasse*. It is to use as a model or analogy the manner in which the anthropologist goes about trying to understand the beliefs of a primitive culture which he himself does not share. For the anthropologist does claim to understand at least to some extent 'concepts' like *taboo*, *mana*, etc., which go to make up such beliefs. Otherwise he would soon be out of business.

The author's balanced and penetrating critical analysis of the different theories of what it means to understand a primitive culture lead him to the following conclusions:

(1) It is true that there is no single abstract norm of intelligibility in general transcending all social contexts, which can serve as an effective criterion for judging the presence or absence of intelligibility in all concrete cases. Hence to understand a given belief in a given culture we must first enter sympathetically into that culture or language-game within the culture to discover what are the criteria of intelligibility accepted within the culture at the time.

(2) On the other hand, the attempt to maintain a total relativism of intelligibility, or an extreme Wittgensteinian theory of language-games as totally self-contained, self-justifying, by their own unique internal criteria, and hence immune to evaluation from without, is also untenable and in fact impossible to follow out. I agree here with the author and I would add to his factual evidence the deeper reason, discoverable also in human experience, that, although there

is no common expressible *formula* for intelligibility among all men, there is at least a common basic *exigency* of rationality in the wide sense, which resides like a hidden compass in the unity of the living consciousness of any person with the use of reason, no matter how varied the ways in which he expresses or lives it out. It is this which enables him to compare critically his own various language-games with each other or with other men's, discover inconsistencies or incoherences within any one, and amend or reject it. Certain concepts or modes of thinking may indeed be difficult or impossible to grasp in their full *positive* content without some kind of special corresponding experience. But at least certain basic *negative* criteria, by which we judge that a given belief is wanting in intelligibility, are by their nature more susceptible of universal application, given sufficient sensitivity to modes of thinking and speaking different from our own.

Mr. MacIntyre then works out some of the main criteria for validly passing such negative judgements. They can be reduced to three : (i) when a belief or concept is no longer relevant to the present social context; (ii) when it is not coherent and consistent both internally and with the facts known to the believer; (iii) when it can survive only in the absence of a wider knowledge of facts or a richer set of categories possessed by the evaluator, especially categories of effectiveness and ineffectiveness built up by the practice of science and technology.

Again I think we have to thank the author for a most helpful and fruitful analysis. It should be noted, however, that his set of criteria permit one only to make negative judgements on the belief being examined, in a word, to *disbelieve* it. They presuppose the positive understanding of its content and give no help for achieving this end. They also presuppose a richer intellectual equipment in the evaluator and disbeliever than in the believer. None the less, if these conditions are all verified, Mr. MacIntyre's set of criteria seems to me to be an excellent tool of analysis, especially for throwing light on the breakdown or decay of a given belief.

Can One be a Believer Today?

My two serious criticisms arise, first, from the manner in which he applies his criteria to the beliefs of primitive cultures and, secondly, from the manner in which he applies them to Christian belief. With regard to primitive cultures, what worries me very much is that nowhere does the author speak of symbolic thinking (or of mythical thinking — I take the former as including but wider then the latter), let alone indicate that it is a mode of thought quite different from abstract thinking in the conceptual and analytic mode so dominant in western culture since the Greeks. Thus he speaks of the 'concepts' of taboo, mana, etc. But from what I understand of the studies made of mythical and symbolic thinking in recent years — and this is the kind of thinking involved in the religious beliefs of most primitive people — terms like mana, taboo, etc., do not stand for concepts in our sense at all. They function rather as 'symbolic formulae' within a holistic, indivisible unit of symbolic thinking. The aim of such thought and language is not to analyse, assert or explain anything in a literal way, but rather to express in a dramatic manner the speaker's existential communion with nature and the forces behind it. The concept seeks clarity by abstracting and dividing off something from the web of reality. The symbol remains deliberately vague, concrete and mysterious so as to be as all-inclusive as possible, to set up resonances on as many levels as possible, to express or stimulate existential participation, not analysis or explanation.

Thus when some Eskimos speak of the great woman who lives at the bottom of the sea and sends them up their food from her bounty, this is less a causal explanation of the source of their food supply than a dramatic restatement of the actual facts of their daily life understood as communion with nature. Hence if one were to ask them whether they really believed there was a real woman who actually lived at the bottom of the ocean and literally sent up seals and other food to them, one would really be forcing them out of the symbolic mode of thinking to which they were giving expression and demanding a literal transcription into our conceptual, analytic and explanatory mode. If they were sophisticated enough, or had had the good fortune to spend a few terms on scholarship at Oxford or Cambridge or Princeton, or the like, they would wisely refuse to answer or would protest against this 'category mistake'. If not, they might feel that they would have to answer 'yes', thus unwittingly betraying the authentic meaning they were trying to express. Similarly, when some primitive peoples say the sun is a white cockatoo, it is possible that such an expression cannot be analysed into three analytic concepts, *sun, white cockatoo,* and *is,* which are then synthesized into a judgement. Rather, 'The-sun-is-a-white-cockatoo' is a single symbolic expression in which all the elements are fused into a single new meaning somehow linked with, yet irreducible to, their ordinary meaning, as though transposed into a new key. In general this new meaning may be a way of expressing the lived intercommunion of all natural forces, or something of the sort.

Now I think it is clear enough that in the presence of such symbolic thinking the application of the norms of inconsistency or incoherence must be quite different from their application to our more literal analytical type of conceptual thinking, or even our self-conscious use of metaphor. The norm of literal verbal contradiction is quite irrelevant and it is no wonder that the primitives who use such a mode of thinking are not bothered at all by such 'contradictions' in their thought and language, even though they might be quite incapable of explaining why in conceptual terms. I suspect something similar might be said about the aborigines who carry around a stick as though it contained their soul. It is thus a very tricky business to apply the negative criteria of incoherence and inconsistency to such symbolic thinking, and I wish Mr. MacIntyre had given more evidence of taking this into account. It is quite true, of course, that a unit of symbolic thought can to a certain extent be transposed into the conceptual mode and its components partially analysed into concepts. But the translation can never be exhaustive; it must always leave behind, unanalysed, a certain irreducible living residue, a unifying existential attitude of communion which must be lived to be understood adequately and is denatured if analysed abstractly. It can, perhaps, be realized by sympathy or empathy from without even by those who do not share it, but it cannot be expressed in abstract, analytic language. This difficulty, of course, would not affect the effectiveness of his other two criteria: namely, relevance to present social context and ability to survive only in the absence of richer sets of categories.

It is important to add here that symbolic thinking by no means exists only in primitive societies, though it is certainly more predominant there. All living religions, it seems, use the symbolic mode of thought and ritual to express the believers' lived personal realization of their dependence on and communion with the divine. But when such a religion is imbedded in a culture which also possesses a highly developed conceptual and analytical mode of thinking, and especially when such a religion has made use of this instrument to elaborate a self-conscious conceptual theology, there is a special danger of overlooking the irreducible core of symbolic language and action which is the living heart of the religion and to attempt to understand and evaluate it purely as a set of concepts united in propositions, as though the belief were a belief primarily in a set of propositions held as true. This danger is still further increased when, as in the case of our contemporary Western culture or, in fact, of any industrialized society, the conceptual analytic mode of thinking has become so predominant that its members have almost lost the feel of the rich existential meaning and power of symbolic thought, language and action. This is the point of the return to Biblical and patristic theology and to the liturgy now in evidence all over the Christian West, namely, to restore to vitality once more the living core of the Christian religion and its symbolic expression as a form of God-directed life, too long overlaid and obscured by expression in the abstract conceptual mode of thought and language. I do not find any evidence of awareness of this fundamental character of religious thought and language in Mr. MacIntyre's paper, though it might possibly be only for reasons of lack of space.

Let us now move on, in the light of the foregoing remarks, to the crucial point at issue, the application of the author's set of negative criteria to Christian belief in the contemporary world. Here I must frankly confess that, although Christians can learn a good deal from Mr. MacIntyre's implied criticism of Christianity as lived in the West, it seems to me that his analogy of the anthropologist obscures more than it illumines its referent.

In the first place, let me smoke out what seems to be an unexpressed implication of the analogy, though Mr. MacIntyre would not perhaps wish to push it this far. The anthropologist is dealing with a more primitive culture than his own, one that does not possess his own richer and more refined equipment of conceptual analysis. Now, for the parallel to be relevant, the modern sceptic should be applying his own presumably richer and more sophisticated intellectual resources to an earlier and less developed state of Christian culture, say the early, or mediaeval, or at least pre-scientific-revolution Church, in which Christians lacked his own superior vantage-point. But the trouble is that the setting to be explained is not some earlier phase of Christian belief, but the contemporary world in which sceptics and believers share the same culture and conceptual instruments. This world contains large numbers of Christians in many countries, including our own, who are quite at home in all the available modern techniques of scientific and analytic thinking in the major fields of thought, and yet consider this kind of critical thinking quite compatible with sincere Christian belief. These believers are just as capable of applying the test of relevance to present social context or inseparability from a past social context as are unbelievers, and it is noteworthy that they consider one of the outstanding characteristics of Christian belief to be its ability to transcend all social contexts and incarnate itself inexhaustibly in ever new cultures and periods of history.

Thus sceptics and believers are not divided into two cultures, one more developed than the other, but into two attitudes towards the same data among equals within the same culture — something relatively new in history, at least on a large scale. Thus for the analogy of the anthropologist to be at all relevant the author would at least have to present impressive evidence that Christians can live intellectually in the modern world and still maintain their Christian belief only at the expense of some sort of schizophrenic split in their consciousness, so that when they enter the latter domain of Christian belief and action they would have to close the door behind them on their habits of critical thinking and regress to an atmosphere inseparable from a more primitive social context and mode of thinking. Such a position would indeed be difficult to establish either on factual or *a priori* grounds, and certainly the author has not tried to do so.

Unfortunately, not a few Christians do seem to live with such a split consciousness. But this is to my mind a mark of the immaturity of their Christian belief and its lack of integration with the rest of their life. There is indeed always a tension between critical analytical thinking and lived Christian belief, just as there is in any man between his critical analytical faculties and his existentially-lived values, especially in the realm of intimate interpersonal relations. But this can and should be a vital and fruitful tension, stimulating the believer to a deeper appreciation of the precarious human condition, itself already illumined by his faith.

Let us now come to closer grips with the core of the author's challenge: namely, that the relevance of Christian belief is indeed tied inseparably to past social contexts and cannot survive their disappearance save as a kind of anachronism to which the believer can adhere only by living in the past. Again the author's general analysis of how concepts lose relevance when their original social contexts are changed seems to me both valid and fruitful. But again, too, the application to Christian belief seems to me to miss some of the latter's most distinctive characteristics. The criticism is indeed quite effective when applied to most primitive religions, and for a very good reason. The content of such religions usually expresses the believer's communion with nature according to the particular concrete mode of relation to material nature proper to this particular culture. In other words, the very content of the religion embodies to a large extent an expression of the concrete social context. Hence when that context or mode of relation to the material world is changed, the belief itself cannot long survive. Thus if the Eskimos mentioned earlier were to be suddenly transplanted to a place where most of their food came from supermarkets, their belief in the great woman under the sea who sends up their food could hardly remain relevant for long.

But one of the most fundamental characteristics of Christianity is that it is precisely not a religion expressing communion with material nature in its ever-recurring cyclic rhythms but a conversion to a spiritual God transcending all of nature, who calls the believer to a new personal *supernatural* relation with him. It implies a rupture with any kind of worship of nature or personified natural forces treated as gods. It is symbolized by the call to Abraham, father of the Chosen People, to rise up, leave his native land and go forth whither God should lead him; by Israel's exodus from Egypt and wandering in the desert; by Christ's call to leave all things and 'Come, follow Me'; and by Paul's exhortation in the same spirit to die to the world with Christ and live now, in the world but not of it, for God alone.

In other words, the content of Christian belief includes an explicit break with the old nature or cosmic religions, with their dependence on some concrete mode of relation to nature, and an explicit orientation towards a universality transcending all cultures: 'Go therefore and teach all nations . . .'; 'There is no longer Jew or Greek', but all are one in Christ, the one mediator for all men, etc. It is true that the Founder of Christianity in teaching its transcultural content used parables and examples drawn from his own social context of Palestine, and that as Christianity takes roots in different cultures or changing phases of the same culture it must incarnate itself creatively in ever new cultural symbols and modes of expression. But when such social contexts change radically or pass away, what is affected, if one has really grasped the authentic living core of Christian belief, is only the particular mode of expression or cultural impact, not the essential content of the belief itself. The discernment of one from the other is not always easy for those immersed in a given culture with little knowledge of any other, especially during a period of cultural revolution or decay. But it becomes clearer once the new incarnation has taken root. And it is much easier for us today to distinguish essential content from accidental and transient form in our more consciously pluralistic and easily intercommunicating world.

Hence I would say, contrary to the author, that, as Christian belief moves down through changing social contexts, its essential religious content does not steadily shrink towards a hypothetical vanishing-point, as is indeed the case with most primitive or nature religions, tied as they are to a particular cultural mode of communion with nature and with the divine immanent in it. I admit, however, that the author has here posed a very crucial and fruitful question that is an excellent topic for discussion. *Something* certainly diminishes in the relation of religion to life when social change occurs in a Christian culture. And this is especially true in the case of that particular type of change which the author stresses so justly: the progressive secularization of areas of human life once directly governed by religious belief. This is the most significant cultural phenomenon of modern times with respect to the place of religious belief in human life. What exactly diminishes here? Mr. MacIntyre would maintain it is the very content of the religious belief itself. I would maintain that the shrinkage occurs in two areas: first, in the direct and explicit *influence* of the belief in the particular areas of the culture, not in the essential content; secondly, in the literal, unconsciously culture-bound interpretation of the rich symbolic language of the primary sources of Christian revelation, the Bible (and analogously in the sacred books of any religion that can successfully survive profound social change).

But it is noteworthy that this kind of diminution in the direct application of religion to life is also accompanied in any vital Christian group by a compensating increase not only in the purity and depth of their comprehension of the content of their belief but also in a gradual positive unfolding or explication of previously unsuspected implications and meanings within this essential content itself. This is called by Catholics 'the development of dogma' and its closest analogue is perhaps the organic growth of a seed or embryo in the direction of fuller articulation of the dynamic 'form' already present within it from the beginning. Or perhaps a still better analogue is the growth of a person or social group in self-consciousness, or self-discovery, as they are forced to commit themselves and express themselves in clearly articulated ways of thinking and acting in response to the varied existential challenges of real life in process. This growth in depth, purity and articulateness of comprehension of the original content of a belief more than compensates, to my mind, for the loss of an earlier more direct, but often naïvely unreflective, conception of the influence of religion on life, as well as for an over naïve, literal and culture-bound mode of interpretation of the original sources of revelation. It is clear that a rigidly fundamentalist, letter-bound mode of religious belief cannot long survive profound social changes, especially among an uneducated population, but speaking for Catholicism (though something similar holds more and more for most other Christian denominations), it has never been rigidly fundamentalist in spirit and is becoming markedly less so at present as it grows in mature and explicit comprehension of the nature of divine revelation as mediated through human channels and of the laws of authentic development of dogma. In the light of the above remarks, the author's example of St. Thomas's Aristotelian-inspired proofs of God loses most of its force and relevance, it seems to me.

This brings us to our final and perhaps most crucial objection to Mr. MacIntyre's challenging analysis. He admits at the end of his paper that in fact Christians of our own day, living in the same culture as disbelievers and equipped with the same intellectual resources, still interpret the same data differently. Hence one of the two parties must be making a mistake or else both differ in their understanding of what Christian faith really means to a mature Christian.

This is indeed the nub of the whole question. And here we return to our first difficulty over Mr. MacIntyre's analysis, the overlooking of the distinctive nature of symbolic thinking and the interpretation of religious belief as essentially a set of concepts joined in propositions held as true. I admit that this is a point easy to miss in the case of Christianity and above all, I fear, in the case of the Roman Catholic Church with its outwardly so forbidding and — so it might seem — adequately conceptualized definitions and formulas of belief, proposed as infallible and immutable.

Yet the living core of Christian belief and the key to the existential process of conversion is not at all, as any competent Christian theologian will explicitly admit, intellectual acceptance of a set of propositions held as true on exclusively intellectual grounds. It is rather first and foremost an existential, global and unconditional commitment of loving trust to a person, that of Jesus of Nazareth, as witnessed to by his immediate disciples in the Gospels and renewed continually in the life of the Church. One first sizes up and accepts the person as manifesting the wisdom, power and love of God to us that we may 'have life and have it more abundantly'. Then the believer decides to 'follow Him', to take Him as the Way, the Truth and the Life in his own life.[1]

This very following of Christ necessarily involves thinking, speaking and acting as far as we can, like Jesus: 'Go . . . and make disciples of all nations . . . teaching them to observe all that I have commanded you'; 'Do this in

---

[1] Thus Jesus constantly appeals to those whom he addresses to 'have faith *in him*'. An excellent and typical example of this process of faith may be found in the dialogue between Jesus and Martha before the tomb of Lazarus: 'Jesus said, "I am the resurrection and I am life. If a man has faith in me, even though he die, he shall come to life; and no one who is alive and has faith shall ever die. Do you believe this?" "Lord, I do," she answered; "I now believe that you are the Messiah, the Son of God who was to come into the world."' John 11: 25-27 (*The New English Bible*, 1962). *Cf.* Jean Mouroux, *I Believe: The Personal Structure of Faith*, Sheed and Ward, New York, 1959.

commemoration of me', etc. This in turn necessarily involves within its total existential, personal commitment a whole set of truths to be intellectually assented to, which are partly explicit, partly implicit, in the teaching *and whole life* of Christ himself.

The Church in its official teaching, as well as theologians in their speculation, strives constantly to reflect on this rich existential treasure of the person, life and teachings of Christ and to unfold it in conceptual explication as far as it can. But the task is an endless one, as it is for anyone in love to spell out what he sees and loves in his beloved. And no amount of conceptual analysis and refined formulation will ever be able to grasp and express exhaustively the living core of existential communion with Christ, through him with his brethren, and through him and in him with the Father and the Holy Spirit. This is a *mode of existence*, of personal existence, and not *primarily* a set of propositions held to be true, though the latter point to and safeguard the former. That is why the ultimate mode of expression of Christian belief as lived, which functions as the point of departure and return of all conceptual and analytic modes, must be the richly concrete, at least partially symbolic language of Scripture and the liturgy, which draws those who hear it with faith into an existential attitude of communion with the divine through Christ, illumined from within by a kind of lived understanding irreducible to adequate expression in abstract concepts and propositions.

To sum it up very simply, the primary and most fundamental question in evaluating Christian belief is not 'What is the meaning and evidence for these propositions in the Creed or in further definitions of doctrine by the Church', but rather, 'What think you of Christ? Are you willing to trust and follow him, take him as the Way, the Truth, the Life for *you*, and as a consequence accept his teachings because you trust him and believe he is giving them to you as God's wisdom for your salvation?' It is this personal core, transcending all conceptual formulations, which makes possible both (1) the organic development of Christian belief from within by a process of explication that is more akin to growth in self-awareness than to logical entailment, and hence is never precisely predictable beforehand, though reasonable after the fact; and (2) the capacity to transcend all particular cultural contexts and culture-bound modes of explication. Perhaps this will serve as an embryonic sketch of an alternative account of the kind of intelligibility proper to Christian belief that Mr. MacIntyre quite legitimately asked for at the end of what I found a most stimulating and fruitful paper.

DISCUSSION

Norris Clarke, S.J.: A Further Critique of MacIntyre's Thesis

After the discussion following Mr. MacIntyre's paper, the nature of the fundamental issue he was raising became clearer to me, and I believe I am now in a position to sharpen up my own counter-challenge more effectively.

MacIntyre's fundamental reason why understanding Christian belief is incompatible with believing in it is that understanding it leads to the discovery that its specifically religious content is relevant only to certain cultural contexts now past. And since the permanently valid moral contributions of Christianity have now become assimilated by secular humanism, the remaining religious content which first gave birth to these moral attitudes has now become vacuous for our modern scientific-minded society.

Now, in making this charge, Mr. MacIntyre has committed himself, it seems to me, to a position that is very hard to defend. For, granted that a given cultural context can make it psychologically easier to believe in the truth of the Christian message, either as a reaction against the culture or as a reinforcement of it, it clearly does not follow that for this reason the message itself is not true but merely a subjective construction whose adequate cause is the pressure to satisfy needs peculiar to this culture. Nor, if a given social context makes it harder to believe, does it follow that the belief is therefore rendered objectively more valid. Otherwise the argument could all too easily be turned against its wielder: since the social context today makes it easier to be an atheist or agnostic, these convictions themselves could thereby be discredited as mere culture-bound attitudes which in turn will lose meaning and relevance as soon as the present social context changes. But this would obviously land us in a hopeless cultural relativism depriving all views of life equally of any truth-value at all. I feel sure Mr. MacIntyre does not intend to commit himself to any such position as this.

If not, then he must be doing one of two things. He might be merely making the quite sound sociological observation that it is harder to believe in Christianity today than in mediaeval or earlier times (though the latter might perhaps be questioned), for the reason that the efficacy of science and technology now makes it harder for many to see the relevance of Christianity to modern life. But such an assertion by no means entails that Christianity is not true or is merely the product of those social contexts more favourable to belief in it; hence such an assertion would be irrelevant to his claim that understanding Christianity is incompatible with believing it. What he must therefore be maintaining is that, in fact, belief in Christianity is a purely human construction resulting from social needs or pressures peculiar only to certain cultural contexts, and is therefore not at all what it claims to be — namely, a response to an objective divine revelation historically communicated to man in the person of Jesus Christ.

Now this charge that belief in Christianity is both culture-caused and culture-bound labours from the difficulty that through its two-thousand-year history Christianity has already survived the passing away of many social contexts and has taken vigorous roots in a wide variety of different cultural contexts, both simultaneous and successive, in Asia, Europe, the Americas, and Africa. Since this process is still operative today, the notion of 'culture-caused' and 'culture-bound' thus becomes so loose and indefinitely elastic as to be rendered worthless as an explanatory category. If the author wishes to hold, as I suspect he does, that the decisive difference between the present and *all* past cultural contexts is the presence of the scientific and technological spirit, and that it is primarily this that renders belief in Christianity no longer relevant to our modern society in scientifically mature nations, then he is forced into the paradoxical consequence of holding that the hundreds of thousands of converts to Christianity every year in such social contexts, including many scholars and scientists, are really the most misguided, self-deceived, intellectually blind, and least excusable of all the long parade of believers in Christianity down to the present day. This is indeed a large order to prove.

In view of all this, it would seem that, if MacIntyre wishes his position to be taken seriously, the responsibility lies upon him to present at least some sample analyses of basic Christian doctrines which are dependent for their intelligibility and relevance upon a social context that has now passed away. But in fact he has presented no such analyses, with the exception perhaps of one brief undeveloped suggestion to the effect that the meaning and relevance of the beatitudes and their opposites in the Sermon on the Mount ('Blessed are you poor . . .'[1] and 'Woe to you rich . . .',[2] etc.) are tied to a social context wherein blessing and cursing are taken seriously as social rituals.

It would not be fair, of course, to make too much of such a brief example. Yet the extreme narrowness and literal rigidity of such an interpretation of this famous text, plus the lack of any feeling for the living understanding of it throughout the long history of Christian tradition, offer, to my mind, modest but very damaging evidence that something is radically wrong with Mr. MacIntyre's own understanding of Christian belief and his manner of reading its primary written source, the New Testament.

To conclude, it seems to me that to bear out his charge that Christian belief is culture-caused and culture-bound MacIntyre is obliged by the nature of the case to present some sample analyses of basic Christian doctrines which fall under this charge, and that he clearly has failed to do so. Until he does this, it seems to me that he has done no more than reinforce what we already know, that *mis*understanding Christianity and believing in it are, or at least should be, incompatible!

As for MacIntyre's original question Is it possible both to understand Christian belief and yet to disbelieve it? it seems to me that it still remains wide open and begging for a solution. In the light of our discussions I would venture the following answer. Although it is not possible to achieve full understanding of Christian belief save through the illumination from within that comes from the existential commitment of faith to the personality of Christ, still a considerable degree of understanding can be achieved, at least enough for intelligent discussion. But the necessary condition is that 'understanding Christian belief' should not be taken as a direct conceptual comprehension, subject to precise and definitive conceptual analysis (i.e. delimitation) of the content of this belief, since it is part of Christian belief itself that its principal doctrines are 'mysteries' revealed as true by Christ but never philosophically explained or justified by internal evidence, nor even accessible to any adequate comprehension by the human mind in this life. Rather it should be taken as understanding how it is possible for a Christian to come reasonably to believe in what exceeds the direct grasp

[1] Luke, 6: 20.   [2] Luke, 6: 24.

of his intelligence. And this requires an analysis of how one can reasonably make an act of total personal commitment to another person and then reasonably accept as true without further evidence that which the latter bears witness to as known by him to be true.

DISCUSSION

Richard Brandt: *Critique of MacIntyre's Starting-Point*

MacIntyre begins by saying that his problem is the dilemma, consisting in the fact that we 'do want to say that a common understanding of religious concepts by sceptics and by believers is both necessary and impossible'.[1] I believe, however, that MacIntyre's suggestion that there is such a dilemma rests on a mistaken assumption: he thinks that people don't share a concept unless they agree 'in at least some central applications of it'.[2]

It must be possible for sceptics and believers to share basic religious concepts, since obviously they often do. Some of the most ardent sceptics are sometime believers, even former students of theology whose mentors in that subject thought they grasped the concepts firmly. It would be absurd to claim that such sceptics do not understand, even quite well, the theological concepts of their former teachers. Of course, not every sceptic need understand the religious language of everyone who meets the loose standards for being a 'Christian' or even of every theologian; but I expect that many sceptics understand quite well what F. R. Tennant meant by 'God', or St. Thomas Aquinas, although they may perhaps be genuinely baffled by the statements of Paul Tillich.

In general, it seems to be a mistake to think that individuals share a concept only when they agree about at least some applications — if by 'application' we mean, as MacIntyre seems to, the predication of the term of some specific individual or situation. For instance, two persons can understand 'courageous' in exactly the same way but never agree about application of the term; for whether an act is to be adjudged courageous depends on how the situation is thought to have presented itself to the

[1] P. 116.   [2] P. 115.

agent, what his values are thought to have been, and so on, and on these matters the speakers may always disagree. One might ask in what sense of 'same concept' two individuals might have the same religious concepts although the one questioned all the existential assertions containing theological terms made by the other. Part of the answer seems to be this. First, in the sense that both would agree about which religious propositions are analytic and which self-contradictory. ('If there is a God, he is omniscient and immaterial.') Next, just as a physicist may think of an electron as a tiny planet with a large electrical charge in comparison with its mass, but with some reservations such as its not being assignable simultaneously both a definite position and velocity, so both the sceptic and the believer may think of God in terms of a human mind with certain limitations removed. Again, the believer and sceptic may agree as to what kinds of fact about the experienced world would support the existence of such a being; for instance, they will think the existence of evil a serious difficulty.

It seems to me possible, then, for a sceptic and a believer to share the same religious concepts. It could be that they disagree only about the force of the supporting evidence or reasons.

It is consistent with this to say, however, as I should be inclined to do, that it is a distinctive feature of contemporary scepticism that there is dissatisfaction with religious language on the point of its meaningfulness. Sceptic and believer may share the same concepts, but the sceptic is apt to make an unfavourable appraisal of the meaningfulness of the language which in a sense he understands (as well as the believer). Because he does, the sceptic may be unhappy about the employment of religious language. Whereas the believer does not make such an unfavourable appraisal. But does this mean, as MacIntyre suggests at the end of the paper, that sceptic and believer necessarily clash over the 'criteria of intelligibility'? I fail to see that it does.

Let me first point out that sceptics about theology need not share the same set of 'criteria of intelligibility': for instance, A. J. Ayer and C. D. Broad. I should imagine the same is true for theologians or philosophers who are believers. There is the much larger question in what sense the general educated public might be said to have 'criteria of intelligibility', and what these are, if there are any. I shall not speculate on this, but rather confine myself to the question whether a person today could be a believer without surrendering the criteria of meaningfulness which a philosopher today must hold, if he is to be reasonable, in the light of the past thirty years. I am not quite sure that

MacIntyre means to take a stand on this question, but I think he does and that his view is that this is *not* possible.

There would be no difficulty if religious language could be construed as purely performatory, ritualistic, etc. MacIntyre seems to me quite right in putting such a possibility aside as not being faithful as an account of the religious language of believers. I hope I am agreeing with him when I say that religious language has to be construed as primarily descriptive or explanatory, like the language of science: explanatory of the existence of a world, of its order, of historical events of large scale, or of significant events in the personal life of the believer. (This is not, of course, to deny that the purpose of making a religious statement in a particular context may be to complete a ritual, or to do any one of very many different things.) If so, our question is whether a believer must surrender the standards of meaningfulness of descriptive or explanatory terms that are reasonably held today.

What is MacIntyre's view about reasonable criteria of meaningfulness? Some of the things he says about 'rules of use' suggest a rather radical form of verifiability theory of meaning. However, I hope he would agree that only a quite tolerant form of verifiability theory is defensible today: something like the view that a statement is meaningful if, and only if, it is well-formed and its non-logical terms are either observation predicates or *predicates which have an essential role in an explanatory theory of the world of experience*. Now such a criterion has the consequence [1] that it is difficult to draw any sharp line between the meaningful and the meaningless, and that it is more useful to grade systems of concepts, as being more or less endowed with meaning, according to the explanatory and predictive power of the system, the clarity of the model and the sharpness of its connection with observation predicates, the rigour of the formulation, and so on.[2]

I see no reason why a contemporary believer need reject a form of meaning criterion roughly along the above lines.

Suppose the sceptic and the believer agreed on the criterion. Is there any way in which we could explain how the sceptic could rate the set of religious concepts low on meaningfulness, whereas the believer could rate them high? I think there is: for the scoring or grading of a system of concepts is not a mechanical matter, and there is room for debate about how well a given system does. I should imagine, for one thing, that there will

---

[1] See Hempel, 'The Concept of Cognitive Significance: A Reconsideration', in *Proceedings of the American Academy of Arts and Sciences*, July 1951.

[2] I do not mean to suggest that Hempel would agree with this, at least as stated.

be differences about exactly what counts as an 'explanation'. Furthermore, and very important, sceptics and theologians can differ on how well a system *might* score, if only it were improved in ways in which excellent minds and time might enable it to be improved. The believer will be more optimistic, the sceptic more pessimistic, on this. For instance, St. Thomas seems to have been aware of the difficulties in the account he gives of analogical predication, but presumably he was able to tolerate it in the thought that future work could make the conception clearer. A candid theologian must admit that MacIntyre is right in thinking that it would have been reasonable to grade St. Thomas's system more highly, in point of meaningfulness, in his day than in our own. For the explanatory work done by his system in his day was greater than it can do today when, for instance, the theory of evolution does in a more detailed way some of the jobs which St. Thomas's fifth argument allocates to God. Moreover, systems of scientific concepts must rate very high in meaningfulness, so that the score of a theological system is now relatively lower, in comparison with large systems of other concepts with which everyone is familiar, than it was in the time of St. Thomas. Still, even if the contemporary believer must in candour rate religious concepts lower than, say, the atomic theory, in point of meaningfulness and lower than they would have reasonably been rated six hundred years ago, he might claim that they do not score too badly considering the problems, and he may construe his job to make the system clearer so that it scores better. If so, we needn't suppose that the sceptic and the theologian necessarily have different criteria of intelligibility, or that the contemporary believer is necessarily making some mistake about criteria of intelligibility.

Perhaps MacIntyre is taking for granted that, at the present day, no person in his senses would seriously regard any theological system as explanatory of anything. At any rate, whether he does or not it rather seems that some theologians would be willing, even eager, to grant this. If one does make this assumption, then I agree that one cannot both construe religious language as explanatory or descriptive language which is meaningful, and also adopt a theory of meaningfulness which is reasonable today. But, to make this dilemma stick, of course, one first has to show the futility of the enterprise of traditional philosophical theology. If one is convinced that traditional theology is futile in this sense, however, it is difficult to see — or at least it is difficult for me to see — what would be one's point in writing a systematic theology, or even in making religious statements.

DISCUSSION

William Alston: *On Sharing Concepts*

Mr. MacIntyre is concerned with failures of understanding in discussions between believers and sceptics. But instead of focusing on specific examples of such failures, he introduces the issue with the following statement of his 'central problem'. '... usually (and the impulse to write "always" is strong) two people could not be said to share a concept or to possess the same concept unless they agreed in at least some central applications of it.'[1] A few lines later he seems to have given in to the impulse, for he writes: 'But two men who disagreed in *every* judgement which employed the concept — of them what could one say that they shared?... It follows that unless I can be said to share your judgements at least to some degree I cannot be said to share your concepts.'[2]

If we include analytic statements, this thesis is undoubtedly true. For if we do not even agree, e.g., as to whether to be omnipotent is to be able to do anything whatsoever, then clearly we are not using 'omnipotent' to express the same concept. But if we restrict the judgements in question to those 'they make in which they assert that objects fall under it', as Mr. MacIntyre seems to want to do, then the thesis is certainly false. We can think of many cases in which two people do not agree in any applications of a term, but nevertheless obviously share the same concept (use the term in the same sense). On a simple level there is, e.g. the concept of a sea serpent. There may have been occasions on which I supposed that there were sea serpents in the vicinity, but you, who were present on the occasions, may deny that what I took to be sea serpents really were, and may furthermore deny that there are any such things; and yet, for all that, we may have exactly the same concept of a sea serpent. Perhaps a better analogy for the theological case is disagreement over high-level theories in science. Consider the concept of the ether as an elastic medium pervading space. I may postulate this, along with various other things, in an explanation of radiation of various kinds, whereas you reject this theory. In this case you do not 'apply' the term to anything, whereas I do, but it seems obvious that we might still have the same concept.

It may be that both of these cases seem unproblematic because of the fact that in each of them the person who doesn't apply the concept to anything can appreciate what it is that

[1] p. 115. [2] p. 115.

leads the other person to do so. That is, he has some idea of what basis the other person has for his application, what data the other person is trying to explain in terms of the concept. And Mr. MacIntyre might want to distinguish his case from these by claiming that nothing of this sort is present in the former. If so, his general principle would have to be severely qualified, and I fear that in evaluating this revised version we would be in danger of plunging into the bottomless abyss of difficulties with the verifiability criterion of meaningfulness.

It is noteworthy that in the body of the paper there seems to be little if any reliance on the principle that two people can share the same concept only if they agree in some applications of it. The problems which do receive an illuminating treatment, e.g., the relation of intelligibility to social context, are not explicitly connected with it. Therefore I suspect that Mr. MacIntyre could deal with his central concerns more effectively by not trying to force things into the impossibly narrow confines of that principle.

IV
IRRATIONALISM IN THEOLOGY

CRITICAL REFLECTIONS ON KARL BARTH

BY

BRAND BLANSHARD

To the philosopher the main interest of Barth lies in his apparent irrationalism. He has had the courage to break with philosophy frankly and thoroughly, and to insist that the knowledge of God, though the most important of all knowledge, is not in the ordinary sense knowledge at all, nor, therefore, subject to the sort of criticism or support that reason has to offer. This is, of course, not a new position in either philosophy or theology. Mystics have often held that they had a clear and certain knowledge of God that was above reason and incapable of expression in thought or speech. In Christian theology the claim of a non-rational knowledge of God is as old as Tertullian; it was accepted by Pascal in his doctrine of 'reasons of the heart that the reason knows not of'; it was developed with vehement verbosity by Kierkegaard, and with logic and eloquence by Dean Mansel. Though Barth lacks the acuteness, scholarship and style of Mansel, there is a Lutheran self-confidence, energy and pugnacity about him that has caught the religious world's attention, and given him the best-known name among living theologians.

I have neither the time nor the competence to discuss Barth's huge *Dogmatik* or the commentary on *Romans* which first brought him to public notice. I will base my remarks chiefly on his Gifford Lectures on *Knowledge of God and Service of God*. That Barth should have been invited or should have consented to give these lectures is something of an anomaly. He began by citing the specification in Lord Gifford's will that the lectures were designed for the 'promoting, advancing, teaching and diffusing' of natural theology, 'without reference to or reliance upon any supposed special exceptional or so-called miraculous revelation'[1] Regarding such natural theology Barth said at once, and with disarming candour, 'I do not see how it is possible for it to exist. I am convinced that so far as it has existed and still exists, it owes its existence to a radical error.'[2] The service he proposed to render to natural theology was to stimulate such life as might be left in it by stating the case for its mortal enemy, 'that totally different theology by which "natural theology" lives, in so far as it must affirm what the other denies and deny what the other affirms'.[3] In the face of all the projectionists who, like Freud and Feuerbach, would make religious 'knowledge' an imaginative fulfilling of need, of all the pragmatists who, like Dewey, would make it merely a means to human betterment, of all the rationalists who, like Hegel, would make it philosophy half grown-up, of all the psychologists, who, with Schleiermacher and Ritschl, would make it essentially a matter of feeling, Barth proclaimed a full-fledged return to the theology of the Reformation, in which God is set over against the world as 'wholly other', known indeed to faith, but unknowable, unapproachable and unimaginable by any natural faculties.

It is this doctrine of God as the 'wholly other', as discontinuous with us in nature, as closed to our thoughts and alien even to our ideals, that has been the arresting note in Barth's teaching; and we shall turn to it in a moment for special attention. But first let us see its place in the wider setting of his theology.

THE NEO-ORTHODOX POSITION

That theology has been rightly described as neo-orthodox. Orthodoxy for Barth, as for the Roman Catholic, is a serious matter; to him the notion is frivolous that each of us can go to the Bible and pick out from it what happens to suit our own taste or temperament. In his early days

---

[1] *The Knowledge of God and the Service of God*, pp. 3, 4.
[2] *Ibid.* p. 5.   [3] *Ibid.* p. 7.

Irrationalism in Theology

he saw this happening among German liberals. Even the great Harnack, who was his teacher and who made so much of objectivity, looked at the Gospel through his own glasses; he saw Jesus as a social reformer in advance of his time, not as incarnate Deity. Now if Jesus is not incarnate Deity, no doubt the liberal approach to him is right. He will then present the tragic figure of a poet and prophet trying to make the world over by gentleness, and subject to many illusions. If this is what he was, the long 'quest of the historical Jesus' by researchers bent on describing, interpreting and amending him will be in order.

But this is not the orthodox view of Jesus. The orthodox view is that he spoke as never man spoke because he was more than man, because he was the embodiment on earth of an eternal, all-knowing, all-powerful, infinite Creator. This Creator made man and enjoined him to obey and glorify his maker. The first man broke this command. In doing so he brought sin into the world. This sin corrupted not only his own nature but also the whole race of his descendants, who therefore stand utterly condemned in God's sight. Only an infinite sacrifice could atone for their guilt. This sacrifice was in fact made when the second person of the Trinity, himself infinite in power and goodness, offered himself as a ransom to the first person, and though living a sinless life on earth, subjected himself to a cruel death. Because of this sacrifice, God has made available to certain men, not through any effort or merit on their part, but through his mercy alone, the gift of grace, which both averts from them the wrath which is their due, and transforms them inwardly so that they become capable again of faith and righteousness.

To ears accustomed to liberal scepticism or rationalistic philosophizing, Barth admits that such language sounds archaic. But it is more important to note, he thinks, that according to the Reformation, according to the church, and according to the Bible, it happens to be true. And if it is true, the work of the Christian is clearly appointed. It is not to hammer out a theology with the crude tools of his own reason, or to exalt the whisperings of his own conscience

Faith and the Philosophers

into the laws of the good life. It is his business, if God has really spoken, to be silent and listen. And the business of the church is not to wrangle with the philosophers or to compete with politicians and economists in social reform. In so doing it would be taking a feeble and febrile stand; it would be throwing away Excalibur and doing battle with an absurd tin sword. The true line for the church is to stand up and say, as its prophets said, and can still say, 'Thus saith the Lord'. This bugle-note of uncompromising confidence and courage has rallied behind Barth's leadership many thousands of persons who were feeling faint of heart about the Christian prospect in the modern world.

For Barth, then, there is one towering fact that stands out in monolithic majesty on the plain of human history: God spoke to man in Christ. Of that revelation we have a witness in the Bible and a further witness whenever God in his mercy gives us grace to believe. It is upon this fact of revelation, therefore, that we must fix our eye. How does Barth know when it is occurring and what it says?

REVELATION *versus* KNOWLEDGE

He gives us his answer through a series of denials. Revelation has been thought to occur in many areas of experience. Many poets, scientists and philosophers have professed to find it in nature. Wordsworth found it in the light of setting suns; Kepler held that in his astronomy he was 'thinking God's thoughts after him', and the evolutionist John Fiske wrote a book charting the passage *Through Nature to God*. But when Emil Brunner ventured to suggest that there was some truth in this idea, Barth answered, '*Nein*'; natural theology 'can only be becoming to the theology and church of Antichrist'.[1] 'God is never for us in the world, that is to say in our space and time, except in this His Word.'[2] There is no road from science to faith.

Is there any road from philosophy to faith? Many of Barth's distinguished predecessors in the Gifford lectureship, for example the brothers Caird, held that there was, and

[1] *Nein! Antwort an Emil Brunner.*   [2] *Theological Existence Today*, p. 12.

Irrationalism in Theology

that our thought of the world, so far as it becomes coherent and comprehensive, is in rapport with a reason immanent in nature; reason rightly used is indeed one with revelation. Barth will have none of this. God is and must remain the unknowable 'wholly other'. As Gogarten puts it, he is 'the Unknown by our knowing, the Unconceived by our concepts, the Measureless for our measures, the Inexperienceable for our experience'.[1] This does not mean that we have no knowledge of God of any kind, for faith is itself the highest knowledge. But having said this, Barth adds at once that this knowledge 'differs completely from anything else which man calls knowledge, not only in its content, but in its mode of origin and form as well'.[2] 'Further, it has been forced down my throat that the Dogmatic theologian is under the obligation to "justify" himself in his utterances before philosophy. To that my answer is likewise, No. . . . It cannot be otherwise than that Dogmatics runs counter to every philosophy, no matter what form it may have assumed.'[3] The very attempt to know God by thought is impiety, since it is an attempt to catch the infinite within the rickety crate of our categories. Though Barth dislikes and distrusts philosophy, he did in his youth study Kant's first critique. For his own position it was a happy choice, since Kant confirmed him in the view that reason is made for nature and cannot penetrate beyond it.

REVELATION *versus* CONSCIENCE

Kant thought, however, that in the experience of duty we did manage to go beyond it, and moralists of such different complexions as Butler, Newman and Martineau have agreed that in some sense the voice of God is to be heard in the voice of conscience. Would Barth agree? His answer again is an emphatic 'No'. For there is really no health in us, and conscience, as an organ of the natural man, is infected by his disease.

Barth is scornful of 'poor present-day man with his

---

[1] *Von Glauben und Offenbarung*, p. 11. [2] *Knowledge of God*, p. 25.
[3] *Credo*, pp. 185-186.

utilitarian notions',[1] and the 'happy gentleman of culture, who today drives up so briskly in his little car of progress and so cheerfully displays the pennants of his various ideals'.[2] He praises the Scottish confession because it 'is opposed, and rightly so, to all talk about the goodness of the Christian life'.[3] There is something startling about a theologian belittling goodness itself, but Barth does not flinch from it. 'In the Christian life we are not concerned with our becoming Christian personalities. . . . All that . . . can be very fine, but yet it looks as if there were already in process here another instance of the idolatry in which man wishes really to make his own achievements the basis of his confidence,'[4] and for Barth man's attempt to justify himself by works is a sin against the Holy Spirit. Between God's goodness and man's there is a deep gulf and it is misleading to say of the sinlessness of Christ that it is an example of what we mean by moral goodness. Douglas Mackintosh and Canon Quick have complained of Barth's speaking 'as though it were treason to the Christian faith to commend the truth of the Christian revelation to non-Christians on the ground that the character of Jesus is surpassingly good and beautiful, and that His life reveals thereby the beauty and goodness of the Godhead'.[5] One would expect Barth to reject the social interpretation of the Gospel, but he seems at times to go further and to disparage the very idea of service; 'speaking generally', he says, 'the Church has not to be at the service of mankind'.[6] She has higher work to do.

REVELATION *versus* THE BIBLE

If we are not to look for revelation in any of these quarters, shall we find it perhaps in the Bible? No again,

[1] Karl Barth, *Knowledge of God*, translated by J. L. M. Haire and Ian Henderson (London: Hodder, 1938), p. 194.
[2] Karl Barth, *The Word of God and the Word of Man*, translated by Douglas Horton (New York: Harper and Brothers, 1928), p. 17.
[3] *Knowledge of God*, p. 146.   [4] *Ibid.* p. 154.
[5] Douglas Clyde Mackintosh, *The Problem of Religious Knowledge* (New York, London: Harper and Brothers, 1940), p. 342.
[6] *Theological Existence Today*, p. 51.

Irrationalism in Theology

if that means that we can hope to find it by analysis or interpretation or any other process of sifting meanings. God does speak through the ten commandments of the Old Testament, but their meaning is not what a moralist could arrive at from reflection on natural rights or through listening to his own conscience.[1] Revelation comes also and comes indeed supremely, through the Christ portrayed in the New Testament. But Barth is quite ready, as Catholic and Protestant fundamentalists are not, to let the critics go ahead with their work of dissecting and reconstructing this portrait, since it is idle in any case to look for revelation in it. God is not revealed to us in the character or mind of Jesus, in anything he did or said or was, so far as this is apprehended with our natural gifts; the Jesus of history is not the Christ; God dwelt in him only incognito. 'The Bible is God's Word . . .' says Barth, 'so far as God speaks through it.' But we shall never find the points at which he is speaking through it by raising questions of authenticity or reasonableness. This is merely one more attempt to appraise divinity by human tests.

REVELATION AND IMMEDIATE EXPERIENCE

Baffled in the search for revelation in any of these quarters, suppose we take the last step open to us. If we look in vain for revelation in nature, in thought, in conscience, in the Bible, in the Jesus of history, may we not find it in immediate religious experience? There is, of course, a vast volume of Christian tradition to the effect that we may. The mystical vision, the Quaker inner light, the Methodist's conversion, the common experience of faith and prayer, have been felt by millions of persons, both simple and sophisticated, to give them contact at first-hand with the divine. May we agree with any of them? Barth's answer is not only uncompromising but startling. He would ask first whether these experiences are genuinely human experiences, the sort, for example, that James described in the *Varieties*, that psychologists are able to

[1] *Knowledge of God*, pp. 127-128.

connect causally with adolescence or sex or emotional need, that are reported in other religions as well as the Christian. If the answer is, Yes, they *are* experiences of this kind, then Barth replies that to take them as revelations is impious. The mystic's claim to union with God is blasphemous. God is never present in the human heart, and it is idolatrous to suppose that he is.[1] Prayer, if a seeking for God's presence, is presumptuous and separates us from him; Barth notes 'how profane a world this world of prayer is'.[2] Religion as such is not spared; 'The Church does not take the slightest interest in religion . . .'[3]; 'the pandemonium of human piety' is dangerous to the God-seeking soul.[4] 'Religion must die. In God we are rid of it.'[5] Thus religion in its most intimate experiences of piety, prayer and mystical exaltation, is set down as dangerous delusion.

Now if revelation is not to be found in any of these areas or experiences, what sort of message does it have for us, and how are we to recognize this when it comes?

THE CONTENT OF REVELATION

To the first question, What does it say?, Barth replies that no answer is possible of the kind that presumably is wanted. If one is asking for a set of commands, ideas or propositions that can be understood, put into words and communicated to other people, one is asking for an impossible translation of the 'wholly other' into human terms. 'When one has stated what Father, Son and Spirit in God mean', says Barth, 'one must continue and add that one has said nothing'.[6] If real revelation occurs, 'before it all words are hushed, and we, when we see Him, can only worship'.[7] To call him wise or good or powerful or just or even gracious, in our senses of these words, to say that he has qualities analogous to these in any sense that we can understand, to draw inferences about him that are based

[1] *Epistle to the Romans*, pp. 33 ff.
[2] *Ibid.* p. 458.
[3] *Knowledge of God*, p. 178.
[4] *Epistle to the Romans*, p. 212.
[5] *Ibid.* p. 238.
[6] Monsma, *Barth's Idea of Revelation*, p. 138.
[7] *Knowledge of God*, p. 75.

Irrationalism in Theology

on these concepts, all these are alike and in principle illegitimate. In talking about revelation, we are using a denotation without any clear connotation. Barth feels free to call it by many names, since none of them are descriptive; in referring to revelation, the terms 'God', 'Christ', 'grace', 'faith', 'the Son', 'the Father', the 'mercy' or 'love' or 'justice' of God, all mean the same thing; even 'the service of God' and 'the knowledge of God', since both mean simply the indwelling God himself, again mean the same thing. To the question what is revealed?, Barth's answer is as succinct as one could wish: 'God himself, God alone'.

THE RECOGNITION OF REVELATION

To the other question, how we recognize revelation when it comes, Barth again admits that he has no answer that will satisfy. What is wanted, no doubt, is a criterion or set of marks by which an authentic revelation can be distinguished from a pseudo-revelation. And there are no such marks. How then is my groping search to proceed? How am I to recognize the boon when it presents itself? The truth is, says Barth, that *I* cannot recognize it. To say that I could would be equivalent to saying that the finite can recognize the infinite, that the temporal, while still sunk in time, can view eternity, that corruption as such can put on incorruption. No, man as he is cannot respond to or even identify revelation. It is only God in him that can rise to so high an occasion and interpret what the testimony for revelation really means. 'How could revelation ever be recognized as the divine content of that testimony except through revelation? But so to recognize revelation through revelation means to recognize it by revelation awakening one's faith.'[1] 'It is faith that knows God as a child knows its father',[2] and faith is an exercise of no human faculty; 'the man who really has faith will never consider his faith as a realization or manifestation of his religious life, but will on the contrary admit that his capacity for religion would

[1] *Ibid.* p. 67.   [2] *Ibid.* p. 30.

in itself have led him to the gods and idols, but by no means to Jesus Christ'.[1] Deep can speak only to deep. In this respect the achievement of an understanding faith is like the achievement of genuine goodness; neither is really an achievement. We must admit that 'what we wish, will, and strive after today, i.e. what we are today, is simply our sin . . .'[2]; on the other hand, 'all our works which proceed from faith will be good works',[3] and only these. The faith that sees and the goodness that embodies that faith are alike the work of Deity, who in his inscrutable grace descends at times into human life.

Barth's view of revelation, though developed to date through approximately fifteen thousand pages, is thus in essence very simple. There is no road from man to God, no way of gaining knowledge or union with God through human experience or through reflection on that experience. There *is* a road from God to man. That road was taken in the incarnation. It is taken now in unpredictable times and places by divine grace, but since the revelation comes from a 'wholly other', discontinuous and incommensurable with all our powers, both that which speaks in us and that which hears it transcend the human level.

THE ACHIEVEMENT OF BARTH

What are we to say of this teaching? Two things we must grant to it without reservation. First, it has achieved a dramatic and unexpected turning of the tables on rationalism and liberalism. In the first two decades of the century, liberalism seemed secure in its ascendancy. I heard an eminent theologian say recently, 'One thing is now clear: liberalism is dead'. I hope he was mistaken, but there can be no doubt that an astonishing change has taken place in the theological climate, and that this change is due to Barth more than to any other living man.

I think too that, whether we are persuaded by it or not, we must admit the adroitness of Barth's strategy. He has chosen his own ground, and for the most part refused to

[1] *Knowledge of God*, p. 106. [2] *Ibid.* p. 96. [3] *Ibid.* p. 135.

meet his critics on ground where he would be at a disadvantage. He is not a philosopher and he knows it. If he had attempted a systematic argumentative defence of his position, he might have been manœuvred into logical disaster by craftier rationalist tacticians; indeed it is imprudent for anyone advancing an irrationalist thesis to rest his case on rationalist weapons. Barth may have learned this from considering the way in which conservatives met the great upsurge of liberal rationalism under Hegel and Strauss in the last century. Kierkegaard met it with a shrewd denial that religious faith was a rational matter at all, and Kierkegaard's voluble ghost is still very much alive in our divinity school quadrangles. Mansel, with a power of mind beyond the range of such as Kierkegaard or Barth, attempted to defend a similar view of revelation by argument. His book had the misfortune to fall under the eye of John Stuart Mill, and 'for once a book got reviewed'. Mansel was crushed, apparently beyond revival. Barth has prudently reverted to the line of Kierkegaard. He says to the philosophers bluntly: I decline to recognize your jurisdiction; my appeal is to a court in which you and your logic-chopping have no standing.

IN WHAT SENSE IS REASON UNTRUSTWORTHY?

Our first step in examining him may well be to ask whether he is entitled to this appeal. Philosophers can admit an appeal from logic-chopping, but not from logic, and when Barth declines to be judged by the standards they employ, we must ask rather more precisely what he means. He might mean any one of three things. He might mean, first, that the ultimate truth about God and the world is so far beyond us that any conceptions of it arrived at with our present powers are bound to fall short. Or he might go beyond this and mean, secondly, that in the picture of the world which we are now bound to accept, taking both revealed and natural knowledge into account, there are genuine contradictions, but that these are rather incident to the process of search than indicative of irrationality in the world. Or he might mean, thirdly, that they do indicate just this, and that we must therefore say that the very attempt to grasp ultimate truth by reason is misguided, since it is bound to be flouted in the end by the object it is trying to understand. Which of these things is Barth saying?

He is obviously saying at least the first, and here we may surely agree with him. The ideas we form of the world always grow out of our experience; that experience is severely limited by the range of our senses, by our flickering attention and vagrant reflection, and indeed on every side by our imperfectly evolved powers of mind. If rationalism implies the claim that our present ideas, even at their best, on the nature of matter, time, life, mind, personality or value, or on the place of any of these in the universe as a whole, are adequate and final, then we may heartily agree with Barth that rationalism is absurd. Unfortunately, the agreement is not very significant, since this is not a kind of rationalism that any responsible rationalist would avow.

KNOWLEDGE AS INCOHERENT

Does Barth then also take the second position, that there are contradictions in our knowledge, though not in reality? He has not discussed, so far as I know, the antinomies in natural knowledge alleged by Zeno, Kant or Russell. But he has held that revelation presents us with insights which, when placed side by side with those of natural knowledge, result in contradictions from which we cannot escape. That revelation is to be considered a kind of knowledge is detected by his entitling one of his books *Knowledge of God*. And he would not deny that science at its best is knowledge. But when we try to put these into one whole, it breaks into contradictory pieces. Barth perhaps takes less delight in dwelling on these contradictions, which he would rather call paradoxes, than Tertullian and Kierkegaard did, and he has never, so far as I know, set them out in formal fashion. But they are there in plenty. For the sake of clearness, I will list a few of them.

First there are the contradictions about original sin.

Irrationalism in Theology

No man can be justly condemned for the deeds of another, but nevertheless man stands under just condemnation for the sin of Adam. Sin is distorted or perverted will; but original sin somehow infects us before we can use our wills.

Secondly, there are the contradictions about God's justice. God is perfectly just; yet we have to ascribe to him acts that appear plainly to be unjust. He has withheld his revelation from some persons and nations and granted them to others in a manner that, for all we can see, is arbitrary; he has remitted punishment that is due to certain men because he is appeased by the sacrifice of another, and has inflicted his punishment or displeasure on persons who, to the best of our knowledge, are innocent.

Thirdly, there is the great nest of contradictions about the incarnation. God really became man. But an omniscient mind cannot also be a mind that is limited and growing. A mind with no evil in it cannot be tempted as we are. A mind that is really eternal cannot be temporal for thirty-three years. A mind that is absolute, in the sense that it is free from finite conditions, cannot be personal, in the sense that it knows, feels and wills what is other than itself. A God who is pure goodness cannot also, in becoming man, share his corruptness and sinfulness. But Barth insists that he does; 'the completeness of God's humiliation . . . lies in His taking upon Himself *everything* which man's rebellion against Him has made inevitable — suffering and death, but also perdition and hell . . .'.[1] To this passage Barth adds in a characteristic note: 'I have received a letter the writer of which maintains that it would be both impossible and incomprehensible that God should suffer death and perdition. To this I would reply that this is the sacrifice of which the Bible speaks.'[2] The person of Jesus Christ is to Barth what it was to Kierkegaard, who regarded it as something logically incredible against which 'reason beats her brow till the blood comes'.

Fourthly, our attainment of goodness is unintelligible. We meditate, pray, resolve and struggle, all to no avail; we are still in God's sight repellent. We are helpless to

[1] *Knowledge of God*, p. 83. [2] *Ibid.* p. 84.

secure his grace; Barth insists that we cannot even cooperate with him in securing it; such efforts are tainted with evil. When we do attain to goodness, it is not we who attain it, but God in us, who, for no reason that our minds can hope to understand, has chosen to descend into us and act through us.

Fifthly, we are told that with God all things are possible. If so, it was possible for him to create a world in which the vast mass of suffering that is morally pointless — the pain and misery of animals, the cancer and blindness of little children, the humiliations of senility and insanity — were avoided. These are not the products of man's free will; they are inflictions from without, and apparently therefore inflictions of the Creator himself. If you admit that, you deny his goodness; if you say he could not have done otherwise, you deny that with him all things are possible.

Here is a long series of contradictions which it would be easy to extend. Barth would say that in some sense we know both sides of each. What can he mean by this? Does he mean that they are temporary confusions that will be cleared up as knowledge increases, or does he mean that the world is really like this, a place of ultimate chaos and incoherence?

BARTH'S INSISTENCE ON REVEALED KNOWLEDGE

Some readers have taken him in the former and less radical sense. Let us see what this would involve. When a contradiction is at issue, there is only one way in which consistency can be saved: if both propositions are to be retained as true, the meaning of one or other (if not both) must be altered; both cannot be taken as true in their contradictory senses. Now the contradictions we have listed are, without exception, cases in which on the one side stands an insight of the natural man and on the other an insight alleged to have come by revelation. If reconciliation is to be achieved, either the revealed or the natural meaning must, as it stands, be given up.

Suppose first that we give up the revealed meaning. This is the line that naturalists would take. But since it would amount to denying revealed truth, Barth would not consider it for a moment. The main point of his thinking and writing is to insist that revealed knowledge is final, that it takes precedence over everything that is or can be set against it, that it is beyond amendment or appeal.

THE ABANDONMENT OF NATURAL REASON DISASTROUS

Very well; let us try the other alternative, and say that what must be given up are those affirmations of our natural knowledge that stand in contradiction to revealed truth; these illusions are the growing pains of knowledge and will disappear as humanity matures. I have more sympathy with this suggestion than some of my philosophic colleagues, for, holding as I do to the theory of internal relations, I would go so far as to say that none of our so-called knowledge is wholly true just as it stands. But this dependence of our concepts and insights upon the changing context of knowledge is itself a matter of degree. To say that the proposition 'colds are produced by a virus' is not true with its present meaning would be a minor shock, but its repercussions would not be nearly so destructive as those of denying that two and two are four. Our question then is, How serious would be the consequences of denying the sort of propositions to which Barth is opposing revelation?

I can only think they would be disastrous. For among the propositions that would have to be given up are some of the central insights of ethics and cosmology. Is there anything clearer in ethics than that a man cannot be condemned as morally evil because his great-grandfather sinned, or that to inflict extreme and gratuitous pain on a child or an animal is wrong? Is there anything clearer in cosmology than that if a mind knows all there is to know, it cannot grow in knowledge; that if it is not in time, it cannot grow older in time; that if it is omnipresent, there is nothing outside itself to know or love? These are the kinds of insight which, in Barth's theology, conflict with revealed truth. They cannot be reconciled with that truth unless their present meaning is revised out of recognition or set down as false. And that would quite simply destroy both ethics and speculative thought. If it were now to be called right to condemn the living for the deeds of the dead and to inflict gratuitous suffering, then anything could be right; the distinction between right and wrong as we know it would have ceased to exist. If a mind could at once grow and not grow in knowledge, grow older and yet not grow older, love others without there being others to love, then anything could be true, and the distinction between truth and falsehood has been blurred irreparably. Natural knowledge would be so confounded that both sides of a contradiction might be true.

Let us see where we are. We have been considering what Barth can mean by denying the jurisdiction of philosophy or natural reason over theology. If it means merely that reason as now exercised falls short of ultimate truth, we can only agree. If it means that the conflicts between revealed and natural insights are such as may be removed by expanding knowledge and are only a temporary veil for a coherent world beyond them, the question is on which side the revision is to take place. That revealed knowledge can be revised Barth would of course deny. What must be given up as it stands is, therefore, natural knowledge. But we have seen that the required revision of natural knowledge would revise it out of existence by denying the truth of insights that are clear and crucial. It would even compel us to accept as true what presents itself as self-contradictory. But to say that a statement, though self-contradictory is still true, is to say that reality itself is incoherent. This second interpretation of Barth's meaning, if thought out, thus carries us on to the third.

BARTH'S IRRATIONALISM

The third interpretation is that the conflict is genuine and beyond remedy. Revelation tells us what is not only unintelligible to natural reason, but is a challenge and offence to it, and before a challenge from an absolute authority, reason can only surrender. This, I think, is what Barth is really saying. In spite of the attempt by some of his followers to tone down his conflict with philosophy and to deny any disparagement of reason, he is surely saying this: revelation is not subject to rational tests, and even if it requires, as it does, that we should abandon some of the most certain of our ethical and speculative insights, or the law of contradiction itself, it is ours not to reason why, but to obey.

There are those who would say that even with this interpretation Barth is no enemy of reason rightly conceived. When in a lecture at St. Andrews some years ago I ventured to describe him as an irrationalist, an eminent Scottish theologian took me to task in the Edinburgh *Scotsman*, insisting to my astonishment that 'Barth stands out in Europe as the great protagonist *against* irrationalism'.[1] His case, as I recall, was this: that the task of natural thought is to conform to its object. If its object happens to be one that does not obey the rules we have set up for the conduct of reason, then the truly rational course is to conform to the object and override the rules. What is really irrational is to try to force reality itself into the rickety procrustean bed of our own logic.

That seems at first sight rather sensible. It has often been suggested that the laws of logic are laws of our thought but not of reality. But consider what that means. Take, for example, the best known law of logic, the law of contradiction. When we say that although thought must conform to this law, things need not, what we must mean is that there may be a being that both has and does not have a certain character. Now if we can really conceive of a being of this kind, we have contradicted ourselves in the very statement of our theory, for that theory was that thought must conform to this law, that it cannot think the self-contradictory, and we are now saying that it can. On the other hand, if a thing's having and also not having a certain

[1] *The Scotsman*, April 1952.

character is truly inconceivable, then our thesis itself is inconceivable and our theory meaningless. One may protest that this is logical hocus-pocus and that it takes advantage of a mere logico-centric predicament. But to philosophers logic is not unimportant, and a predicament from which it is impossible to conceive what an escape would mean is not a predicament in which it is very tragic to be caught.

BARTH'S PRACTICE INCONSISTENT WITH HIS CONCLUSION

When Barth says that, illumined by revelation, we must accept things as true which mere reason would call false, he is implying that the standards of reason are invalid. This view, as just suggested, seems incapable of clear statement. We may add that no one, Barth included, can live up to it in practice. He prefers, as we have seen, not to rest his case on argument; he appeals straight to absolute authority. Still he does write theology indefatigably, and just what is theology? As practised by Barth, it seems to consist of statements written in German or English and professing to be true statements of historical fact, of the meaning of Biblical passages, of the relation of rational to revealed knowledge, of conjectures and conclusions innumerable about nature, grace, sin, miracle, creation, judgement, life and death. Barth plainly expects us to accept his statements as true, his exposition as relevant, and his conclusion as valid. He expects us to accept all this while accepting at the same time his indictment of natural reason as unreliable, while believing that some of its clearest and most certain insights are false, while questioning even its simplest and most universal demands. Are we not justified in saying to him: You cannot have it both ways? If reason at its best and clearest is an unsafe guide, then your theology, dependent at every step on the exercise of that reason, is itself a journey over quicksands. On the other hand, if the guide that has taken you over the vast theological mileage you have travelled is as reliable as you

Irrationalism in Theology

plainly assume, then you can hardly turn, at the threshold of revelation, and dismiss him as a blind leader of the blind.

Barthians would no doubt reply: We have every right to do that. We are not denying the validity of reason generally; we are admitting its competence in its own field, which is that of nature, and denying its jurisdiction only beyond that field, in the region of the supernatural. Surely that gives you philosophers room enough. Why are you not content?

PHILOSOPHIC DISCONTENT

We are not content because in the area thus forbidden to us lie many of the problems which a deep concern and an old tradition have made specially our own. Philosophers for some thousands of years have been searching into creation, immortality, God, freedom, evil. They have not, perhaps, been notably successful, but they have closed many misleading trails and achieved, as they thought, some glimpses of the summit toward which they have been struggling. You now tell them that, with supernatural aid, you have been privileged to see the summit, that it is not in their world at all, that there is no road to it from where they stand, that all the trails they have been exploring wind up in swamps or deserts, and that they had therefore better cease and desist in their misguided effort.

Now it is not very likely that on receipt of such instructions philosophers will lie down and roll over. Except in authoritarian communities, ecclesiastical or political, they lack practice in such obedience, and besides they have much at stake. If their occupation is to be so largely gone, they will want to know what precisely Barth has seen during his sojourn on the hilltop which vetoes their attempt on the summit from another side. When they ask this question, they receive, as we have seen, a most disconcerting answer.

The answer is that there is no answer they could understand. Even in his revealed essence, says Barth, God is '*unenthüllbar*'; even as *Deus revelatus* he is *Deus absconditus*; he is the absolutely other; he is 'pure negation'; he cannot be described or thought in any terms available to our human faculties. 'Revelation', says Kraemer, 'is by its nature inaccessible and remains so, even when it is revealed.' Brunner agrees: 'In the person of Jesus God tells us what no man can know, what is in no kind of continuity with our human ideas, no, not even with the best and highest we possess'.[1] The content of this revelation cannot even be recognized as such by human faculty; if I do recognize it, it is not I but God in me that does so; if I converse with you about it, it is not you but God in you that understands. Now surely the appropriate mode of expression for such a revelation is silence. What has been seen is more ineffable than the mystic's vision. When the mystic comes down from his hilltop, he comes as a rule with a smile, but a smile means that something in our sense good has been experienced, and the transcendentalism of Barth and Brunner outsoars all human good. The life of the religious man, in Brunner's striking image, is a wheel whose spokes all radiate from a hub — only the hub is hollow. Man's highest hopes and efforts are bent toward reaching a shrine whose doors are at last flung open only to reveal to his straining sight that it is empty.

But if it is thus empty, what are those fifteen thousand pages about? Barth says that though the content of revelation is wholly beyond us, there are *witnesses* in the way of scriptural texts, the words and acts of Jesus, the history, liturgies and sacraments of the church, that are relevant to this revelation. I do not see how they could be. To say that they are relevant to the truth, or a witness to it, in the sense of offering evidence for it, is to bring this truth within the field of rational thought where one belief confirms or disconfirms another. To say that in the character of Jesus we have a suggestion or an adumbration of the Divine character is to say, if anything at all, that the character of Jesus is more or less like the Divine character, and then the contention that God is wholly other has been abandoned. Sometimes Barth qualifies his agnosticism by admitting that we can make the acts or deeds of Deity the objects of our

[1] *The Word and the World*, p. 45.

thought, but not Deity himself, since he is a subject; and it is true that I shall never know you or make you my object if that means that I shall sense or directly perceive you. But that does not imply that I cannot know you in another and perfectly relevant sense. Even if, in order to reach each other, we must cross a bridge of inference, we may know each other very well indeed. Of course Barth may mean by 'subject' something wholly different from what the term commonly means. If he does, the argument ceases to be invalid and is merely unintelligible.

UNINTELLIGIBILITY RAMPANT

There is a certain advantage in asserting the existence of the unintelligible. For you can then say unintelligible things about it, and to any objection you can reply that it is unreasonable to insist that the unintelligible should appear out of character. We have already found suggestions of this procedure in Barth. In endeavouring to communicate the incommunicable, he uses many descriptive terms as somehow appropriate to revelation. It is a message or a word; it is also the person of Christ himself; it is a state of faith; it is a state of knowledge; it is a decision or act, though also an influx received passively; it is truth; it is the service of God; though this is the same as the knowledge of God, and the same again as the justice, mercy and grace of God. What is Barth trying to tell us by all these characterizations? If revelation is utterly discontinuous with all we know, they can mean nothing, and why mislead us by using them? If they are really descriptive of revelation, even by metaphor or analogy, then God is not discontinuous with us after all. And since in that case they bear meanings that we can make sense of, should not some regard be paid to those meanings when the words are put together? To say, as Brunner does, that 'only by this act does man become a person' and then to add that faith is a free gift in which man does not act at all; to say, as Barth does, that revelation is truth (that is, a relation between proposition and fact), but also somehow a person, though it is really also a state of knowledge which somehow is also a decision — to say these things is to offer for our belief an incoherent patchwork. If a philosopher were to say them, he would be dismissed as gabbling, since they cancel each other out. And he is disposed to wonder, perhaps naïvely, why that which would be gibberish in his own mouth should be profundity in another's.

NON-DIALECTICAL THEOLOGY

Barth calls his theology dialectical. To the philosopher dialectical thinking means thinking that takes us slowly nearer to the goal through a series of zigzag steps. We are now told that this is just what thinking cannot do. The thinker can no longer take a 'position over against God so that from this he may form thoughts about God which are in varying degrees true, beautiful and good'.[1] 'The value of what theology has to say is measured by no standard except that of its object',[2] and that object is separated by an impassable chasm from even our highest thought. He is thus compelled to relinquish a powerful means of persuasion to be found in much theological writing, the value of a felt approximation to an immanent ideal. Though there is much in Hegel's reasoning that seems to me invalid, there is something most impressive in the widening sweep of vision as he climbs the ladder of his categories toward the absolute idea; it is not hard to feel, as one follows him, something of the excitement that Spinoza felt as he approached his third kind of knowledge, that Newton felt as he found himself drawing nearer to the supreme law of the physical universe. The steps of the intellectual dialectician may be halting and his progress slow, but his quest itself is not misguided; indeed it is the inevitable expression of 'the intellectual love of God'. But if theological thought disclaims what is so natural and inevitable, if it insists that progress toward the end of knowledge brings us no nearer to God at all, then in emancipating itself from human nature, it is also emancipating itself right out of human interest.

[1] *Knowledge of God*, p. 103.   [2] *Credo*, p. 156.

Irrationalism in Theology

When the dialectical pursuit of truth can promise no better knowledge of ultimate things, even at the end, than irremovable illusion, why travel the stony road at all?

NON-ETHICAL ETHICS

Something similar must be said about ethical thinking. The character of Jesus is for me, as for so many millions of others, a source of recurring wonder and fascination. When it is put forward as the flawless ideal to which all human conduct should try to approximate, I take the claim seriously, though I cannot simply shut my eyes and swallow it. I try to understand it; I try to test its claim by noting whether, as my moral insight matures, I find myself closer to it, and whether, as I read expositions of it by preachers and theologians, I can say, 'Yes, on this point and on this, I now see that you are right'. The most powerful plea for moral authority is one that, forgoing all appeal to authority, asks only the ratification of reflective conscience; does the ideal, if it is lifted up, draw to it all honest and thoughtful minds? Some expositors make a powerful case by revealing, perhaps unconsciously, what life in that personal presence has done to them. To take a few examples that may mean less to others than to me: when one comes in touch with the singular moral grace of Dean Church, or the inexhaustible affection for his fellow men of Scott Holland or Charles F. Andrews, or the sunny serenity of Phillips Brooks, or the ethical sensitiveness of James Martineau, or Schweitzer's sense of fellowship with even the humblest life, one may feel a little like Adams and Leverrier when they marked the aberrations of Uranus from its orbit; they were sure that there was a tremendous unseen body farther out that was pulling the planet towards it. Perhaps by reason of my own obtuseness, when I read Barth I feel nothing of all this. I hear the bleak, strident voice repeating that the Wholly Other is over all, that we have no claim on his mercy, that though he has made us he finds us hateful, that he commands absolute acceptance, unquestioning obedience, unconditional abject surrender. It is as if the harsh voice were determined, in demanding this surrender, to beat us down still further by insisting that there is and can be no earthly reason for it. If one is attracted by the kindness or courage or tenderness of the Jesus who loved children and would break the Sabbath for an ox in distress, one is attracted by the wrong things, the kind of virtues that mere natural man can respond to and hope to attain, whereas the Jesus to whom surrender should be made is the incognito Jesus who was wearing these virtues as a disguise. One of the most persuasive arguments in the old theological armoury was that in Christianity we find life and find it more abundantly, and that its way of life alone can satisfy our native moral sense. To Barth this argument is without force.

STRANGE AFFINITIES

Because of this uncompromising distrust of the thought and conscience of the natural man, Barth has strange philosophic affiliations. In the theory of knowledge he shares important convictions with the positivists. He holds, with Ayer and Carnap, that the attempt by rational thought to go beyond nature to the supernatural is inevitably defeated, though of course he draws a different inference from the defeat. He concludes that since we cannot reach a knowledge of God through rational means, we must do so through non-natural means; the positivists conclude from the same premise that the attempt itself is meaningless. But as to the futility of metaphysics, the two schools join hands.

In ethics, Barth has a striking affinity with Stoicism though at one of its weakest points. The Stoics taught that virtue and vice were not matters of degree; if you were guilty of one peccadillo, you had broken the moral law as truly as if you had murdered your mother, and there was no health in you. Barth talks at times in a curiously similar vein. 'Either we love God and our neighbour or we hate them both. Either we are obedient or we are not. There is no possibility here of a third, middle course, consisting of some sort of approximation. . . . Man with all his outward and inward achievements . . . stands in the presence of that Law as one who is unthankful and impenitent, and who, since he does not love God or his neighbours, must hate them. . . .'[1] There is much that is admirable in Stoicism, but its black-and-white notion of goodness is surely inhuman. It seems likewise inhuman in Barth. If anything can be said with confidence about human nature, one would have supposed it to be that we are neither saints or satans, that we are all blends of aspiration and sordidness, in short that we all fall in that third class which to Barth is a null class. To say that if we lack his kind of faith, our attitude toward our fellow men must be one of hatred suggests that he is adjusting his facts to his theology rather than his theology to the facts.

THE MORALITY OF THE SPHINX

Because of this alienation from humanity in both senses of 'humanity' Barth's ethics seem to me strangely sterile. It is hard to deduce anything helpful from a conceptual blank. At first one is impressed by the high line taken. To the question, How should I live? Barth gives the same answer as to the question, What is revealed? — simply 'Jesus Christ'. 'The law, the rule and the first principles underlying all service to God are — Jesus Christ.'[1] '*Was sollen wir denn tun?*' he asks in the *Römerbrief*, and answers: 'We can, indeed, do one thing, not many. . . . For what can a Christian do in society other than follow attentively the doing of God?' No one wants to be put in the position of criticizing action from such a source, but one does need more than a name; one wants guidance; one wants to know how Jesus would deal with a communist, whether he would approve the professional artist, soldier or athlete, what he would say to a confused youth about sex. To all such questions Barth's answer seems to be the same, Act out the indwelling Christ. But since the Christ who may dwell in us is discontinuous with us, both psychologically and ethically, it is hard to see how any inference can be drawn from his presence as to what a human being in a given

[1] *Knowledge of God*, pp. 138-139. [2] *Ibid.* p. 135.

position would or should do. If, in our eagerness for some cue, we were to look at Barth's own life, with its curious mixture of courage toward the Nazis, complaisance toward the communists (he maintained a loud silence throughout the Hungarian crisis) and arrogance toward critics (anyone who ventures to criticize 'should have read me completely'), the light gained is flickering.

Brunner takes the same puzzling line. 'We never know what is right for us,' he says, 'nor what is best for the other person. We go astray when we think we can deduce this from some principle or other, or from some experience. . . .'[1] Both men are clear enough about what non-Christian living means; it means everything that in our own persons we do, from holding up a bank to rescuing a drowning child. But genuinely Christian living is far more difficult to detect, since it is apparently beyond identification by the natural man. Christian action springs from love, but this is not the sinful love felt by unregenerate man for his fellows. How we are to recognize a Christian when we meet him, I do not know. We can be fairly confident, I suppose, that if he is as much of a Hindu as Gandhi or as much of a humanist as Schweitzer, he is not a good man in the true sense; one must be a Christian in the transcendental sense in order to be that. But is the man who robs a bank also beyond the pale, along with the Gandhis and the Schweitzers? How can one tell? If human virtues may disguise sinners, may not human vices disguise saints? If the centre from which a man's actions proceed and the standard employed in those actions are discontinuous with our natural ones, it is hard to see how any judgement is possible. The courts indeed might have something to say, but they are administering mere human justice, which we are assured is corrupt. If Barth means what he repeatedly says, it seems to follow that our jails may be filled with Christians under aliases, just as our churches and humane societies are filled with people suffering from sinful human kindness.

I do not suppose that Barth actually thinks in this way.

[1] *The Divine Imperative*, p. 120.

Irrationalism in Theology

The absolute wall of separation between natural and supernatural is like the 'absolute' American wall of separation between church and state, or the wall in Berlin between East and West; there is a continual osmosis through it. Does Barth really feel natural love and selflessness to be as little irradiated by the divine presence as hatred or malice? That is hard to believe. His transcendence tends, in spite of itself, to melt into moral immanence. There is a similar welcome inconsistency in his account of the approach from below. He is constantly using terms in his theology that seem to bear more meaning than they ought to bear if his theory is true. He remarked in the first of his Princeton lectures (recently published in book form): 'the God of the Gospel has a genuine interest in human existence'[1]; 'The God of Schleiermacher cannot show mercy. The God of the Gospel can and does . . . God is father, brother and friend.'[2] If such statements do not imply that our thought of God as a person is justified, that we are right in ascribing to him the sort of interest, mercy and kindness that we know, their meaning is lost on me. In most of his writings Barth repudiates the applicability of such concepts to God. In one of his Princeton lectures he seemed to acknowledge the harshness of this position by making a distinction, not developed, between 'theanthropology', which he considered permissible, and 'anthropotheology', which he did not.[3] This distinction I have failed to grasp.

BARTHIANISM AND THE MODERN TEMPER

Still, discontinuity has been the most conspicuous point in his teaching. It is on this, rather than on his departures from it, that we must fix attention. And I should like now to say something about the relevance and opportuneness of this teaching in our present situation. I cannot think that the future is on its side. Not that this would disprove it; truth and success are different things, and the truth of a speculative doctrine is not to be tested either by the range

---

[1] Karl Barth, *Evangelical Theology: An Introduction*, p. 8.
[2] *Ibid.* p. 11.   [3] *Ibid.* p. 12.

of its acceptance or by the good or ill effects of accepting it. But Christianity is more than a speculative doctrine; it is also a way of life; and in appraising a way of life, we cannot be indifferent to its working in society. Christianity, as Barth interprets it, involves an attitude toward thought and action that impinges on the culture of our time in significant ways.

NEO-ORTHODOXY AND THE NON-CHRISTIAN WORLD

Consider first its impact on the non-Christian world. Our mastery of space is crowding us so closely together that we are now less than twenty-four hours away from great centres of Hindu, Islamic and Buddhist population. Since our ties with these cultures are bound to grow closer, the need for understanding and friendship is also growing. Scholars are discovering in the faiths of the world many areas of resemblance and finding the same sense of dependence on the unknown, the same universal yearnings for light, security and guidance. These other religions are the product of many centuries of what we may call religious experimentation in the way of thought, ritual and practice; they have the deep respect and allegiance of their followers; indeed the people of India are disposed to think that, whatever the advantage of the West in material wealth, they themselves have been more sensitized by their religion to things of the spirit than we have by ours. What is the neo-orthodox attitude towards these faiths?

'The God of Mohammed', Barth answers, 'is an idol like all other idols, and it is an optical illusion to characterize Christianity along with Islam as a "monotheistic" religion.'[1] All other religions are the product of the natural man, the sort of religion, one gathers, of which he says that 'the Church does not take the slightest interest in religion'[2] and 'religion must die'.[3] With such faiths the true faith cannot compromise. Revelation has been given through

---

[1] *Knowledge of God*, p. 21.   [2] *Ibid.* p. 178.
[3] *Epistle to the Romans*, p. 238.

one man only, Jesus of Nazareth, and through him only to the eyes of the elect; to say that it was in this sense present in any degree in the Buddha, for example, is blasphemy. If the people who follow Buddha do not see this, it is because God has withheld from them that power to do so with which he has favoured so many people in the West, and there is no effort on their part that can hope to open their eyes or secure a similar blessing.

What is the likelihood that Christianity, so interpreted, will be heard gladly or with conviction by the people of other faiths? Surely not very great. They will suspect, and with some reason, a hidden link to that Western arrogance of which they carry long memories. They are invited to accept, without argument and in scorn of argument, a deity who has focused his favours on a fraction of the race — and not their fraction. They do not see why revelation should come through one scripture only, or one life only, or why the miracles of one faith should be true miracles and those of all others fraudulent, even when equally well attested, or why religious experiences that seem qualitatively very much alike should be revelatory in Basel and illusory in Bombay. The Christianity that is a gospel of love, overflowing boundaries of race, class and colour, they understand, and their Gandhis and Tagores and Suzukis have listened to it and gratefully borrowed from it. But when offered this exclusive transcendentalism with the take-it-or-leave-it postscript, they may be expected to return it to the sender with the endorsement, 'Thank you very much; on the whole, we prefer to leave it'.

THE FUTILITY OF MORAL AND RELIGIOUS EFFORT

Consider, secondly, how the temper of this teaching suits that of our newly emerging world. The new atmosphere is one of hope, based on effort plus the increasing mastery of nature. Since the United Nations was founded, literally scores of new nations have been added to its list, most of them exultant over their freshly-won freedom.

Faith and the Philosophers

These peoples are trying to absorb the ambition, energy and self-reliance that have made the more advanced nations what they are. The Russian experience in particular seems relevant to them, because in a single generation the Russians have lifted themselves by their own rough boots from poverty and ignorance to some degree of prosperity, and to impatient eyes that means hope. The fact that Russia has chosen to make its effort without benefit of clergy is not lost on these observers. They are not indifferent to the things of the spirit; they long for them. But they hold increasingly to a conviction, now orthodox among the Russians, that the spirit has long roots in the body, and that if it is to produce its proper flowers, those roots must be studied and watered and nourished. The precipitate progress of the last few decades has come through a new mastery over natural processes, including that mastery over the body that has added so many years to our lives. There is a restless and urgent hope in the air, the hope of emergence into a larger life through the control of its natural conditions.

On this sort of hope neo-orthodoxy throws a douche of cold water. Through its doctrine of discontinuity it declines to admit that the spirit, in its true sense, has its roots in the body at all. The goods that are so rooted and that may therefore be gained by cultivation are constantly disparaged. Barth has been particularly critical of American 'materialism' and its goals, while Brunner pours scorn on all merely natural morality. Of the morality in which we judge conduct by the natural goods it produces he says: 'this whole moral gradation which for us is absolutely necessary, simply does not count ultimately, that is, in the sight of God . . .',[1] indeed he goes so far as to say, 'in the last resort it is precisely morality which is evil'.[2] And beyond all this is the iteration that, valueless and sinful as man's whole natural life is, there is nothing, absolutely nothing he can do to lift himself out of it. 'We have as little share in our rebirth,' says Barth, 'as we have in our being created . . .;'[3] 'man's salvation

---

[1] Emil Brunner, *The Divine Imperative* (Philadelphia: Westminster Press, 1947), p. 175.   [2] *Ibid.* p. 71.
[3] Karl Barth, *Knowledge of God*, p. 107.

is the work of God *exclusively*, and to say anything else is to blaspheme against Jesus Christ.'[1] This is a chilling gospel for a world of rising hope in what man can make of man.

Its bleakness has repelled many even of those brought up in the Christian tradition. Professor Marion Bradshaw has written of it with feeling: 'when I find a theology advocated by its adherents because it makes men feel their helplessness and the worthlessness of even the best that men can think and do, it is simply impossible for me to regard it as "more desirable and profounder". Reading much more of it could easily have led me into a measure of sympathy with Whitehead's dictum that Christian theology is one of the great disasters of the human race.'[2]

Barth would probably deny that his theology is incongruous with the time, and would like to think it equally relevant to all times and places. But it is hard for an energetic American or an aspiring African of the present day to feel its relevance or to forget that it is the product of a very different moral climate from his own.

We cannot understand Barth's teaching unless we remember the mood of reaction from which it sprang. In his youth he had shared the generous enthusiasm of the labour movement, and had looked to it to secure the peace of Europe. The War shattered all hope in man and man's achievement. Henceforth it must be utter despair or else reliance upon God alone.[3]

Of Barth's *Romans*, the same writer adds, 'everything human in it is scorned and condemned, and, not least religion, man's approach to God'.[4] 'A religion', says John Baillie, 'that refuses to exhibit its own reasonableness is fellow to a political regime that refuses to submit to a free referendum, and it is no accident that the two are products of the same age.'[5] But that age is not our age. Authoritarianism no longer commends itself to free minds in any field. Trust in man's power to shape himself and his future is returning, and a wave of awakened life is rolling over people who fifty

[1] *Ibid.* p. 91.   [2] *Advance*, June 13, 1956.
[3] Sydney Cave, *Hinduism or Christianity?* (New York: Harper and Row, 1939), p. 37.   [4] *Ibid.*
[5] John Baillie, *Our Knowledge of God* (New York: Charles Scribner's Sons, 1939), p. 16.

years ago would have seemed buried centuries deep from civilization. For such people, the new theology is an anachronism. To faces turned toward us in hope it is preaching despair of human aspiration and effort.

NEO-ORTHODOXY AND SCIENCE

Consider, thirdly, the attitude of this theology toward science. There is no need in our day to stress the importance of science, which has been done to the point of weariness; if one wants some measure of its improved position one need only compare a college catalogue of 1862 with one of 1962 on the relative places of science and the classics.

When I speak of science, I mean both the results and the methods of scientific study. As for the first, the results of science, the neo-orthodox attitude seems to vary. Sometimes it takes the line that revealed and natural knowledge are in hopeless conflict, but that this does not really matter, since the supernatural is beyond our logic. We have dealt with that line already. Sometimes it insists rather that between revealed and natural knowledge there can be no conflict because the realms are different. The devotees of neo-orthodoxy are not fundamentalists. They can read Darwin, Freud and Einstein without alarm; they have no aversion even to the criticism of the scriptural record by linguists, anthropologists and archaeologists. Still, their readiness to approve such criticism is not based on any sense of its importance for their own province. On the contrary, their tolerance springs from a serene conviction that the results of such criticism are irrelevant to anything of real importance in religion. The human body, even the human mind, may have evolved from the inorganic; a new gospel of St. Thomas and new scrolls from the Dead Sea may revise our records of the life and times of Jesus; all this matters little. For the planes on which faith and science move are discontinuous with each other. Nothing central to the Christian position could possibly be touched by these researches. With this insight, the theologian remains above 'the conflict between science and religion', which is only an illusion anyhow; what has occurred is a tiresome clash of zealots, ignorant on both sides of where the real boundaries lie.

This is an attitude that wears on its face a certain respect for science. But is it really more respectful than that of the fundamentalists? The fundamentalists fought Darwin at Dayton, Tennessee, because they saw, or thought they saw, that he was saying something important for faith as well as for science; Genesis and *The Origin of Species* could not both be true, and if they were forced to choose, they were going to stay with Genesis. Astronomy was important, for if it succeeded in proving that on a certain day in the first century darkness did not cover the earth, then the New Testament was at one point (Luke 23 : 44) unreliable, and it might be so in others. Science was thus paid the respect due to a formidable foe. To neo-orthodoxy in one of its standard moods, science is not sufficiently relevant even to be an enemy. The evolution of body and mind may be a fact; the received history in the New Testament may be through and through inaccurate; but the truth that God exists, that he created the human soul and that he revealed himself to this soul, are untouched by these or any other scientific theses. And the liberals are just as wrong as the fundamentalists. For the liberals, also frightened by the alleged conflict, try to make peace not by adjusting science to dogma, but by adjusting dogma to science. But what is called for is neither war with science nor surrender to it. Rightly conceived, science is no menace at all. It never penetrates beyond the purlieus of the temple; it deals with accidents not with essence, at best with more external witnesses to the faith, not faith itself. As neutrals, we should allow it to go its own way, without either fright or provocation.

SCIENCE *IS* RELEVANT TO RELIGIOUS BELIEF

I do not think this high line will stand examination; there are too many holes in the fence that Barth and Brunner have tried to erect between faith and science. The liberals,

I think, have been right in their sense of the importance of scientific advance for theology. If one sits like Canute and ignores the rising tide of science, one is only too likely to be drowned in it. To say that the evidence for man's ascent from the inorganic or for the dependence of mind on body has no relevance to the nature or destiny of the soul seems to me plainly untrue. That evidence may be indecisive, but if so, it will be shown to be so by further evidence, the evidence brought to light, for example, by the psychical researchers, who are fighting their own courageous battle with the fundamentalists of science. Dean Inge was surely right in thinking that the second law of thermodynamics is a serious threat to the belief in a God who loves mankind, and in writing a book to consider gravely whether there is any way out for the theologian. The anthropologists of religion like Frazer, and the psychologists of religion like James and Freud, who have offered naturalistic explanations for religious beliefs and experiences, can be met if at all only by a more thorough criticism than any they have yet received from neo-orthodoxy.

And it is not only science but the philosophy of science that needs consideration. Barth can afford to be disinterested about this or that miracle because he is so certain that the Christian revelation is one great miracle, and he could conceivably be right that those who have eyes to see will simply see this to be true without aid from evidence or argument. But for those who doubt it or deny it or think it a partial truth, some clear discussion of the meaning and probability of miracle in a world of science is surely called for. Barth's way of dealing with such questions, I take it, is to say that the certitude possessed by the man of faith about the occurrence of this great miracle is supreme and not really comparable with the confidence of the scientist that it does not occur; that if one has the insight of faith, argument is unnecessary and that if one lacks it, unprofitable. One can understand the persuasiveness of this attitude for anyone in the inner circle. But it leaves those outside of it singularly cold.

Irrationalism in Theology

BARTHIAN AND SCIENTIFIC METHOD

Science, however, means more than a set of conclusions; it means also a set of methods and intellectual habits. The most important of these habits is adherence to a rule that is felt to be at once intellectual and moral, the rule of adjusting one's assent to the evidence. This rule is not a restriction on intellectual freedom. It says nothing against our entertaining the wildest of hypotheses; one of the heroes of science, Darwin, admitted that he had taken seriously many more theories than he would care to confess. But on the assumption that we are interested above all in truth, the rule does forbid us to commit ourselves intellectually without grounds, or to withhold assent where sufficient grounds are present. The wild hypothesis may be entertained, but must not be believed before we have evidence for it, and if the evidence makes both ways, we should accept such probability as the evidence warrants; desire or fear that something should be true is no basis for assenting to it. This principle of intellectual rectitude is spreading steadily into other areas and is making itself felt increasingly in religious and political discussion.

Now the Barthian would reject this principle at the outset. To chain belief to the evidence in the field of religion would seem to him an absurd restriction, in that it doubly begs the question. It assumes, for one thing, that religious belief is the kind of belief that rests on empirical or rational evidence, and this he denies. Secondly, it assumes that such belief is an intellectual act, which can be willed or inhibited, and one of his main points is that it is no act of ours at all, but an uncovenanted, uncontrollable descent of grace. These are large issues which cannot be dealt with in passing. Suffice it to make two further remarks.

First, we must frankly admit that when the Barthian takes this attitude, it is unfair to charge him with the irresponsibility that a scientist would exhibit by a like attitude in his own province. The Barthian is not denying that the principle of mental rectitude is sound for inquiries into nature, and if confronted by persons who stubbornly adhered to the flatness of the earth or flew to a belief in centaurs and leprechauns for which they could produce no evidence, he would feel as the rest of us do. But he insists that if a belief is such that scientific evidence can have no bearing, one way or another, upon its truth, then to charge him with illicitly exceeding the evidence in the same fashion is false and unjust. There is nothing wrong in ignoring evidence known to be irrelevant. And, of course, if it is known to be irrelevant, he is right.

But here we must add our second remark. In spite of his protestations of neutrality toward science, he is clearly hostile to its own conception of its work. He is claiming a knowledge of objects that it cannot see, by means of faculties that it does not recognize. He would no doubt reply that for science to question the existence of objects and faculties merely on the ground that it has failed to observe them is the sort of arrogance that appears in Russell's calm remark that what is knowledge is science, and what is not science is not knowledge. And if it is true that science is only a set of statements about what is or may be given in sense, as some positivists have maintained, there is force in this reply. But science is not necessarily to be identified with myopia. It is a systematic attempt to explore and understand every kind of fact. It does not object to anyone's announcing the discovery of a new kind of fact or faculty; what it does insist on is that there should be some means of checking or verifying the alleged discovery. Not that the new object must be a public and physical thing like the sun and moon, but at least that if it is private, like a pain or an emotion, it must have some sort of continuity with the experiences of other persons, or some sort of generic resemblance to them, so that reports about it will carry meaning. I do not think that science would deny the possibility of an insight so exceptional that it could not be communicated to others, but it would deny that the occurrence of such an insight imposed any obligations on others to accept it so long as it remained for them without content.

Irrationalism in Theology

Science does not consider this attitude dogmatic or negative. It is at least hospitable to any belief that can show itself in any degree probable to normal minds. Of the major beliefs of neo-orthodoxy, however, it seems to be admitted and even insisted that no such account can be rendered and that they remain nevertheless the most luminously certain and overwhelmingly important of all beliefs. And we are called on to honour this certainty and importance even though we have never had the sort of experience out of which they arise. To be sure we cannot have faith, for with that our wills have nothing to do. But Barth does not speak only to the converted, and when he announces to scholars and scientists what the Scripture really means, he seems to be asking them to lay aside that intellectual pride which asks for evidence in advance; they should rather follow the principle he quoted [1] from Calvin, 'omnis recta cognitio Dei ab oboedientia nascitur'.[2]

This makes a demand of the scientist to which he finds it very hard to accede. For implied in the demand is the rejection of that very principle of intellectual rectitude by which he has lived, through which he has gained his successes, and through which he justifies himself in his own eyes. He is assured that from time to time there are lodged in men a set of faculties so discontinuous with their other faculties as to be undiscoverable by observation or introspection, by means of which they can apprehend truths beyond the range of merely human verification. The majority of men, even of educated men, though they bent their attention assiduously to what was being said to them, could not understand it, nor could they hope to do so by any earnestness of research, reflection or sympathy, though something might at any moment be done to them from outside nature, for no reason that they could discover, which would flood the hitherto unintelligible with supernatural light. I have said already that I do not think this view can be worked out in detail without conflicting with the conclusions of science at many points. But even if such

---

[1] In his book, *Evangelical Theology: An Introduction*.
[2] 'All true knowledge of God is born out of obedience.'

collisions could be avoided, the Barthian would still be asking of the scientist an ethics of belief, an attitude toward the use of evidence and a conception of what evidence consists in, that would require him to set firmly aside his scientific way of thinking.

PRIDE

What if he declines to bow at the altar of an unkown God? What if he asks for reasons why he should worship where he cannot see? That, he is told, is pride, and pride is a very great sin. At an accusation of pride from this particular source, he is apt to blink a little. If his bedside reading includes theology, he may recall a letter of Newman's to Cardinal Manning: 'I do not know whether I am on my head or my heels when I have active relations with you. . . . Meanwhile I propose to say seven masses for your intention. . . .'[1] Consider what is being said to him. It is not pride for a man to dismiss the scientific view of the world and the entire succession of rationalist philosophers from Plato to Whitehead, and to report that he has received a revelation from Omniscience which is true beyond all possibility of criticism from either science or philosophy. That is quite consistent with modesty; 'evangelical theology', Barth told his Princeton audience, 'is *modest* theology'.[2] On the other hand, to look before one leaps and ask for light before committing oneself, to display the kind of integrity that tries to hold its belief strictly to the evidence, to adhere to what philosopher and scientist alike regard as a primary virtue, that is pride and sin. Is there not here some lapse of humour? I am tempted to call in aid two honoured former teachers of mine. 'Humour and humility', said C. C. J. Webb, 'are qualities apt to go together; and one misses both when called upon, with no hint that the invitation has about it anything strange which might require apology or explanation, to express a certain truth not "in the language of our experience" but "from God's stand-

---

[1] Quoted by Lytton Strachey, *Eminent Victorians*, p. 92.
[2] *Ibid.* p. 7.

point"!' If that is humility, one wonders what higher standpoint is left for pride to occupy: 'A very little modesty', says Professor H. J. Paton, 'might suggest to the prophet that to question the truth of his message is not the same thing as to sit in judgement upon God. Theological ignorance can also be a form of sinful pride.' [1]

THE TEMPTATION OF IRRATIONALISM

It must be admitted that the appeal to reason is not an exciting appeal, and that when some short-cut to absolute truth has been offered in tones of authority, men have often shown a delighted alacrity in throwing down the laborious tools of intelligence and trooping after the prophet. Our own generation has seen millions of people following political leaders who refused ostentatiously to be judged or guided by reason. Such irrationalism is perhaps easier still in religion, since its dogmas are so little susceptible of familiar kinds of check. And so Tertullian and Luther and Pascal and Kierkegaard and Barth each gain a fervid following when they raise their voices against the presumptions of reason. Even in a communion as comparatively generous to reason as Catholicism, the tendency has often been manifested. We have just mentioned the fascinating Newman. Many commentators have pointed out that Newman's appeal, subtle as his intellect was, was not essentially to reason. 'Dissenting altogether from Bishop Butler's view that reason is the only faculty by which we can judge even of revelation, he set religion apart, outside reason altogether. From the pulpit of St. Mary's he told his congregation that Hume's argument against miracles was logically sound. It was really more probable that the witnesses should be mistaken than that Lazarus should have been raised from the dead. But, all the same, Lazarus was raised from the dead: we were required by faith to believe it, and logic had nothing to do with the matter.'[2] And even the young intellectuals of Oxford, we are told, began to go about murmuring 'credo in Newmannum'. We have something similar in today's

---

[1] *The Modern Predicament*, p. 54.   [2] Herbert Paul, *Life of Froude*, p. 25.

outbreak of theological irrationalism. As Anders Nygren puts it, 'there is coming to be a regular cult of the paradoxical and irrational, as though irrationality and lack of clearness were a hall-mark of Christian truth'. Reinhold Niebuhr, whose politics are as much the admiration as his theology is the despair of some liberals, can write: 'the canons of logic and rationality are transcended when reason attempts to comprehend the final irrationality of things'. And Niebuhr and Barth have voices that are heard in the land; they have even achieved the secular canonization of appearance on the cover of *Time*, as mere philosophers like Whitehead and Russell never did.

What is a person to do who has had respect for reason bred into his bone? He does not want to be *der Geist, der stets verneint*. He knows that science and philosophy too have their dogmatisms, and he may recall the remark of Bradley that 'there is no sin, however prone to it the philosopher may be, which philosophy can justify so little as spiritual pride'.[1] He knows that even logic has had its history, indeed that it has shown extraordinary changes in his own lifetime. And if he is the son and grandson of the parsonage, as the writer happens to be, he will have too many memories of the power and attraction of the religious life to wish to line up with its enemies, even if much that was credible to his parents is no longer credible to him. The humility, the capacity for reverence, the high concern for ends neither material nor selfish, the morality touched with emotion, which religion has stood for over the centuries are priceless still, and deeply needed in our troubled time.

THE INNER RESISTANCE TO IRRATIONALISM

On the other hand when invited to let all holds go by which he has clung to his standards of reasonableness and to commit himself to a world discontinuous with everything he knows, in which paradoxes are absolute truth, ethics prides itself on leaving reason behind and all activities of the natural man, including religion itself, are set down as

[1] *Appearance and Reality*, p. 7.

sinful, he feels bound to reflect before accepting the invitation. If he is told that what to his reason is contradictory may still be true, he will see and say at once that this is nonsense which cannot even be clearly thought. On the other claims of the new theology he will judge more tentatively. He knows that many of its claims, like those of miracle and revelation itself, are incapable of conclusive disproof and must be dealt with by considering their probability in the light of systematic knowledge and reflection. If he is told that such tests are invalid, he will reply that they are the best he has, and that according to his theological advisers themselves he cannot hope by any effort to gain higher ones. When the theology offered him is thus set in the common daylight of philosophy and science, it tends to disintegrate. The experiences reported as unique and ineffable take on a family resemblance to others that are intense and exalted indeed, but still natural. The inconceivable dogmas begin to look less like flashes from the superrational than like the vaguely formulated beliefs of natural minds, suffused with passionate conviction. The central experience, instead of being an inexplicable, vertical descent into the natural order from an utterly foreign realm, begins to seem like many another supposed visitation which appeared on retrospect to be explicable after all by the dark forces of man's own mind, not least of which is his desperate desire to escape from them and gain a foothold on a firmer shore.

It has been said that in religion men tend to divide by nature into the children of Luther and the children of Erasmus. I belong to the Erasmian household. I am content to take my stand with those unromantic liberals who, before they give assent to a doctrine, ask what it means. One of these was my honoured colleague Douglas Clyde Mackintosh, who though no lover of Hegel, loved still less that Hegelianism in reverse to which neo-orthodoxy tends, in which the real is the irrational and the irrational is the real. Another is Professor H. J. Paton, who has rightly warned us that 'to declare war upon reason is to alienate all who care for truth and to hold open the door for the impostor and the zealot'.[1] Still another is Professor C. A. Campbell, who has used words that I should be happy to make my own: 'The philosopher *must* claim, I think, that wherever the question of objective truth arises, whether it be the truth of religion or of anything else, it is for reason, and for reason *alone*, to carry out the assessment of the evidence, and to make the final adjudication upon it. . . . What is there save reason, the philosopher asks, to perform this office?'[2] To that question liberals would answer, Nothing. Some of them would go further and hoist a danger signal. That lifelong student of religion, James Bissett Pratt, wrote: 'The position taken up in certain passages of Kierkegaard and in some of the Barthian writings is sheer defeatism. It is a notification to the enemy and to the world at large that Christianity is no longer logically defensible, that it is frankly unreasonable, and that no one who respects human intelligence can consistently or conscientiously remain within the Christian fold.'[3] These are strong words from an exceptionally sane critic. They call for a better answer than they have yet received.

[1] H. J. Paton, *The Modern Predicament* (London: Allen and Unwin, *also* New York: The Macmillan Company, 1955), p. 58.
[2] *On Selfhood and Godhood*, pp. 14-15.
[3] *Can We Keep the Faith?*, p. 80.

'BUT IS IT BARTH?'

BY

EDWARD A. DOWEY

THE lack of discrimination of Mr. Blanshard's critique of Karl Barth reflects a good deal of exasperation that so much attention is paid to a writer the substance of whose thought is anachronistic, whose method is an 'incoherent patchwork', and whose language is 'gibberish'. Certainly 'The Achievement of Barth' has never been more tepidly described than in Mr. Blanshard's paragraph of that title.[1] And the secret of Barth's success, or notoriety, he estimates to be found in his 'Lutheran self-confidence, energy and pugnacity'.

Before proceeding to a more substantive matter, I mean to call attention to several respects in which I think Mr. Blanshard fails to take his subject, Barth, seriously enough to make all his comments interesting. For instance, the 'neo-orthodoxy' described on pp. 160-162 contains nothing 'neo-' at all, nothing noticeably Barthian, but a list of doctrines held traditionally as the common possession of most Christian theologians. Also the 'contradictions' listed for Barth[2] bear no marks of Barth at all. I suggest that some attention to Barthian nuances — incipient universalism, his rejection of the appeasement theme of the atonement, and his utter disinterest in the proposition, 'with God all things are possible' — might have placed both the doctrines and the contradictions in a quite different light.

Further, it seems that Mr. Blanshard has so thoroughly convinced himself of Barth's irrationality that he does not feel bound by the usual amenities of criticism and dialogue. The first amenity, that of reading Barth extensively, is

[1] Pp. 168-69.   [2] Pp. 170-72.

willingly excluded by us all, for to read Barth extensively is to do little else. The choice of the 1937 Gifford lectures, however, which in Barth's case are a brief and non-technical 'paraphrase'[1] of the Scottish Confession of 1560, was not a good one for a critic interested seriously in Barth's method. There is nothing here of 'Dogmatics as a Science'[2] and the like. Also Barth's development is overlooked. He now professes to see only his own ghost in the terms 'wholly other', 'discontinuity', 'infinite qualitative distinction between God and man', which are the refrain of the present critique.[3] Some theological critics are now saying that Barth is unduly bound to a rational consistency involving a Hegel-like metaphysic that practically removes sin from the plane of theology.

More captiously, this criticism occasionally damns Barth by quotations torn from context. Two of these are the substance of Mr. Blanshard's paragraph on the content of revelation. The remark that 'When one has stated what Father, Son and Spirit in God mean, one must continue and add that one has said nothing'[4] is here alleged to mean that revelation has no content. Where Barth wrote it the meaning is that the method of beginning with three and proceeding to one in Trinitarian discourse is a wrong method, and therefore 'says nothing'.[5] There is a section on 'The Meaning of the Doctrine of the Trinity',[6] and that is the place to find the subject discussed. So also the remark that 'if revelation occurs, "before it all words are hushed, and we, when we see him, can only worship"', is not taken from a place where Barth is discussing content, but belongs to the familiar theme of awe and silence before divine grace. Elsewhere, it is said to be 'startling' to find a theologian

---

[1] 'The brevity is regrettable', writes Barth. 'But I have been detailed enough elsewhere and no doubt shall be so again.' Each lecture was read in German, together with a running English translation, within the length of a classroom hour. They were published as delivered without footnotes and precurses. See the preface to the German edition, *Gotteserkenntnis und Gottesdienst*, pp. 4-6. Why he 'paraphrased' the Scottish Confession is explained in the first lecture.   [2] *Church Dogmatics*, I/1, pp. 315-330.
[3] From Barth's preface to the English translation of Otto Weber's handbook entitled, *Karl Barth's Church Dogmatics*.   [4] Quoted from Monsma, p. 138.
[5] *Church Dogmatics*, I/1, p. 422.   [6] *Ibid.* pp. 431-440.

'belittling goodness itself'.[1] But in the place cited Barth was only enlarging on a saying of one of Mr. Blanshard's favourites, Jesus, who appears guilty of the same thing: 'When ye shall have done all those things which are commanded of you, say we are unprofitable servants'.[2] Again, Barth is caught allegedly rejecting goodness in the words, 'In the Christian life we are not concerned with our becoming Christian personalities'. But in context Barth is arguing that faith is not a private affair, not primarily a matter of self-cultivation, but that it issues in a life in community.[3] The apparently negative reference to 'becoming Christian personalities' taken in this context, is an ironic reference to faith individualistically conceived. So presented, Barth has a right to sigh as he once did: 'All in all, "neo-orthodoxy" with a faint flavour of nihilism! What else? Shall I weep or laugh?'[4]

Lastly, Mr. Blanshard's exasperation causes him to hint that Karl Barth of the 'bleak, strident voice'[5] might disapprove of kindness to little children or willingness to rescue an ox on the Sabbath as Jesus did. And no doubt Barth cannot distinguish between Albert Schweitzer and a jailbird.[6] It may be enough to report here that Barth is a spectacularly successful grandfather, and it has been his practice for years to preach in the Basel prisons.

The comments so far are not intended to dismiss the critical content of the paper before us, but to indicate what I take to be the less valuable type of material in it. We turn now to a different issue.

II

The basic point of Mr. Blanshard's critique is that the claim of supernatural revelation is inadmissible to rational man because it does not fall under the adjudication of reason. Barth, having exempted revelation more completely than others from the judgement of reason, is a theological 'irrationalist' who requires the 'surrender' of

---

[1] P. 164. [2] *Knowledge of God*, p. 146. [3] *Ibid.* p. 154.
[4] *Loc. cit. supra*, n. 3. [5] P. 181. [6] P. 184.

reason. It is thus perverse of Barth to reason or rant his way through 15,000 pages *about* revelation. Even more, 'we' who do not have the experience out of which neo-orthodox doctrines arise are 'called on to honour this certainty'.

Barth does not speak only to the converted, and when he announces to scholars and scientists what Scripture really means, he seems to be asking them to lay aside the intellectual pride which asks for evidence in advance. . . .[1]

And Barth, like Calvin, makes obedience a component of the knowledge of God.

There are, among others, three questions here: (1) Does Barth's view of revelation actually require him to surrender all rational activity? (2) Does Barth perversely cross over the 'wall of separation' he is supposed to have built between reason and revelation? (3) Does Barth actually, as theologian, demand a sacrifice of the philosophical intellect?

(1) Does Barth's view of revelation require him by the consistency of his own 'irrationality' to quit being a theologian and content himself with a benign mystic smile? I think the Edinburgh theologian who took Mr. Blanshard to task in *The Scotsman* may have had a point. He, whoever he was, apparently held that reason should conform to its object, and in this case it should be conformed to the content of revelation.[2] This is the place at which Barth 'adjusts assent to the evidence'. This I take to be a crucial issue on which Barth and practically all Christian theology can be mortally wounded. The commentaries on ancient philosophical treatises that made them in the past variously serviceable to theology witness to the long history of this problem. Mr. Blanshard's brief argument concerning the law of contradiction[3] does appear to me to be, as he suggests it may, hocus-pocus.

What can one really say as logician to a theologian who starts with divine revelation and believing obedience? And how many Christian theologians do not finally have recourse to both? If revelation of this kind is reflected upon by those who claim it and the result is called theology, where

---

[1] P. 195.   [2] *Church Dogmatics*, I/1, pp. 340 f.   [3] Pp. 175-76.

is there access for the non-theological critic? The method and structure of theology, thus conceived, can be criticized only in intra-theological debate, which is what Barth intends. He may thereby be wrong or irrelevant, but the present issue of whether it is inconsistent of him to reason at all does not appear subject to Mr. Blanshard's formal critique.

(2) Does Barth illicitly cross the line and make use of rational and ethical insights not actually derived from his theological criterion, the 'Word of God'? It would be a mistake here to regard Barth's work as mere loose talk. He makes quite clear that theology consists of words in various languages and does not constitute a sacred grammar and logic. He writes:

> The Church in fact is also a sociological entity with definite historical and structural features. Preaching in fact is also an address. Sacrament in fact is also a symbol in compromising proximity to all other possible symbols. The Bible in fact is also the document for the history of the religion of a tribe in Nearer Asia and of its Hellenistic offshoot. Jesus Christ in fact is also the Rabbi of Nazareth, historically so difficult to get information about, and when it is got, one whose activity is so easily a little commonplace alongside more than one other founder of a religion and even alongside many later representatives of His own 'religion'. And let us not forget that theology in fact, so surely as it avails itself of human speech, is also a philosophy or a conglomerate of all sorts of philosophy.[1]

That which is uttered, the Word of God, must be uttered through forms unsuitable, the words of men. The Bible, too, which until the nineteenth century offered a relatively safe precinct of sacred statements, enshrining sacred truths, is not so regarded by Barth.

This issue of Scripture may be a good one on which to test Barth's procedure, or at least to present an issue on which he might be tested. One of Barth's vaunted achievements, deplored by Mr. Blanshard who thinks the fundamentalists took Darwin more seriously, is that he has constructed a doctrine of revelation in such a way as to exempt it from all science implied in historico-critical Bible study.

[1] *Church Dogmatics*, I/1, p. 188, *cf.* pp. 321 f., 325 ff.

Faith and the Philosophers

On the face of it, there appears to have been a retreat in the nineteenth century from equating the biblical canon with the Word of God. Were this the case, Barth would be the end of this retreat. Having abandoned all shaky positions in cosmology, psychology, biology, he holds the fort of a quite minimum *kerygma*. If this is what happened (and certainly it is what happened to the 'old' orthodoxy) then Barth was actually letting secular reason, scientific and philosophic, function as a judge in matters of theology. But what Barth *claims* is that revelation properly understood is of such a character that it excludes these matters. Orthodoxy erred by confusing natural or rational theology with its central task of church dogmatics: dogmatics determined by its object, revelation. The thought of Luther and Calvin serve as forerunners for Barth's position from the pre-scientific era. That is, while not actually abandoning the venerable conception of an unimpeachable text, they made their case for faith and even for the Bible on quite other grounds, namely, the Word understood as the promise of redemption in Christ. Now if Luther, Calvin and Barth do actually derive their faith from the Word thus grasped, rather than from the formal authority of Book or Church, from the Christocentricity of the *kerygma* even before the days of Darwin and Freud — then Barth's thought on this subject may be appreciated as following a rationale derived from the Word and from the theological tradition. He can only with great difficulty be forced into the dilemma, Genesis or Darwin, fundamentalist or scientist, where Mr. Blanshard has to have him in order to deal with him. This procedure of Barth's may not have been a success, but it is on this level, I think, that his success or failure is to be judged, not with the epithet 'irrationalist'.

(3) Does Barth as theologian actually demand a sacrifice of the scientific and philosophical intellect? Barth as theologian does not address the scientist and philosopher as such. Nor does he answer their scientific and philosophical questions as such. Barth's *Church Dogmatics* is offered as a self-criticism of the church, by and for the church with reference to its preaching language, that is, its language

about God's redemption. Since 'dogmatics' is not a part of revelation and is not the Word of God, it of course falls under the criticism of being, as Mr. Blanshard points out, a product of man's pride. Barth writes:[1]

> A kind of solemn elevation in the common utterances of the philosopher, and a kind of kerygmatic urgency in those of the theologian, in no way alter the situation that neither is in any position to speak as it were out of heaven either to himself or to the other.

There is, says Barth, an inevitable conflict between theology and philosophy that has a two-fold ground: (1) both philosophy and theology share the same problems as they stand before the same single whole of relatively accessible truth — this holds them together; (2) the primacy, order and sequence of treating these identical problems is radically different in the two enterprises — here their inevitable conflict arises.

The strife between philosophy and theology must come and should not be shirked or avoided by either some narrow division of labour or a friendly peace treaty. The role of each field is to hold the other responsible for dealing with the whole, even if by mutually unacceptable approaches. The resulting conflict can, in fact, be carried on hopefully, if the 'one single whole truth' is the persistent aim of both, despite their different paths of approach.

The primacy of revelation which characterizes theology and sets it off from philosophy is a necessary primacy. It is of such a quality that the theologian may finally look in astonishment at the philosopher for not availing himself of it. However that may be, the philosopher cannot be expected, as philosopher, to abandon the ground on which he stands and adopt revelation as the base of his work, for then he would become a crypto-theologian, which is Barth's term for *philosophia christiana*. Theology, on the other hand, should not allow philosophy to become merely *advocatus*

---

[1] Most of the following comes from Barth's short essay, 'Philosophie und Theologie', pp. 93-106, in the Festschrift, *Philosophie und Christliche Existenz*, published in honour of his brother Heinrich, professor of philosophy in the University of Basel.

diaboli, something to be guarded against and a set of methods to be avoided. Rather the theologian should listen to the philosopher and be thankful for him as the *advocatus hominis et mundi*, as the truly wise of this world.

The theologian and the philosopher cannot really 'sit down and converse' because their paths cross or intersect rather than run together. But they can and should 'discuss and debate'.[1] Barth does not profess to know how the philosopher likes this role, since it is described from within 'church dogmatics' and he finds it not in his province to say what the philosopher is likely to gain from this discussion. But Barth suggests that 'quite unexpectedly and contrary to programme' either the theologian or the philosopher may in fact find something profitable for his own enterprise. It is, says Barth, their common humanity that should keep the philosopher and theologian on speaking terms professionally, however they may differ in their paths toward the 'one single whole truth'. For scientist, philosopher and theologian are all *men*. This means *fellow* men (*Mitmenschen*), and their differing occupations and interests should not be allowed to deny this, in fact cannot deny it without the man becoming inhumane (*ein Unmensch*).

The access to theology, however, for the fellow man who is a philosopher or scientist, does not derive from theology proper, or from a technical '*Auseinandersetzung*' between philosopher and theologian. In 1949 Barth and a Roman Catholic theologian were among those who addressed an international congress of scientists and philosophers in Geneva. The theme was 'The New Humanism'. Barth's approach was typical and revealing of the position of his thought over against science and philosophy. His Roman Catholic colleague took generally the same approach. Barth spoke of the gospel as the 'humanism of God'. He described his theological project, but affirmed at the beginning and the end of his address that the actuality of the message would be lost because he had been asked to lecture, not to preach:

---

[1] Barth makes an untranslatable play on words, '*zusammensetzen*' (sit together) as opposed to '*auseinandersetzen*' (a synonym for 'discuss' with the implication of divide or 'sit opposite').

Irrationalism in Theology

I cannot point out the actuality of the Christian message or present it, as it were on a platter. And with any effort of this kind I would only distract you from it. Were I here to preach, then I would go on with the challenge, 'Repent and believe the gospel'. But I must not preach here, rather I must bring this lecture to an end. . . . [Again] a treatment of this subject to become 'actual', would have to begin by praying together the 'Our Father' and celebrating the Lord's Supper . . . and beginning here to think and to speak. . . .[1]

It would seem that Barth does not wish to ask that philosophy bend or break into theological moulds, and that he expects discussion in the form of conflict will and should take place hopefully, and with respect for mutual integrity. All the while he holds that the man who is philosopher or scientist, like the one who is theologian, is fair game for preaching about the grace of God.

Since philosophers, I suspect, generally prefer lectures to sermons, it may be that they will never even hear Barth's preaching. If so Barth's programme for evangelism may be much more successful in the jails of Basel than in the University of Basel, where he lectured through the whole *Dogmatik*.

[1] 'Die Aktualität der Christlichen Botschaft', in *Humanismus, Theologische Studien*, Heft 28, 1950, p. 12.

ON BARTH, THE PHILOSOPHER

BY

GEORGE S. HENDRY

THEOLOGIANS have been exposed to this kind of critical attack by philosophers ever since the apostle Paul had the temerity to address a congress of Epicurean and Stoic philosophers (at their invitation) on the Areopagus (Acts 17: 16-34). Despite the fact that on this occasion he adopted a conciliatory manner of approach, which stands in puzzling contrast to the extremely negative attitude to philosophy expressed in some of his Epistles, he seems to have had only limited success. This appears to have been the general pattern. The theologians of the early centuries followed the path of conciliation for the most part; they strove to come to terms with the main currents of philosophical thought which they encountered, and they made copious use of philosophical conceptualities in the elaboration of Christian doctrine, but, though they won some converts from the ranks of philosophy, most philosophers, and the most eminent among them, remained aloof. A good example of the failure of conciliation was the school of Alexandria, one of the most ambitious attempts to create a philosophical theology which, however, failed to impress the philosophers it was designed to conciliate. It is not surprising, therefore, that some should have come to the conclusion that philosophy is the bane of theology. These are a small minority, but they include some famous names. The most famous in the ancient church was Tertullian, who declared war *à outrance* on philosophy and consigned Aristotle to outer darkness. He had a successor in Luther who sometimes denounced reason in intemperate terms. And in our own time the succession has

Irrationalism in Theology

descended to Karl Barth. Barth has expressed the view that theology is most likely to win the respect of the philosophers when it goes about its own business according to its own methods with no thought of conciliating them, and he alleges that the theologians who have been most eager to conciliate the philosophers have received the least attention from them; he points to the succession of theologians in the nineteenth century who courted philosophical approval by pouring their theologies into Hegelian moulds.

It is evident, however, that Barth is mistaken; for he has signally failed to impress Mr. Blanshard. Mr. Blanshard charges Barth with flagrant disregard, or defiance, of the laws of rational thought, and he supports this with a bill of particulars which add up to a formidable indictment indeed. Barth seems to be left without a leg to stand on. If Mr. Blanshard's standards of rationality are valid, Barth has been demolished. The only thing left to do would be to gather up the fragments and carry them out for burial.

This paper will not attempt to refute the charges brought against Barth. It will merely plead some extenuating circumstances in the hope that the court may be induced to reduce the sentence.

(1) It is not always clear who the target of Mr. Blanshard's attack really is. Ostensibly it is Barth who is charged with irrationality, but at times the charge is directed against the whole theological tradition in which he stands. In the latter case it is hard to see why Barth should be singled out for special attack; for if the material with which he deals is inherently irrational, he has little choice but to be irrational himself.

A discussion of the rationality of the Christian faith would take us too far afield and would raise issues which it would hardly be profitable to pursue within the framework of this conference. One thing should be said, however. Before such a discussion could be undertaken, it would be desirable to ensure that the Christian doctrines are fairly, if not sympathetically, presented, and this, I fear, is something which Mr. Blanshard has failed to do. In his paper he passes in review a series of Christian doctrines, all of which he find to be riddled with contradictions,[1] and here, it seems to me, he has abandoned the role of a philosophical critic and assumed that of a prosecuting attorney or a minister of propaganda.

The doctrine of original sin, which he cites first, has always affirmed that all men stand in a natural, and not merely a juridical relation to Adam; and surely it is not difficult to see in its 'mythological' terms an attempt to express the trans-personal dimension of responsibility and guilt. The doctrine would be indeed absurd if it could be assumed that responsibility is always neatly packaged in individual lots and that a man could be judged to 'render to every man his due' while the majority of his fellow citizens are condemned to a condition of servitude. Courts of law find it convenient to operate with this fiction, but they are frequently made aware of its limitations, as the Nuremberg trials showed. There may be less rationality, but there is surely more wisdom in the words of Father Zossima, that 'we are all responsible to all for all, apart from our own sins'.

Mr. Blanshard also find 'a great nest of contradictions about the incarnation', and in the end he finds the idea of incarnation itself contradictory, if it is taken to mean the involvement of God in the sin and corruption of men. But this is the mystery of grace which Christian faith confesses, though it has never succeeded in formulating it in terms which are invulnerable to rational criticism. Here one can only invoke the ancient rule: *in scholis contra negantem principia non disputatur*.

Finally, a brief comment on Mr. Blanshard's conception of divine omnipotence, which he uses to introduce the classical dilemma regarding God's goodness and his power. Is it profitable to speculate whether it was possible for God to create a world without problems and mysteries? Is it wise to vote him out of office because the world he created does not meet our specifications at every point? If faith in God fails to solve the problem of pain, does the rejection of faith make it less painful? If it is a mystery why some have to bear suffering which they have manifestly

[1] Pp. 170-72.

Irrationalism in Theology

not deserved, is it not also a mystery why so many more are spared the suffering they have manifestly deserved? If rationality demands a world in which happiness varies in direct ratio to morality — if it is rational to speak, as Mr. Blanshard does, of 'suffering that is morally pointless' — would it not be more rational to follow Kant and postulate a future life in which the imbalances are corrected?

(2) In so far as Barth is the specific object of Mr. Blanshard's attack, two observations may be made.

(a) The charge of irrationality, brought against Barth, might be even more heavily weighted, on the ground that he has developed his theological systems in philosophical moulds, which are *ex hypothesi* rational. He has, so to speak, laid his theological eggs in philosophical nests. This is true of both the earlier and the later Barth, though it is more openly avowed by the earlier than the later, and it is true in a deeper sense than avowed. Barth has often confessed that theology cannot do its work without conceptual tools provided by philosophy. But if this suggests the old picture of philosophy as the handmaid of theology, the picture is not quite accurate; for philosophy is, to Barth, something more than a handmaid who hands him his tools, it is a mistress with whom he goes to bed.

The framework of the first system, which is found in the *Römerbrief*, is transparently Kantian (and/or Neo-Kantian). The frequent designation of God as the 'Origin' is derived from Cohen, whom Barth studied at Marburg, and who tried to remove one of the difficulties of the Kantian system by virtually dropping the Aesthetic and transforming the Logic into a 'logic of origin'. God as Origin represents the hidden unity that lies behind the dualities of experience, and as such he is 'the wholly other' (meaning the 'non-given'). The subject-object split is the model of Barth's interpretation of fallen existence; it is existence that has fallen out of its primordial unity with the Origin. Indeed, the predicament of fallen man in the *Römerbrief* is basically epistemological: he is condemned to live in a world in which God (like the thing-in-itself) cannot be known. Religion represents a vestigial recollection of that original unity or immediacy from which man has fallen. It is essentially a vacuum; and in so far as it tries to bridge the gap and recover the unity, it only intensifies the crisis by offering man an illusory knowledge of God which is only a projection of himself (Barth has a veritable obsession with Feuerbach). The crisis is resolved, not by religion, but by revelation, i.e. by the action of God himself. But God is so wholly other that his action in the world cannot take the form of intervention. Revelation registers in the empirical world only in negations, culminating in the death of Jesus. Its decisive impact is in the transcendental realm, and it can only be apprehended by faith. Its paradigm is the resurrection, in which, as he puts it, the world is 'moved' by God, as from an Archimedean point. The revelation of God effects a 'transcendental disposition' or 'transcendental pre-determination' of human life, and, as such, it is apprehended by the transcendental self, where Barth locates the work of the Holy Spirit. Faith, then, is primarily a transformation of our thinking (*Umdenken*), and it expresses itself, not so much in action, as in demonstration. He compares the Christian ethic to a May Day parade in which the demonstrators carry placards with such slogans as 'No mixing of heaven and earth' and 'Call God God and man man'; if they were also to carry portraits (which he does not suggest), Kant's would no doubt be much in evidence. The real inspiration of the 'dialectical theology', as it was called at this stage, was the transcendental dialectic of the first *Critique*.

This will probably strike philosophical students of Kant as a charade — or a nightmare.

The later system, which is developed at prodigious length in the *Church Dogmatics*, is cast in a more Hegelian mould. The 'wholly-otherness' of God is now replaced by the 'humanity of God'. The Creator-creature relation is no longer represented as the dissolution of a primordial unity but as an (analogical) expression of the being of God, who, as the Father and the Son, contains the original (idea?) of the self-other structure within himself. The ultimate destiny of the creature is pre-figured in the Son, who, in his descent and ascent (in traditional language, his humiliation and exaltation) dramatizes both in the derivation of the antithesis from the thesis and its ultimate resolution in the synthesis. The end is in the beginning (Pre-destination). Barth's system has been aptly characterized by a Dutch theologian as 'The Triumph of Grace'. If Hegel could say, 'the real is the rational', Barth says, 'the real is the gracious'; and if Hegel's reason, in its cunning, could harness the irrational to its all-embracing purpose, Barth's God, in his grace, can negate the negation of sinful men and bring all safe home at last. Theology, with such a theme, cannot but be a 'happy science'.

It would be interesting to know how students of Hegel would regard this attempt to transpose his philosophy back to its original, theological key, and how they would estimate its rationality.

(b) When a man is grinding an axe, the friction generates a shower of sparks, which, if allowed to fall on combustible material, can cause a fire. A man who allows this to happen may be careless, but it would be manifestly unfair to brand him an incendiarist. In the same way I think it is unfair to brand Barth an irrationalist without a more patient consideration of the axe he is grinding. For Barth is certainly a man with an axe to grind, and if he has caught the religious world's attention — and even 'made' the cover of *Time*[1] (a fact which seems to annoy Mr. Blanshard, surprisingly enough, since it surely signifies nothing *sub specie aeternitatis*) — it is because he convinced the religious world, or a large part of it, that this axe needed grinding, and not because the religious world took an immature delight in the incendiary sparks that accompanied the process. Barth has recalled theology to what he regards as its proper theme, viz., revelation or, to be more specific, the revelation of God in Christ. The question is whether theology can apply itself to its proper theme without coming into conflict, or at least tension, with reason.

Mr. Blanshard discusses various possible ways in which this may happen.[2] His whole discussion, however, appears

[1] P. 198. [2] Pp. 162 ff.

to be informed by the assumption that revelation (if there be such a thing) consists in the disclosure of 'truth' or 'knowledge' which, though inaccessible to reason, is of the same order as rational knowledge and is therefore susceptible of formulation in propositions which are subject to rational tests; or, in his own variation of a traditional figure, revelation is a 'supernatural aid', like a telescope or a pair of binoculars with which theologians are privileged to see the summit of the mountain which philosophers are painfully struggling to ascend with unaided reason. This is a Roman Catholic conception, which has also, to be sure, been widely received in Protestantism, but from which Protestant theology has been striving to extricate itself ever since the Enlightenment. To the rationalist eye the whole movement may well appear to be a flight from reason or a quest for an asylum where theology would be safe from the attacks of reason. But though apologetic motives were undoubtedly at work, they are not sufficient to account for the movement as a whole, which was rather the fruit of an awareness that the reality of revelation, as it is apprehended by faith, is something other than the communication of knowledge, that though theology can only conduct its business in propositions which raise *prima facie* pretensions to rationality, they are not, and can never be, identical with the reality of revelation itself.

If the philosopher asks, 'What then is revelation?' he receives 'a most disconcerting answer';[1] he is told, in effect, that the question is unanswerable. This may strike him as 'unintelligibility rampant',[2] if he takes the position that revelation, to be intelligible, must be describable, and that if it is indescribable, it is unintelligible. But are these the only alternatives? If instead of demanding that the theologian stand and deliver an answer to the question, What is revelation? we ask, What is the status of theological propositions in relation to revelation? certain other possibilities suggest themselves.

The two alternatives correspond to two strains which have always been present in the theological tradition, a

[1] P. 177. [2] P. 179.

positive (kataphatic) theology which holds that theological propositions are commensurate with the truth of revelation and which can therefore speak of 'dogmas divinely revealed', and a negative (apophatic) theology which holds that the truth of revelation is so 'wholly other' that we can never say what it is, only what it is not. A more extreme form of negative theology holds that the truth of revelation is literally ineffable and would deny the competence of theological propositions altogether; Simonides, whose theology of silence was admired (but not practised) by Calvin, would have endorsed Wittgenstein's dictum, 'Whereof one cannot speak, thereof must one be silent'. Echoes of the negative theology are to be heard in Barth in his earlier, more Kantian, period, from which most of Mr. Blanshard's quotations are taken. The truth of revelation is like the thing-in-itself; we know it is there, because it makes its impact in the empirical world, but we do not know what it is: 'The very attempt to grasp ultimate truth by reason is misguided.'[1] In his later, more Hegelian and, as some would say, his more orthodox phase, Barth has moved toward a more positive view of theological propositions and tends therefore to show a greater concern for preserving at least the semblance of rationality. But he is not overmuch concerned with the rationality of the individual propositions in which the system is set forth, since for him, as for Hegel, 'the truth is the whole'. He would therefore not be unduly disturbed by Mr. Blanshard's exposure of his illogical utterances; for 'the whole' is a movement in which logical contradictions will be resolved, like the discords in a musical composition (especially one by Mozart). He employs the Christological analogy and argues that, just as the eternal Son of God assumed our flesh into the unity of his person, so God in his grace assumes our concepts into union with his truth. This does not mean that they are identical or commensurate with his truth, but they are enabled to participate in it and approximate to it.[2] Reason, therefore, is no longer consigned to utter darkness in relation to the truth of revelation; it is given a role somewhat similar to

[1] P. 170. [2] *Church Dogmatics*, II/1, especially para. 27.

that which Hegel gave it in philosophy: it is the owl of Minerva which starts its flight at dusk and, so to speak, reflects on the events of the day. It follows at a distance and seeks to express the truth of revelation in analogies. Philosophers, of course, are not all content that reason should have only this modest role; they prefer to see it as the eagle which soars up into the light with unblinking eye. But can reason sustain this role? It is significant that philosophy has for some time had to reckon with the presence of irrationalists in its own household, one of whom has gone so far as to say: 'Thinking only begins at the point where we have come to know that reason, glorified for centuries, is the most obvious adversary of thinking'.

Mr. Blanshard concludes his paper with the suggestion, which he supports with a series of quotations from philosophers, that we have to choose between reason and unreason, between Erasmus and Luther. I doubt whether this is the real choice and I would suggest it is more reasonable to ask, What is the role of reason in religion?

DISCUSSION

Linwood Urban: *Barth's Epistemology*

There is an important aspect of Barth's thought which was not discussed either in Mr. Blanshard's critique or in the rejoinders. This omission comprises Barth's remarks about the nature of knowledge and his justification for the claim that 'no more objective and strict form of knowledge can exist, and no type of knowledge can lay claim more definitely to universal validity than the knowledge of faith'.[1] Barth's statements on these issues would be significant in themselves, but their importance is enhanced by the fact that they play a central role in Barth's thought. They show that Barth does give reasons for what he believes, that he does follow a consistent methodology, that he is not precluded in principle from a consistent methodology, as Mr. Blanshard seems to think.

A useful point of departure for considering Barth's position

[1] Karl Barth, *Knowledge of God and Service of God*, Hodder, 1938 *and* Scribner, 1939, p. 25.

on the nature of knowledge is the following quotation: 'The knowledge of God is a knowledge completely effected and determined from the side of its object, from the side of God. But for that very reason it is genuine knowledge.'[1] This claim must be explicated with two issues in mind. First, we must explain why Barth believes that the knowledge of God is completely determined and effected from the side of its object. Secondly, we must consider why this 'knowledge of faith' is to be taken as 'genuine knowledge', and moreover as the most 'objective and strict form of knowledge'.

Let us look at the first issue. Barth does not believe that one can come to a knowledge of God by rational argument from the empirical world. This is part of what is meant when he says that 'it differs completely from anything else which man calls knowledge, not only in content, but in mode of origin and form as well'.[2] 'Differs completely', says Barth in this work. Certainly, as we shall see, this phrase is much too strong for what he has in mind, and Barth himself modifies it in other writings. The knowledge of God is not reached by argument, but comes from a sense of God's presence which is so powerful that one feels grasped, possessed and overwhelmed. One is gripped with such force that the attempt to derive the content of the revelation from logical arguments seems not only superfluous but absurd. Furthermore, the experience is such that the appropriate reaction is one of wonder, awe, a sense of mystery and fascination. It also has about it the quality of moral demand which requires unconditional obedience. Under these conditions doubts about the existence of the Being the experience heralds do not even seem a possibility. The conviction that God exists is not the result of a judgement of man's but is thrust upon him, wrung from him in such a way that he does not voluntarily contribute anything to it. We cannot help believing it.

But, furthermore, Barth has asserted that this experience of religious men is genuine knowledge. How does he justify this claim? First of all, Barth notes that most of our knowledge is determined in part by the object and in part by what we bring to the apprehension of the object. Thus, scientific theories about the structure of matter are the result of both observation and the rules of logic. They also include hypothetical constructs in the form of laws and theories. In this kind of knowledge the content of our knowledge is not wholly determined from the side

[1] Karl Barth, *Dogmatics in Outline*, Harper, 1959, p. 24. Cf. *Against the Stream*, Allenson, 1954, p. 207 f. *Church Dogmatics*, Vol. I, Part 1, 1955, p. 214 f. *Knowledge of God and Service of God*, p. 25 f.
[2] *Ibid.* p. 26.

of its object; we bring a great deal to it. However, this is not the only way in which we come to know things in the natural world. There is another kind of knowledge in which the observer brings less to the apprehension of the object. He is simply confronted by an object in such a way that he cannot think it away. In the knowledge of theoretical entities he can think away the construct without falsifying his immediate experience. But when faced with a physical object the readers cannot, in Barth's words, 'withdraw into themselves in order from there to affirm, question or deny it. Its trueness has come home directly to them personally, has become their property.'[1] Here the knowledge is almost completely effected by its object. Now of the two kinds of knowledge, the one determined to a lesser, the other to a greater extent from the side of its object, Barth believes that we universally recognize the second to be more truly knowledge than the first. *A fortiori*, then, a knowledge wholly determined from the side of its object would be supreme knowledge, and thus knowledge of universal validity.

But although knowledge by direct acquaintance is a much closer analogue to the knowledge of God than is the knowledge of a scientific hypothesis, there is still a most important difference between it and the knowledge of God. We are certain that this is a book because we have a set of criteria to which we can subject the data of our experience, and the criteria are satisfied. But the knowledge of faith is not the result of a judgement but something wrung from men. How then can we be certain that it is genuine knowledge? How can we know that it is determined wholly from the side of its object?

It is clear that Barth does not intend to make a claim that the knowledge of faith is caused by God in the usual sense. If he did this, he would contradict himself. The claim would have to be established in the usual way, by seeing if the ordinary criteria for such a claim were satisfied. But Barth has already precluded himself from attempting to answer in this way. He himself admits, 'the real believer will be fain to acknowledge that even his consciousness of faith is human darkness'.[2] Why is it, then, not to be taken as an irrational hunch, if even a cause for it is not to be discovered? How are we justified in considering it to be determined wholly from the side of the object so that it can be considered knowledge of universal validity? To this important question Barth gives the following answer:

If it is the case that a man really believes (1) that the object of faith is present to him; (2) that he himself is assimi-

[1] *Church Dogmatics, op. cit.* p. 214.   [2] *Ibid.* p. 278.

lated to the object, the conclusive result is, thirdly, that his being a believer is wholly dependent upon this object. By believing he can regard himself as based not on himself but only on his object, in fact as existing only through his object. He has not personally created his faith himself; [God's] Word has created it. He has not reached faith, faith has reached him through the Word. Moreover, he has not taken faith unto himself; faith has been gifted to him by the Word.[1]

What Barth claims is that if a man cannot help believing, if, as he says in other places, 'in spite of all that may be said against it' he finds himself still believing, and if he has satisfied himself that his faith is not based on anything in himself or in the material world, there cannot be any other conclusion than that this belief is determined by its object, God.

Certainly a host of perplexing problems remain. Many will be convinced that Barth has not succeeded in making his case. If he is to do so, additional arguments will be necessary. At the very least he has been guilty of occasional lapses. He cannot claim that the meanings of the words used to express the faith are determined from the side of the object, although the choice of words may be. We may feel compelled to express the faith in a certain way, but the words are ordinary words and, more often than not, the meaning is to be taken as closely related to its ordinary meaning. Furthermore, Mr. Blanshard has accused Barth of serious inconsistency, of failing to practice wha he preaches, of using rational argument to establish the truth of the Gospel. Again Barth has left himself open to misunderstanding. He has said that the knowledge of faith 'differs completely from anything we call knowledge' and yet in the long quotation cited above he gives what looks to be an attempt to persuade by rational discussion.

In answering this criticism, there are two points which should be kept in mind. First, Barth believes that the methods of ordinary knowledge are to be used to remove false faiths. In just this way his followers argue that Zarathustra cannot be considered a true prophet, since his conception of God is in part based on considerations derived from moral philosophy. His concept of God is not determined from the side of its object. The Barthians do not appeal to revelation to establish this conclusion, but do so by ordinary philosophical analysis. Much of Barth's argumentation can be construed as the attempt to destroy false faiths. Even the requirement that we be satisfied that our belief in God is not based on something in ourselves is

[1] *Ibid.* p. 280.

to be taken as an examination of the possibility that we may have a false faith. The requirement is thus merely a necessary, but not a sufficient, condition of true faith. It does not establish the content or the truth of faith.

Secondly, in matters of the content of the faith, Barth cannot be accused of inconsistency in his use of rational argument as long as he does not claim that we should believe his theology *because of* the arguments. As long as he insists, as he does, that the only reason he, or anyone else, ought to believe what he says is because that belief is determined as to its content from the side of God, he is not inconsistent.[1] In so far as rational argumentation in theology is justified, it is because of the nature of the object of faith. It is not justified by an appeal to general epistemological consideration. 'The element of reason in the knowledge of faith consists in the recognition of the rationality that is peculiar to the object of faith.'[2] It is only from the side of the object that we can tell when rational argumentation is justified and when it is not, and when it ought to be pursued and when it ought not.[3] Barth's position is certainly out of the ordinary, but it is not in principle inconsistent.

There is reason to believe that other apparent inconsistencies might also be eliminated by considering more carefully the implications of Barth's central principle that the knowledge of faith is the highest exemplification of real knowledge and is wholly determined as to its content from the side of its object. It might have been used by Mr. Hendry in giving substance to his remarks that for Barth 'God is just there', and by Mr. Dowey when he sought to support the Scottish theologian's remarks about the status of logic. Of course there are still a great many problems. However, the importance of Barth's claims about knowledge make it necessary for his supporters as well as his critics to investigate thoroughly their implications and possibilities.

DISCUSSION

Malcolm Diamond: The Pragmatic Validation of Religious Assertions

Mr. Blanshard describes Karl Barth's thought as a tissue of contradictions that conveys a number of deplorable moral

[1] Cf. Barth, *Anselm: Fides Quaerens Intellectum*, S.C.M. Press and John Knox Press, 1960, p. 50.   [2] *Ibid.* p. 50.   [3] *Ibid.* p. 15 f.

attitudes. Barth himself is more concerned with proclamation than ratiocination. He has not and will not address himself to the intellectual difficulties that his thought raises for non-believers. For this reason, any effort to explicate his thought in terms that are independent of his powerful rhetoric and vast scholarship may clash with some of his central emphases. The risk is worth taking because, as Mr. Hendry observed, Barth does not stand alone; he is part of a tradition. Barth proclaims the truth of Christianity and neither he nor his many followers regard his exposition of Christian truth as morally vicious. I should like to suggest that in Barth's thought there are some implicit justifications of his claim that Christianity is true, and also to indicate the sort of moral value that Christians may find in it.

One of the contradictions that Mr. Blanshard cited in his indictment of Barth was the latter's statement that 'the completeness of God's humiliation . . . lies in his taking upon himself *everything* which man's rebellion against him has made inevitable — suffering and death, but also perdition and hell . . .' Yet here Barth is speaking in a way that is strikingly similar to the language of an important New Testament passage: 'Have this in mind among yourselves, which you have in Christ Jesus, who, though he was in the form of God, did not count equality with God a thing to be grasped, but emptied himself, taking the form of a servant. . . . And being found in human form he humbled himself and became obedient to death, even death on a cross' (Phil. 2:5-8). The late H. Richard Niebuhr told a story which shows how this New Testament passage, echoed in Barth's teachings, might function in a situation of religious intensity. Shortly after the Second World War, a conference between French and German theologians took place. At the outset the Germans were very much on edge because they expected to be indicted for the horrors of the Nazi era. Instead, the French, who at that moment certainly held the psychological whip-hand, humbly confessed their own sins. The Germans were deeply moved and they in turn confessed their sins so that a genuine reconciliation ensued. Jesus first established the pattern of the strong party manifesting its strength in the seeming weakness of humility and the French theologians acted this out. And, in the Letter from which I have just quoted, that is what Paul himself urged his readers to do. Karl Barth stands in this tradition.

Although neither Barth nor his followers would have any use for talk about the pragmatic validation of religious assertions, this sort of validation is implicit in his thought. The claim is that the kind of reconciliation that took place among the theologians is possible only because the forgiving love of the God revealed in the person of Jesus Christ is the ultimate power in the universe. A claim of this kind, whether made by Barth or any other Christian thinker, is subject to a momentous qualification: its validation is inter-subjective, but not public. It is inter-subjective in the sense that the religious assertions are meaningful, and the 'fruits of faith' that validate them are accessible to the community of the faithful and not merely to the isolated individual. Nevertheless, the claim and its validation are not 'public' because they are not accessible to people who stand outside the circle of faith. Non-believers often cannot even understand the language of faith, much less the correlation of this language with recognizable human virtues.

This pragmatic mode of validating religious assertions is inadequate, but I must defer a discussion of this in order to deal with a different point. Even if the pragmatic validation were successful, it would not of itself explain why theologians continually make assertions that strike the non-believer as outright contradictions. I submit that theologians talk this way when they find evidence piling up on both sides of an issue. To indicate this in sketchy form we might use the example of grace and freedom. Many theologians have insisted that man is free but that he can do nothing to achieve his salvation because salvation is a gracious gift offered to sinful men by a merciful God. The two assertions appear to be in total opposition. If man can in no way contribute to his own salvation then he is not free in the most significant sense of the term. Mr. Blanshard insists that a contradiction is involved in the simultaneous affirmation that a man is saved by God's grace alone and that he is free. The theologian calls it a paradox.

The theologian makes this paradoxical assertion because he is confronted by inescapable evidence of his own freedom and yet of God's limitless power. Therefore he would claim that his use of paradoxes of this kind is not like the case of asserting that there is a round square; he would claim rather that the impasse to which he is driven is like that between the wave and the particle theory of light in contemporary physics. Show him the way out of the impasse and he will accept it. In fact for centuries theologians themselves have searched for a way out of it. There is nothing sacred about the paradox; it simply expresses the evidence of man's freedom on the one hand and of God's power on the other, both of which work for good (pragmatically) in the life of the community.

Here then is one mode of validating religious assertions, even the 'contradictory' ones of Karl Barth; but this pragmatic approach is inadequate. Even if we assume that love, the enrichment of the inner life, the struggle for social justice and other virtues are all manifested within Christendom, before conceding that their manifestation validates Christian claims we might ask: 'Do these virtues manifest themselves to a greater degree among Christians than among adherents of other faiths?' 'Do they manifest themselves to a greater degree among people who associate themselves with some religion than among secularists?' It would seem that a high degree of correlation should be manifest before one could say that the fruits of faith provide pragmatic validation of the assertions of faith.

Yet, even if one discovered that superior virtue was emphatically associated with religious faith in general, and to a superlative degree with Christian faith, one might still raise questions as to the meaning of the propositions with which virtue was thus associated. A pragmatist might conclude that religious indoctrination is beneficial for all sorts of reasons without being persuaded that the reasons for its beneficial results were the ones advanced by Christians who attribute their virtue to the grace of God. This would certainly be true of a pragmatist who had difficulty finding a consistent and significant meaning for the term 'God' as used by the faithful.

Objections of this kind have often been advanced. Barthian theologians and other contemporary religious thinkers might find them more telling if they themselves were trying to demonstrate the truth of religious claims on pragmatic or any other grounds. However, they do not try to prove that Christianity is true because it, and only it, can account for the state of things; rather they witness to the work of God among men. Their claims are not cast in terms of proof but in the language of faith. This involves the distinction — so often invoked in recent discussions of religion — between 'belief that' and 'belief in'. Many religious thinkers regard the language of personal relation as the most appropriate expression of their experience of God. They claim that one believes in God in the sense of trusting a person who is directly encountered, but one does not thereby claim to believe that a certain being exists and that this being may be characterized by various qualities.

There are a number of problems raised by this approach. One is that it would seem impossible to dissociate belief in a person, divine or otherwise, from belief that such a person exists in a sense that is more than fictitious. Furthermore, in *Christianity and Paradox* Ronald Hepburn has argued convincingly that the language of encounter, to which advocates of the 'belief in' approach appeal, is grounded in straightforward observations of an everyday order. Taking the subtleties of love as an example, we come upon involved questions that are similar to those of the language of faith: 'How can I be certain that she loves me; she often acts that way, but how can one be sure?' These questions are cogent because we can point to the persons in question and not merely to statements about them. But this, as Hepburn noted, does not apply to the Person the man of faith 'believes in'. In the face of this sort of criticism (to which I have yet to see an adequate reply), it does no good to say that one is nevertheless speaking meaningfully because one is believing in God rather than believing that certain things about him are true. Thomas Aquinas insisted that one could not make sense of a nonsensical proposition by ascribing it to God; for example, you cannot make a round square into a real possibility by saying: 'God can make a round square'. The same would seem to apply here; if a proposition is intrinsically meaningless one cannot pour sense into it by saying 'I believe in' instead of 'I believe that'. If one is to pursue the analogy from human relatedness to relations between man and God, it must be done on adequate metaphysical grounds and not on the basis of one mode of belief rather than another.

This question of meaning undermines the foundations of a great deal of religious thinking. Theologians must realize that criteria of meaning cannot be defined in terms of the 'circle of faith'. It is obvious that believers in any religion whatever are capable of communicating with one another in the language of faith, but to regard that ability as a sufficient criterion of meaning is to advocate the corporate solipsism of the religious cell group.

Yet if one were dealing with an idea of God that was intelligible, it would surely be appropriate to go beyond the 'hard' evidence in affirming him. Mr. Blanshard's invocation of Clifford's point that one must 'adjust one's assent to the evidence' is misguided when dealing with faith. The great men of the spirit have not measured life with an eye-dropper of a burette.

DISCUSSION

Alvin Plantinga: *The Sceptics' Strategy*

I wish to comment on what I take to be the strategy of some of the sceptics at these meetings. They keep insisting that we believers must offer *reasons* or *evidence* for our belief. And they insist further that we must show that what we take to be reasons for a given belief *really are* reasons for that belief, really do support the belief they are taken to support. And finally they seem to suppose that if we are unable to produce reasons for our beliefs or (what is much more likely) are unable to show that what we regard as reasons for them really do support them, then we have no right to the beliefs in question; we must give them up if we wish to be rational men. The sceptic evidently takes it that we can rationally accept religious beliefs only if we can give reasons and show that the reasons really are reasons.

But this procedure is unfair and discriminatory. For there are many beliefs we all hold, and hold with no detriment to our rationality, for which we cannot produce both evidence and proof that the evidence really is evidence. Indeed, some of these beliefs are such that to *show* that our reasons for them are good reasons, we should have to provide solutions to certain philosophical problems which (to my mind, at least,) have not yet been solved.

Suppose, for example, that on a given occasion I believe that someone other than myself is in pain; and suppose that my reason for so believing is that the person in question utters certain words and behaves in a certain characteristic fashion. To show that my reason for thinking that he is in pain really is an *adequate* reason, or a *good* reason for my belief about him, I should have to have a solution to at least a part of the traditional problem of other minds. Now I don't have any solution to that problem. And the fact is, I don't think anyone else does either. But nonetheless my belief that someone else is in pain might well be as rational as you please. Of course, I may be wrong in thinking that no one has a solution to this problem. But even if someone did, the rest of us who don't wouldn't automatically be guilty of irrationality in holding such beliefs. And even if someone proved that no one could *ever* discover a solution to the problem of other minds, we should all go on holding beliefs about other minds without in the least compromising our rationality.

Even in physical science, that austere bastion of rationality, there is a similar state of affairs. At present there is no satisfactory account (so far as I know) of the nature of theoretical entities — atoms, electrons and the like — or of the way in which propositions about macroscopic objects constitute evidence for propositions about such theoretical entities. Yet presumably one needn't defer accepting what the scientists tell us until this problem is solved. So why do the sceptics keep insisting that if we can't solve the corresponding problems about religious belief, our belief must be irrational?

DISCUSSION

Cyril C. Richardson: *The Sceptics' Myths*

I think it is clear that everybody entertains myths of one kind or another. They are saving myths in the sense that whether one is a sceptic, an atheist, a rationalist or a Christian, one has a certain outlook upon life which involves some mythological structure. In the course of our discussions we would do well to urge sceptics to bring out their myths so that we could understand the point of view from which they look at life. I do not think philosophy of religion can proceed until we all recognize there is an area of discourse in which we use pictures, images and analogies in order to express our total view of human existence. It often happens that the sceptic thinks he is in a privileged position because he does not have any myths and he therefore attacks Christians for seeming to be irrational in a use of analogical and picturesque language. This involves a fundamental misunderstanding. The kind of talk in which Christians engage about God, redemption, eschatology and so forth has its parallel in whatever way a sceptic looks at human existence. It is impossible to talk about the world in general and the meaning of life without using analogical categories. Indeed sceptics have their own mythological structures, and they are not in any privileged position. The weapons they use in attacking Christian positions could equally be directed against their own. It is, in consequence, of great importance in discussions of philosophy of religion for us to look at the character of mythological statements and to appreciate that all human beings indulge in them in order that they may give expression to the meaning of human existence. The fact that all such talk is not literal and is not open to the kind of verification appropriate to scientific and historical statements by no means invalidates that kind of discourse.

This leads me to say a word about the relation of reason to revelation. I think that reason can be regarded as superior to revelation in so far as it has the function of purifying myth. Even Karl Barth, while he does not explicitly elevate reason to this high place, does in fact exercise reason in just that way. He knows that the 'forty days' of which he speaks so much are not literal. Perhaps it would be wise if Barth were more explicit in formulating the canons under which he does so much of his writing. I think indeed we should all agree, whether we are Christians or sceptics, that reason similarly has a primacy in the investigation of historical facticity. The historical study of the scriptures in our day has operated upon that principle.

Irrationalism in Theology

While it is true that some types of historical criticism do involve metaphysical presuppositions, none the less where evidence clearly opposes what has previously been believed, there is an attempt on the part of Christians to revise their beliefs and to be rational in that respect.

The second area in which it can be said that reason has a priority is in the consideration of the canons of logic under which analogical discourse can operate. Granted that one comes to acknowledge and confess certain basic statements of faith in virtue of revelation, one is none the less compelled to think through the significance of analogical structures and what rules there may be for discussing their validity. This should be one of the primary tasks of philosophy of religion, and it is an unhappy circumstance that so much of philosophy of religion does not even get to that point but is rather concerned with sceptical attacks on religious belief. Once we recognize that all human beings are involved in the process of analogical thinking when they consider the question of the meaning of human existence, we may be able to reflect significantly together about the character of analogical discourse and the rules under which such discourse can validly operate.

Lastly, I should like to point out that everyone adduces reasons for the saving myths which he embraces. But these reasons never really reach to the heart of the matter. If one loses an argument one goes home and thinks up some more reasons; and similarly if one's opponent loses an argument he does precisely the same thing. This ought to lead us to recognize that the grasping of religious truth does not occur on the plane of pure rationality. Religious conviction occurs at a much deeper level of consciousness and it is indeed this level that religious people have in mind when they talk about revelation.

To summarize I should say that there are three relations of reason and revelation. First, reason has primacy with respect to historical and scientific fact. Second, reason has a primacy in so far as it attempts to investigate the appropriate canons of analogical discourse. Thirdly, saving myths cannot be handled purely in the terms of the reasons that we adduce for them.

DISCUSSION

Kai Nielsen: A Sceptic's Reply

I want to make some remarks about two comments made from the floor. Someone argued that not only theologians but philosophers as well have their commitments, their 'saving myths'. The example of a philosopher's 'saving myth' or commitment that was trotted out was something like this: one ought to weigh up the evidence for something before claiming it to be true.

It is indeed true that a philosopher is committed to this. Indeed, I do not see how any rational man could *not* be committed to it. In fact, given the use of the word 'true', I cannot declare something to be true and in the same breath declare I have no grounds for it. If I am talking about some question of fact, if I assert that something is true, I imply that I have evidence for what I claim to be true. And if I assert that a moral claim is true I imply that I have reasons for my claim. In short, this 'commitment' is not something that I can deny without saying something that is nonsensical. This being so, we all are in a very obvious way committed to reasoning in this way. Where considerations of evidence are relevant, a rational man is indeed committed when he can to weighing up the evidence before he makes a claim that so and so is true. And if *that* is having a 'saving myth' then I confess to having a 'saving myth'.

I do, however, most strenuously object to such an arbitrary, stipulative re-definition of 'saving myth'. 'Myth' is not used in that way. A myth is some legendary or traditional story, frequently about some legendary hero or some superhuman being. More generally, and derivatively, it can be said to be any kind of invented story. We even frequently use 'mythical' in a rather broader way; we make the concept 'mythical' cover all claims or beliefs which are imaginary or fictitious. In none of these ways is it a myth — saving or otherwise — to assert or believe that we ought to weigh up the evidence for something before claiming it to be true. There is nothing fictional about such a belief and it is patently obvious that believers and non-believers alike must use such a principle in their daily affairs if any kind of truth at all is to be attained. There is surely no intelligible sense in which we can say that 'We ought to weigh up the evidence before making judgements of truth and falsity' is a myth. And if it is replied, 'Not a myth but a commitment all the same', then it should be plainly stated that this is a commitment all rational men must hold. (The force of that last 'must' is logical.)

It may well be true that certain naturalistic and rationalistic philosophers of the Enlightenment and certain contemporary naturalists have had mythical elements in their thought (myths about progress, for example), but modern linguistic philosophy has increasingly purified itself of such mythical elements. Precisely what myths have MacIntyre and Blanshard appealed to

Irrationalism in Theology

or surreptitiously relied upon? What articles of faith did they appeal to that are even remotely comparable to Barth's appeal to Revelation? There are — taking all of the religions of the world into account — literally thousands of claims to Revealed Truth. Barth admits that Christian revelation can in no way be shown to be unique or authoritative among these frequently conflicting revelations, yet, as both Hendry and Dowey show, the appeal to revelation remains central for Barth's thought. But Barth is quite aware that we can in no way justify this revelation. We must simply, as knights of faith, accept it. But this makes the 'Christian story' look like a saving myth of a decidedly irrational kind. Is there anything even remotely like this in what MacIntyre and Blanshard have been telling us? More generally, what are the comparable sets of mythical beliefs that philosophers are somehow committed to? I do not see that either Blanshard or MacIntyre have appealed to any saving myths at all. More generally, I do not think there are some mythical set of beliefs that philosophers *qua* philosophers are somehow committed to. If some philosophical claim is indeed shown to be mythical, a philosopher must, to be true to his calling, immediately give it up. 'A belief that is *known* to be mythical but still held as philosophical' is, as philosophy has developed, like a 'round square'. Philosophers cannot knowingly have saving myths, and no one has shown that the present critics of theology and religion have any saving myths at all.

The second general remark I want to make turns back to a very interesting point made by Mr. Plantinga. He argued that in many areas philosophers are in a very similar pickle to the pickle the theologians are in. It is indeed unclear what could count as evidence for the existence or love of God, for the very concept of God is troubling; but it is also unclear what would count as evidence for the existence of other minds or for the existence of theoretical entities in physics. If philosophers admit this and yet are content to speak of other minds and photons, why shouldn't they have the same attitude about religious belief? This is an interesting and significant remark, but I think Plantinga overlooks an important difference between the cases. All of us can agree, at least for a large range of cases, whether somebody is in pain, whether he's thinking, feeling anxious or the like. We do in general agree about these things. Only a madman would claim that no one is ever in pain or that no one ever knows that another person is in pain. The same is true for thinking, feeling anxious or sad and the like. The first-order discourse here is in place. Our puzzlement is about the correct *analysis* of what it is like to be in pain, to think, to feel sad and the like.

We are concerned to know whether sensations are brain processes; we want to know whether one has privileged access to one's feelings and to what degree and in what way. In short, our perplexities are about the second-order discourse. But we are perfectly content to go on operating with the first-order discourse. No one dreams of saying it is irrational, somehow unintelligible or without justification or point. Similar considerations apply, though not quite to such a stringent degree, to physics. Physicists, when they turn to the philosophy of science, may dispute about the logical status of electrons, but they agree to a very large degree about how to operate with these concepts when they are actually doing scientific work. It is when they began to talk about, operate upon, the discourse that trouble about theoretical entities arises.

Now the situation is very different in religion, though as Mr. MacIntyre in effect pointed out, this wasn't so in the Middle Ages. During that 'Age of Faith' within Christendom (though surely not throughout the world), most people more or less agreed, at least in some fundamental respects, about first-order religious discourse, though they hotly disputed about the correct analysis of this same first-order talk. But in the last few centuries this agreement about the first-order discourse itself has evaporated, and it is this big difference that Plantinga fails to notice and that wrecks his analogy. There are Jews, Christians of various shades, Hindus, Zen Buddhists, agnostics, Neanderthal atheists who believe 'There is a God' is simply false, and non-Neanderthal atheists who reject the very concept of God as somehow unintelligible. In short, there are all sorts of people with various kinds of belief and disbelief. There is a literal and live dispute, not only about the correct analysis of religious concepts but also about the very legitimacy and intelligibility of the first-order religious discourse itself — 'the language of faith' as it has been called. This crucial dis-analogy seems to me to ruin Plantinga's case.

DISCUSSION

Dennis O'Brien: On the Limitations of Reason

It seems to me that the attack on the 'irrationality' of Barth which Mr. Blanshard has launched, and which has been cheered on so enthusiastically by the philosophers present, is very short-sighted historically. One would be led to believe that the whole of the philosophical tradition was swelling up in angry chorus against a theologian like Barth who suggests that reason has some radical defects. But we all know, of course, that there has been a long *philosophical* tradition attacking reason for its pretensions. The philosophical tradition with which I would suppose most of our analytically inclined friends here feel most at home mounted a considerable attack upon vain reason and insisted that only sensible evidence could give access to reality. Considering the idealist-rationalistic cast of Mr. Blanshard's own work it must be gratifying to him to find so many latter-day empiricists suddenly thronging to his side.

Remember that it was David Hume who said, 'Reason is and only ought to be the slave of the passions'. Reading that sentence out of context one could easily say, 'Here is a man opening the door to all kinds of fanaticisms'. One might believe, as Mr. Blanshard believes about Barth, that Hume was issuing an open invitation to babble. Yet, whatever one's ultimate evaluation of Hume's philosophy, it is clear that after sober reflection he decided that reason, since it could neither appropriate sensations nor put those sensations together to form a world, was consigned to be a slave to the passions which, happily, always call us back from the sceptical dissolution of mere reason to the world as custom and practical use regard it. Reason, for Hume, fails to give us contact with the ultimately real things, simple impressions, and it fails as a principle of connection and construction which would yield complexes we could regard as real. Hume found the world as seen by pure reason full of paradox: 'As the sceptical doubt arises naturally from a profound and intense reflection on these subjects, it always increases, the farther we carry our reflections, whether in opposition or conformity to it. Carelessness and inattention alone can afford us any remedy. For this reason I rely entirely on them. . . .'[1]

I would suggest that one of the reasons that 'person' has become such a central category in modern theological discussion is that it has become clear that the 'reality' with which the theologian is concerned is one that cannot be grasped immediately by reason or argued to by reason. The person of the Lord, like the simple impressions of David Hume, constitutes the really real, and can only be appropriated by a kind of immediate experience. When the theologian says that reason is incompetent to do this job he should be understood to be making a judgement about the *specific* functions and capabilities

[1] *Treatise on Human Nature*, Selby-Bigge, p. 218.

of reason as contrasted with some other faculty or faculties. If, however, 'reason' is understood as a blanket term for the sound functioning of our mental capacities, then one who attacks the competence of reason is committing himself not to the Church but to the asylum. A rational reconstruction of the notion of 'person', like Hume's attempted rational reconstruction of 'the world' or 'the self', reveals profoundly disturbing paradoxes which reflection necessarily produces and which it cannot possibly remedy. The believer convinced by the force and vivacity of his immediate awareness of the person in the community of faith 'abandons' reason and decides that he should not only be a philosopher, he should also be a man. Perhaps this is 'carelessness and inattention', or perhaps faith is the only alternative to scepticism.

CHAIRMAN'S RETROSPECT

SCEPTICS AND BELIEVERS

BY

JOHN HICK

THE Conference discussions revolved, in some four or five different orbits, around the question of the reality or existence of God. The conception of God in use throughout the Conference was that of the biblical and Christian tradition. Those of the philosophers who were sceptical concerning the existence of such a Being posed a question to the religious believers. They asked them to indicate how, or in what sense, they could hold it to be reasonable or rational to believe that God exists. The sceptics were not seeking to impose any controversial or arbitrarily narrow definition of reasonableness. They were not, for example, demanding a demonstrative proof of the existence of God; and indeed it is worth noting that the familiar theistic arguments played practically no part in the discussions. The sceptics were not demanding that religious belief be justified under some canon of rationality that is peculiarly their own, but wished to learn what kind and degree of rationality a believer claims for his belief, and how he professes to justify the claim.

The nature of the challenge emerged in the opening session. Mr. Price, in his paper, focused attention upon the fact or state of religious faith as this is exhibited in one who 'cannot help believing in God'. Such a man — as Price presented him — has not arrived in this situation through being convinced by arguments, whether cogent or otherwise, but as a consequence of some moment or period of religious experience which he cannot help taking to be a consciousness of the presence and love of God. In this kind of experience it is evident to the experiencer that he stands in a relationship of mutual awareness and concern with the divine Thou. This is as evident to him as it is at other times evident to him that he stands in a comparable 'I-thou' relationship with various human beings. That is to say, he is aware of the other, aware that the other is aware of him, and aware within this mutual awareness of personal attitudes, such as love or hatred, respect or fear, well-wishing or ill-wishing. Mr. Price spoke of the consciousness of God in terms of inner experiences enjoyed by the individual in the privacy of his own mind. Others added the more communal experience of congregational worship and responses to 'divine revelation' coming through the Bible, the Church's preaching, or communion with nature. Along any of these, or perhaps yet other routes, people arrive at the point at which they cannot help believing in God.

Thus, instead of beginning, in more traditional fashion, with a deployment of reasons which would lead from outside the sphere of faith to a point within it, the discussion began with a directing of attention upon the state of faith itself as this is described from within. From this starting-point the older issue of the adequacy or inadequacy of reasons for adopting a set of religious beliefs gave way to the question whether or not it is rationally permissible for an individual to live on the basis of a putative religious awareness which he finds that he has.

Accepting this re-definition of the issue, the sceptics did not question that there are indeed people who cannot help believing in God. But they pointed out that it is logically possible that someone should be in this state of mind and yet that there be no God for him to believe in. One's being unable to help believing in God does not guarantee that God exists — unless the existence of God is reduced to the fact that he 'exists for me' in virtue of my belief. In view of this, the sceptics asked, does the believer at this point have anything more to say; or is he content simply to report the biographical fact that he is unable not to believe in God?

Sceptics and Believers

One possible way of meeting this challenge, a way which was in evidence at several points during the Conference, was in effect to repudiate it in the name of the autonomy of religious language. In trying now to formulate this autonomist position (as I shall call it) I am relying more upon remarks made in the course of the discussions than upon the now published papers. This view draws its inspiration, philosophically from the later teachings of Wittgenstein, and theologically from the Barthian emphasis upon a self-authenticating divine revelation which neither seeks nor permits rational support. I do not know whether the position which I am about to describe coincides fully with that of any of the Conference participants; but it is strongly suggested by thoughts expressed by several of them.

From the autonomist standpoint, 'believing in God', together with the religious modes of speech in which it expresses itself, proceeds without raising the question of the existence of God. This view focuses attention upon the person who has a use for, and accordingly finds meaning in, distinctively religious language and who engages in distinctively religious practices. He feels grateful to God for all that is good in his experience and penitent for his own shortcomings and failures; he is released from anxiety by the thought of God's sovereign rule, and filled with awe when he joins in the worship of the 'almighty and everlasting God' who is 'Maker of heaven and earth, and of all things visible and invisible'. To some degree at least he lives the life and speaks the language of faith. But — and here the puzzling side of this position appears — such a man does not necessarily hold that 'God exists'. Consequently, it is not proper to ask him how he knows, or why he believes, that God exists; nor to enquire what experiencable states of affairs are entailed by God's existence, such that their occurrence or non-occurrence might yield confirmation or disconfirmation of this belief. Questions of this kind are ruled out as having no place within authentic religious language. The believer talks *to* God, not *about* him; or if he does talk about him, for instance in the recitation of the creeds, this is a liturgical act and not an exercise in metaphysical discourse. There are no connections of logical implication between the realms of religious and philosophical language. Religious premises do not entail philosophical conclusions; for example, 'God is gracious and long-suffering' does not entail that 'God exists'. Religious language is autonomous, as the linguistic aspect of a distinctive form of life; and modes of question, distinction, affirmation and denial which have their proper places in other 'language-games' (for instance, those of the sciences) will if intruded here only give rise to false problems. The religious life, including its appropriate modes of speech, observably exists, and the external observer must be content to say, with Wittgenstein: *dieses Sprachspiel wird gespielt*.[1]

One effect of this position is to make religious utterances immune to philosophical criticism. It is now not appropriate to ask for *grounds* for religious belief. Neither is it appropriate to ask for the *meaning* of 'God exists' if the request implies that there might be some other answer than a spelling out in religious terms of the respects in which God is real — as 'almighty Father', 'a very present help in trouble', etc. Again, it is not appropriate to ask how religious beliefs might be verified or falsified; for they are not that kind of belief. As Mr. Malcolm says, 'There are beliefs and beliefs. Some of them do not issue in expectations in such a way that their fulfilment or non-fulfilment would be a verification or falsification of the beliefs.' Such beliefs may indeed 'make a difference' to the believer. 'The man who believes that his sins will be forgiven if he is truly repentant might thereby be saved from despair. What he believes has, for him, no verification or falsification; yet the belief makes a difference to his action and feeling.'[2] But to enquire about other kinds of differences would be to violate the special nature and proper autonomy of religious language.

From the point of view of the dominant concern of the Conference, the most distinctive feature of this view is that religious language is autonomous, so that statements made within it are invulnerable to external criticism.

Commenting briefly upon this autonomist position, I

[1] *Philosophical Investigations*, para. 654.   [2] P. 110 above.

want to suggest that taken as a whole it must be quite unacceptable to the Christian believer, although there is one aspect of it which will appeal to him.

The unacceptable feature of the position is that by treating religious language as autonomous — as a language-game with its own rules, or a speech activity having meaning only within its own borders — it deprives religious statements of 'ontological' or 'metaphysical' significance. The ordinary religious believer has always supposed that such a statement as 'God loves mankind' is a true declaration concerning an ultimate order of fact which sustains and governs all the more proximate types of fact. The religious worshipper has always supposed that God exists independently of anyone's believing or disbelieving that he exists, and that he is a personal Mind who can know and enter into personal relationship with his creatures. But this supposition is one to which a variety of considerations are logically relevant. For example, the fact of evil tells against it; whilst the fact of Christ and of the deep impression which he has made upon the human soul tells in favour of it. A conviction as to the reality of God is, Christian faith will insist, either a response to fact, rendered appropriate and rational by its conformity with fact, or it is delusory and is rendered inappropriate and irrational by its divergence from fact. The autonomist rejects this traditional position when he confines religious truth-claims within the enclosed realm of the religious speech activity itself. Given the circumstance that 'this language-game is played' there is no way in which it can be logically inappropriate or impermissible to engage in it; nor, however, is there then any way in which it can be logically appropriate or proper to engage in it. If it is not to the point to criticise talk about God on the ground that God does not exist, neither is it to the point to commend it on the ground that God does exist and that what is being said about him is true. The logical implications of religious statements do not extend across the borders of the *Sprachspiel* into assertions concerning the character of the universe beyond that fragment of it which is the religious speech of human beings.

Religious language becomes a type of 'protected discourse',[1] and forfeits its immemorial claim to bear witness to the most momentous of all truths.

Consider the statement that God exists, or is real. To be sure, this is not an item in first-order religious language. The *homo fidei*, as such, probably has no occasion to say 'God exists' — any more than in our ordinary daily commerce with our material and social environments we have occasion to say 'the world exists' or 'people exist'. But there are two possible reasons for not saying that 'x exists'. One is that we do not in fact believe that x exists, and the other is that we take the reality of x so much for granted that there is no need to assert it. We do not declare our faith in the reality of the material world when we arise each morning, for we have no sufficient motive to affirm something which we have never had any inclination to doubt. Nor, for the same reason, do we daily assert the real existence of other people. And it is surely clear that such exemplars of faith as Jesus and his apostles, or the prophets of the Old Testament, lacked incentive to assert that God exists because they (at least sometimes) seemed to themselves to be as conscious of God as they were of their physical environment or their human fellows. It was for them pointless and even absurd to say 'God exists', and this for the same sort of reason that it is pointless and absurd for a husband to affirm the existence of the wife and children who are so much a part of his life. But of course both husband and religious believer do respectively believe (if this word is here strong enough) that the family does indeed exist and that God does indeed exist. That Amos or St. Paul believed in the reality of God is strongly indicated by the way in which they conducted their lives and by their expectations concerning the future. When Amos said, 'Hear this word that the Lord has spoken against you, O people of Israel . . .',[2] and when St. Paul said, 'But God showed his love for us in that when we were yet sinners Christ died for

---

[1] *Cf.* R. E. Allen's criticism of this position in 'The Ontological Argument', *The Philosophical Review*, LXX, 1 (January 1961), pp. 65-66.

[2] Amos, 3: 1.

us'[1] or 'And God raised the Lord and will also raise us by his power',[2] they were presupposing the reality of God as a living Being whose existence and activity are no mere epiphenomena of our religious language, but who is the creator and judge of men, the determiner of our destiny, the final source of our good. I do not know how it could ever be demonstratively proved that Amos and Paul and the other biblical writers presupposed the real existence of the God whom they worshipped; but I also think that anyone who doubts that this presupposition operated in their minds must be blinded in a very sophisticated way to the natural and ordinary meanings of words.

But if such first-order religious utterances as 'God showed his love for us . . .' do presuppose and imply that God exists, then religious belief cannot after all be immune from the familiar questions concerning grounds, meaning and mode of verification.

There is, however, another respect in which, as it seems to me, the 'autonomy of religious language' theory is importantly right. It is right in recognizing a foundational situation beneath which one cannot dig with ratiocinative tools — namely, the fact of religious faith, with religious language as its expression. This does not mean that reason is unable to perform any legitimate apologetic function. It can do much to remove intellectual blockages which inhibit religious faith. It may thus sometimes even play the decisive part in a move from scepticism to belief. But nevertheless faith stands ultimately upon the ground of religious experience and is not a product of philosophical reasoning. There are indeed no logical demonstrations of God; and if there were they would remove the possibility of a free faith-response to him. Various 'theistic proofs' have of course been offered in the history of Christian thought. But the fact that none of these arguments, ancient or modern, has been widely convincing to sceptics suggests that some other factor in the believer's mind has lightened the task of such an argument so that it may succeed, and by its absence from the sceptic's mind leaves the argument to

[1] Rom. 5: 8.   [2] 1 Cor. 6: 14.

carry a burden of proof beyond its strength. This other factor can, I think, safely be identified as religious experience, if we understand that term in the widest sense, including not only the inward apprehension of the presence and love of God of which Mr. Price speaks, but also religious responses to the various media of special revelation — Bible, Church and tradition. Without this there would be no such phenomenon as religion; and the justification of religion must be a justification of the practice of treating some form of religious experience as veridical and of proceeding to live upon the basis of it.

How is such a justification to be provided? A constructive alternative to the autonomist theory did not emerge at all clearly or fully during the Conference, although there were several valuable hints in the direction of one. In what follows I am building upon some of these hints, although not necessarily in a way that would appeal to any of those whose remarks at the Conference I found especially congenial.[1]

It may be profitable to consider the similarities and the differences between taking religious experience as cognitively veridical and taking our perception of the world, including our awareness of other persons, as cognitively veridical.

What are the similarities?

First, in each case there are certain data, and our interpretation of these data in terms respectively of a spatio-temporal world, and a divine Creator of this world who is related to us in and through it. In normal sense perception we are not conscious of sense data as such, or of the habitual interpretative activity which issues in our perception of physical objects. Likewise the man of faith, whilst he is conscious of standing directly in God's presence, is not aware either of 'raw' religious data or of his own interpretative response to them. We have no special name for the interpretative element in our cognition of the world; however, the equivalent element in our cognition of God is traditionally termed faith.

---

[1] The view presented in these pages is developed more fully in my *Faith and Knowledge*, Cornell University Press, 1957.

Sceptics and Believers

What are our religious data? Are they data intuited by a sixth sense, some special organ, physiological or psychological, of religious sensibility? Leaving aside here the special phenomena of mysticism, the answer would seem to be that the data of religious experience are for the most part the same as those through which we know physical objects and other human beings. They consist in the ordinary human experience which is common to believers and non-believers — together with further experiences which are open to everyone but which are not in fact sought by everyone, experiences enjoyed in individual prayer and public worship, in Bible reading and religious meditation, and in the life and work of a community of faith. (These latter are not in principle more private or of more privileged access than the special experiences characteristic of, say, philosophers — experiences of prolonged philosophical reflection, of the reading of a distinctive literature, of participation in the activities of a closed professional association.) Concentrating our attention, however, upon the field of experience which is common to believers and non-believers alike, we may say that the same data are being used in two different ways, ways which are not mutually exclusive or competitive but which operate upon two different cognitive 'levels'. An individual's religious interpretation of his experience presupposes his more primitive interpretation of it in terms of physical objects constituting a natural order. So far as the material aspects of his environment are concerned the man of faith lives consciously in the same world as the atheist; but as a further characteristic superimposed upon its material structure he experiences it as mediating the presence and activity of God. For example, the Old Testament prophets lived amidst events which the secular historian would describe without reference to God but in which the prophetic mind saw the hand of the Lord moving powerfully and purposefully within human history. At the same time it is to be noted that this religious mode of apperception did not blind them to the proximate causes of events in human motives and policies and the operations of the palpable forces of nature. Again, the central figure of the New Testament can be seen either as a purely human individual, the carpenter of Nazareth, or as one in whose actions God himself was acting, so that here 'The Logos became flesh'. Once again, however, this religious mode of seeing and responding to the person of Christ did not cancel or dim the disciples' perception of the genuine humanity of their Master.

Second, in neither case can we prove demonstratively, or even show it to be probable, that the object of our 'cognition' exists independently of those states of mind in which we suppose ourselves to be cognizing it. If anyone were seriously inclined to interpret his sense experience solipsistically we could not expect to argue him out of this. If anyone failed to see other 'human' bodies as centres of consciousness, feeling and purpose like himself we could not demonstrate to him that he is misinterpreting them. The experiential data as such are able to be interpreted in either way. And likewise the atheist, interpreting his experience of human life naturalistically, cannot be shown by any conclusive philosophical argument to be blind to further dimensions of his environment. As human animals we find ourselves interpreting in the way which we describe as perceiving a three-dimensional physical world; and we are not inhibited from living in this world by our inability to prove that our interpreting at this level is not misinterpreting. As religious believers we likewise find that we cannot help interpreting in the way which we describe as being aware of God. Again, we cannot prove that our interpreting at this further level is not misinterpreting. However, the great biblical exemplars of faith were in no way troubled by this theoretical difficulty as they went about their business of serving God in the midst of human life. Ought they, nevertheless, to have been inhibited from trusting their religious experience, and ought we to be inhibited from trusting ours, by this admitted lack of reasons and evidences drawn from outside the realm of religious experience itself?

In order to face the full force of this question we must now acknowledge certain important differences between sense perception and religious perception, which are readily discernible within the more basic similarities just noted.

(*a*) Sense perception is coercive. The perceived world has an objective character and structure and impresses itself upon our consciousness whether we like it or not. When we open our eyes in daylight we cannot help seeing what is before us. If we try to ignore the perceptible world, for instance by treating a brick wall as though it were not there, we quickly learn that we must take account of the actual features of our physical environment, or be eliminated from it.

Religious perception, however, is not coercive. It is indeed a commonplace of contemporary theology that God does not force an awareness of himself upon men, but leaves them free to become conscious of him by an uncompelled response of faith.

(*b*) Sense perception is universal amongst mankind, and the world which it reveals is public to all men, i.e. the sense experiences of any two individuals can be correlated in terms of the hypothesis of a common world which they jointly inhabit.

Religious perception, on the other hand, is not universal amongst mankind. Not all men appear to have it. Nor can the religious-experience reports from different cultures easily be correlated as reports of the same religious reality.

(*c*) Sense perception is highly coherent, in that the perceived world exhibits continuity and order both in space and time. It forms a systematic whole, changing in accordance with discernible laws upon which accurate predictions can be based.

In contrast, the religious awareness of different individuals varies greatly in degree of coherence. At one extreme it is spasmodic, diverse and wavering; at the other extreme (perhaps an ideal limit) it is present throughout life, colouring uniformly the whole continuum of experience.

In view of these striking differences, it might well be said, reliance upon sense experience stands justified, whereas reliance upon religious experience requires further justification. Our reality terms — 'real', 'exists', 'fact' — are modelled upon the kind of reality exhibited by the material world, and it may well seem that these terms are not properly applicable to the supposed object of theistic religious experience.

It is true that religious experience varies far more widely in intensity than does sense experience. We find it present in some, absent in others and fluctuating greatly within most of those in whom it is present. However, at the top levels of intensity religious experience *is* coercive. It gives rise to the situation of the person who *cannot help* believing in God. The apostle, prophet or saint is (sometimes, not necessarily always) so vividly aware of God that he can no more doubt the veracity of his religious awareness than of his sense experience. During the periods when he is living consciously in the presence of God, when God is to him the divine Thou, the question whether God exists simply cannot arise. The awareness of God, for those who have it, can be as coercive as our ordinary awareness of other human persons and of our material surroundings. The difference, so far as coerciveness is concerned, is not in the vividness of the two types of experience themselves (when the religious experience is considered in its strongest instances), but in the fact that whereas everyone is compelled to have sense experience, no one is compelled to have religious experience. God does not force himself upon our attention as does our physical environment. The individual's own free receptivity or responsiveness plays a part in his dawning consciousness of God, even though once he *has* become conscious of God that consciousness may possess a coercive and indubitable quality.

The other two differences which we have noticed between sensory and religious experience arise from the same circumstance. Since the apprehension of God is not forced upon mankind it is perhaps not surprising that many are entirely or almost entirely without it. Again, the lack of coherence among men's religious experiences is a corollary of the variation in degree of this form of experience both from person to person and from time to time in the same person. (It also seems, however, to be due in part to real differences

Sceptics and Believers

in the nature of what, within different religions, is claimed to be apprehended in religious experience; and there is an important problem here which I shall not even attempt to consider in the present paper.)

Thus, underlying the three differences listed above are the two more basic differences, (i) that although the awareness of God is coercive to one who has it in the highest degree, no one is coerced into having it, and (ii) that short of this coercive (but not coerced) awareness of God there is a long descent of degrees of religious consciousness, dwindling down to zero.

Do these two basic respects in which sensory experience differs from religious make it reasonable to trust the former but unreasonable to trust the latter? This is a major question in the philosophy of religion, and one concerning which general agreement will not soon, or perhaps even ever, be forthcoming. As an approach to this crucial issue I would suggest that the believer is entitled to claim the right to trust his religious experience if the following two points can be established: (*a*) these two epistemological differences can be seen to arise out of a prior difference in the natures of the objects of cognition posited in each case, namely, the world and God; and (*b*) this prior difference, although sufficient to account for the differences in modes of cognition, is nevertheless not such as to remove God altogether beyond the scope of the cognitive uses of human language.

(*a*) Christian thought, especially in its more recent emphasis upon the personal nature of God and of his dealings with mankind, does suggest a reason why religious cognition should have this non-compulsory and (consequently) bewilderingly variable character. The suggestion is that this characteristic makes possible man's existence as a finite personal being in the presence of the infinite personal God. Only if man exists as a relatively independent and autonomous moral agent can he enter into a genuinely personal relationship with his Maker. Therefore, God has made his human creatures organic to a world, with its own structure and laws, which he has set forth in relative independence of himself. He has made room for man as an autonomous personal being by creating him at a 'distance' from his Creator — not a spatial but an epistemic distance, consisting in the circumstance that man's first object of awareness is not God but the world, and that the consciousness of God is not forced upon man but awaits his own uncompelled response to non-coercive modes of revelation.

Viewed in the light of this theological suggestion, the epistemological situation would seem to be as follows. Man's awareness of God consists in his experiencing the events of his life and of the world as events in and through which God is having to do with him and he with God. That is to say, a person becomes conscious of God by interpreting his mundane experience as mediating the divine presence and activity. Further, man has been so made that he has an innate tendency to interpret his experience religiously, a tendency, however, which operates only as an 'inclining cause' that can readily be resisted or suppressed. Some reasons why it might be suppressed are suggested in Mr. Price's paper.[1] The sense of God, in its fully developed monotheistic form, is the sense of an incomparably higher Being who must be worshipped and obeyed with one's whole nature; and this is a dawning awareness which, so far from welcoming, we may instead resist or hold at bay. Pascal well expresses this view of religious knowledge when he says, speaking of God's self-revelation in the person of Christ:

> It was not then right that He should appear in a manner manifestly divine, and completely capable of convincing all men; but it was also not right that He should come in so hidden a manner that He could not be known by those who should sincerely seek Him. He has willed to make Himself quite recognizable by those; and thus, willing to appear openly to those who seek Him with all their heart, He so regulates the knowledge of Himself that He has given signs of Himself, visible to those who seek Him, and not to those who seek Him not. There is enough light for those who only desire to see, and enough obscurity for those who have a contrary disposition.[2]

(b) In thus stressing the immense difference between God and the world, such that our status as responsible

---

[1] See p. 12.   [2] Pascal, *Pensées*, No. 430.

persons is not undermined by a compelled awareness of the latter, but would be undermined by a compelled awareness of the Supreme Being, the argument may now be in danger of running into an opposite difficulty. For if God is so utterly different from the world and from our fellow humans, perhaps there is after all no proper question concerning his existence or non-existence. Perhaps then the proper function of statements about God is not to make factual assertions of any kind, but rather to express some inner state of the religious mind, perhaps an ethical intention or a way of feeling about the world. In this case talk of 'knowing' God would be symbolic rather than literal, and the biblical belief in a really existing personal Being who loves us and who can receive and respond to our worship would require to be radically reinterpreted.

As against this possibility I want to suggest that the Christian belief in the reality of God, when taken in its context of associated and corollary beliefs, is — whether true or false — a genuinely factual belief. It is not empirical, if the empirical realm is confined by definition to the material universe. But it is factual, if we use this as a wider term than 'empirical' and define the factual in terms of the making of an actual or possible difference within human experience. For the Christian belief in the reality of God lies at the centre of a system of beliefs which has to be taken substantially as a whole, and which includes the belief that God holds men and women in being, or reconstitutes them, beyond bodily death, so that they shall participate in the final fulfilment of his purpose. This eschatological element is quite inseparable from any conception of God and the universe which is to be recognisably Christian, and it is at this point that the corpus of Christian belief lays itself open in principle to experiential verification — though not, in view of the peculiar asymmetry of predictions concerning continued existence after death, to falsification. If one is willing to allow experience itself to show what different kinds of experience there are, one cannot dismiss *a priori* the Christian prediction of a future experience of participation, beyond death, in the Kingdom of God. However, the further specification of the way in which the Christian eschatological predictions meet the criterion of experiential verifiability is a complex task which cannot be pursued here.[1] What I have sought to do in these brief reflections upon the Conference is to suggest a direction in which it might perhaps be profitable to look in the continuing search for an answer to the philosophical sceptics' questions.

[1] I have endeavoured to do this to some extent in 'Theology and Verification' (*Theology Today*, XVII, 1, April 1960, reprinted in *The Existence of God*, ed. John Hick (New York: The Macmillan Co., 1964)).

THE CONTRIBUTORS

VIRGIL C. ALDRICH is Chairman of the Department of Philosophy at Kenyon College, Gambier, Ohio, and a past President of the American Philosophical Association (Western Division). He is the author of *Philosophy of Art* and of numerous essays in collaborative volumes and articles in the philosophical journals.

WILLIAM ALSTON is Professor of Philosophy at the University of Michigan, Ann Arbor, Michigan. He is the editor of *Religious Belief and Philosophical Thought* and (with G. Nakhnikian) *Readings in Twentieth Century Philosophy*, and author of *Philosophy of Language* and of numerous essays in collaborative volumes and articles in the philosophical journals.

BRAND BLANSHARD is Professor of Philosophy, Emeritus, at Yale University, New Haven, Connecticut, and a past President of the American Philosophical Association (Eastern Division) and the American Theological Society, and a Corresponding Fellow of the British Academy. He is the author of *The Nature of Thought, Reason and Goodness* (Gifford Lectures) and *Reason and Analysis*.

RICHARD BRANDT is Professor of Philosophy and Chairman of the Department of Philosophy and Religion at Swarthmore College, Swarthmore, Pennsylvania. He is the author of *The Philosophy of Schleiermacher, Hopi Ethics: A Theoretical Analysis* and *Ethical Theory* and of numerous articles in the philosophical journals, and editor of *Value and Obligation* and *Social Justice*.

W. NORRIS CLARKE, S.J. is Associate Professor of Philosophy at Fordham University, New York, and a past President of the Jesuit Philosophical Association. He is American Editor of the *International Philosophical Quarterly*, and the author of numerous essays in collaborative volumes and articles in the philosophical and theological journals.

MALCOLM DIAMOND is Assistant Professor of Religion at Princeton University. He is the author of *Martin Buber: Jewish Existentialist*, and of a number of articles in theological journals.

EDWARD A. DOWEY, JR., is Professor of the History of Christian Thought at Princeton Theological Seminary. He is the author of *The Knowledge of God in Calvin's Theology* and of numerous essays in collaborative volumes and articles in theological and historical journals.

KEITH GUNDERSON is Assistant Professor of Philosophy at the University of California, Los Angeles, and the author of articles in the philosophical journals.

Faith and the Philosophers

CHARLES HARTSHORNE is Professor of Philosophy at the University of Texas, at Austin, Texas, and a past President of the American Philosophical Association (Western Division), the Metaphysical Society of America and the Charles Peirce Society. He is the author of *The Philosophy and Psychology of Sensation, Beyond Humanism, Man's Vision of God, The Divine Relativity, Reality as Social Process, Anselm's Discovery, The Logic of Perfection* and of numerous essays in collaborative volumes and articles in the philosophical and theological journals.

GEORGE S. HENDRY is Charles Hodge Professor of Systematic Theology at Princeton Theological Seminary. He is the author of *The Holy Spirit in Christian Theology, The Gospel of the Incarnation* and *The Westminster Confession for Today*, and of numerous essays in collaborative volumes and articles in theological journals.

JOHN HICK is Stuart Professor of Christian Philosophy at Princeton Theological Seminary. He is the author of *Faith and Knowledge* and *Philosophy of Religion*, and of articles in philosophical and theological journals, and editor of *The Existence of God*, and *Classical and Contemporary Readings in the Philosophy of Religion*.

ALASDAIR MACINTYRE is a Fellow of University College, Oxford. He is the author of *The Unconscious: A Conceptual Analysis, Marxism: An Interpretation* and *Difficulties in Christian Belief*, and editor of *Metaphysical Beliefs* and (with Antony Flew) *New Essays in Philosophical Theology*, and has written numerous articles in the philosophical journals.

NORMAN MALCOLM is Professor of Philosophy at Cornell University, Ithaca, New York. He is the author of *Ludwig Wittgenstein: A Memoir, Dreaming* and *Knowledge and Certainty*, and of numerous articles in the philosophical journals and essays in collaborative volumes.

KAI NIELSEN is Associate Professor of Philosophy at New York University. He is the author of numerous articles in philosophical and educational journals.

GEORGE DENNIS O'BRIEN is Assistant Professor of Philosophy, and Assistant Dean of the College, at Princeton University. He is the author of several articles in philosophical and theological journals.

ALVIN PLANTINGA is Associate Professor of Philosophy at Calvin College, Grand Rapids, Michigan. He is the author of numerous essays in collaborative volumes and articles in the philosophical journals.

H. H. PRICE is Wykeham Professor of Logic, Emeritus, in the University of Oxford. He is a Fellow of the British Academy, and a past President of the Mind Association, the Aristotelian Society and the Society for Psychical Research. He is the author of *Perception, Hume's Theory of the External World* and *Thinking and Experience*, and of numerous articles in the philosophical journals, and was Gifford Lecturer in 1949-1950.

CYRIL C. RICHARDSON is Washburn Professor of Church History and Director of Graduate Studies at Union Theological Seminary,

The Contributors

New York. He is the author of *The Christianity of Ignatius of Antioch, The Church Through the Centuries, The Sacrament of Reunion, Zwingli and Cranmer on the Eucharist* and *The Doctrine of the Trinity*, and of numerous articles in the journals and contributions to composite volumes.

LINWOOD URBAN is Assistant Professor in the Department of Philosophy and Religion at Swarthmore College, Swarthmore, Pennsylvania, and is the author of a number of articles in the professional journals.

INDEX

This is an index of names; the topics discussed in the book are indicated in the Table of Contents and in the sub-headings of the longer articles.

Aldrich, Virgil, 38 f., 53 f.
Allen, R. E., 240 n.
Alston, William, 44 n., 52, 53, 63 f., 103 f., 110, 154-155
Amos, 240
Aquinas, St. Thomas, 144, 150, 153, 226
Argyle, Michael, 93-94
Austin, J. L., 42, 44 n.
Ayer, A. J., 151, 182

Baillie, John, 189
Barth, Karl, 130, 159 f., 201 f., 210 f., 228, 237
Berkeley, Bishop, 43
Blanshard, Brand, 159 f., 201 f., 218, 221, 222 f., 230-231
Bradley, F. H., 198
Bradshaw, Marion, 189
Braithwaite, R. B., 125
Brandt, Richard, 150 f.
Broad, C. D., 151
Brunner, Emil, 162, 178, 179, 184, 188, 191
Bultmann, Rudolf, 31-32, 36
Butler, Bishop, 163, 197

Calvin, John, 195, 204, 206, 217
Campbell, C. A., 200
Carnap, Rudolf, 118, 182
Cave, Sydney, 189

Darwin, Charles, 190-191, 205, 206
Descartes, René, 86
Dewey, John, 160
Diamond, Malcolm, 222 f.
Dowey, E. A., 201 f., 222
Durkheim, E., 129 f.

Evans-Pritchard, E. E., 118 f.

Feuerbach, Ludwig, 160
Flew, Antony, 34

Flugel, J. C., 71
Freud, Sigmund, 12, 64 f., 103, 108, 110 f., 160, 190, 192, 206

Gellner, Ernest, 115 n.
Gogarten, F., 163
Gunderson, Keith, 57 f.

Hartshorne, Charles, 26 f., 33 f.
Hegel, G. F. W., 132, 160, 180, 214 f.
Hempel, Carl, 152 n.
Hendry, George, 210 f., 222, 223
Hepburn, Ronald, 57 n., 225
Hitler, Adolf, 131
Hume, David, 233 f.

Inge, W. R., 192

James, William, 98, 100, 103-104, 165, 192
Jesus, 109, 145, 161, 164, 165, 178, 181, 182, 187, 190, 203, 244
Jung, Carl, 71

Kant, Immanuel, 163, 170, 213, 214
Kierkegaard, Søren, 85, 100, 130, 132, 159, 169
Kraemer, Hendrik, 178

Leach, E. R., 124 f.
Levy-Bruhl, H., 117 f.
Luther, Martin, 206, 210

MacIntyre, Alasdair, 52, 53, 110, 115 f., 134 f., 154-155, 230 f.
Mackintosh, Douglas C., 164, 199
Malcolm, Norman, 47 n., 103 f., 111, 238
Malinowski, B., 126
Manning, Cardinal, 196
Mansel, Dean, 159
Marcel, Gabriel, 130

Martineau, James, 163
Mill, J. S., 169
Moore, G. E., v

Newman, J. H., 17, 55, 60, 163, 196-197
Niebuhr, H. R., 223
Niebuhr, Reinhold, 198
Nielsen, Kai, 229 f.
Nygren, Anders, 198

O'Brien, G. D., 232 f.
Ostow, M., 72, 88

Pascal, Blaise, 20, 36, 159, 248
Paton, H. J., 197, 199
Paul, St., 142, 210, 240
Plantinga, Alvin, 226 f., 231, 232
Plotinus, 88
Pratt, J. B., 200
Price, H. H., 3 f., 26 f., 38 f., 57 f., 111, 235, 236, 242, 248

Quick, O. C., 164

Reik, T., 71, 74, 77, 93
Richardson, C. C., 228 f.
Ritschl, A., 160
Russell, Bertrand, v, 170, 198

Scharfstein, B., 72, 88

Tennant, F. R., 150
Tertullian, 159, 210
Tillich, Paul, 81, 129, 132, 150

Urban, Linwood, 218 f.

Webb, C. C. J., 196
Weil, Simone, 132
Winch, Peter, 115 n., 119 f.
Wittgenstein, Ludwig, v, 41, 42, 44, 45, 135, 217, 237-238

Zossima, Fr., 212

THE END